The Ethical Journalist

THE COVER PICTURE

The cover photograph shows two journalists discussing the merits of a story. It is a promotional picture for the 1930s radio series *Big Town*, which starred Edward G Robinson and Claire Trevor as a pair of New York journalists. It was not the only time that Robinson, a classic Hollywood 'hard man', took on the role of a journalist. In *Five Star Final*, a 1931 movie about unethical journalism, he played a newspaper editor who finally salved his troubled conscience by walking out on his job.

The purpose of this book is to encourage discussion among journalists. The aim is a newsroom culture that requires nobody to choose between having a job and having a conscience.

The Ethical Journalist

Tony Harcup

SAGE Publications
London • Thousand Oaks • New Delhi

First published 2007

SAGE Publications Ltd
1 Oliver's Yard
55 City Road
London EC1Y 1SP

SAGE Publications Inc.
2455 Teller Road
Thousand Oaks, California 91320

SAGE Publications India Pvt Ltd
B-42, Panchsheel Enclave
Post Box 4109
New Delhi 110 017

British Library Cataloguing in Publication data

A catalogue record for this book is available
from the British Library

ISBN-10 1-4129-1896-0 ISBN-13 978-1-4129-1896-1
ISBN-10 1-4129-1897-9 (pbk) ISBN-13 978-1-4129-1897-8

Library of Congress Control Number: 2006926612

Typeset by C&M Digitals (P) Ltd, Chennai, India
Printed and bound in Great Britain by TJ International Ltd, Padstow, Cornwall
Printed on paper from sustainable resources

To Terry, Bill and Francis

CONTENTS

ACKNOWLEDGEMENTS

Special thanks must go to everyone who agreed to be interviewed for this book: Eric Allison, Andrew Gilligan, Janet McKenzie, Steve Panter, Ryan Parry, Kevin Peachey and Michelle Stanistreet.

Many people gave up their time to read draft chapters and provide invaluable feedback. Grateful thanks to: Bill Carmichael, Peter Cole, Jackie Errigo, Alice Griffin, Mark Hanna, Jackie Harrison, David Holmes, Helen James, Jennifer McKiernan, David Molyneux, Ralph Negrine, Liz Nice, Karen Sanders, John Steel, Ajay Thakur, Granville Williams, Terry Wragg.

Others have contributed to the contents of this book in a variety of ways, from taking part in earlier research to simply discussing journalism with me over the years. They include: Chris Atton, Miles Barter, Andrew Bibby, Vanessa Bridge, Paul Brown, Sev Carrell, Liz Curtis, Ed Davie, Tom Davies, Caroline Deacon, Jeremy Dear, Lindsay Eastwood, Richard Edwards, Michael Foley, Paul Foot, Nigel Fountain, Bob Franklin, Chris Frost, Sue George, Trevor Gibbons, Kevin Gopal, Tim Gopsill, Carmel Harrison, David Helliwell, Julian Hendy, Steve Henwood, Michael Higgins, Mike Jempson, Pete Johnson, Richard Keeble, Martin Kielty, Peter Lazenby, Tim Lezard, George MacIntyre, Louise Male, Jane Merrick, John Millward, Michele Moss, Deirdre O'Neill, Stephen Overell, Susan Pape, Angela Phillips, Ronan Quinlan, Sue Roberts, Mike Studley, Abul Taher, John Toner, Bob Wade, Martin Wainwright, Sarah Walsh, Chris Wheal, Brian Whittle, Dave Woodhall, Waseem Zakir, colleagues in the Association for Journalism Education, and staff and students at both Trinity and All Saints College and the University of Sheffield.

Finally, many thanks to everyone at Sage past and present, including: Jamilah Ahmed, Rosemary Campbell, Julia Hall, Tanja Lederer, Gurdeep Mattu, Fabienne Pedroletti, Wendy Scott, Sandra Jones, and Kate Legon.

Responsibility for the contents rests entirely with me.

1 INTRODUCTION TO ETHICAL JOURNALISM

It was a small story in a local newspaper. It began:

> Mrs Hattie Carroll, 51, Negro waitress at the Emerson Hotel, died last week as a result of the brutal beating by a wealthy socialite during the exclusive Spinsters' Ball at that hotel.
>
> (Wood, 1963)

That article, published in the *Baltimore Sun* in February 1963, went on to explain that Hattie Carroll had been hit with a cane by farm owner William Zantzinger. Mrs Carroll was a black woman with 10 children. She died in hospital from internal haemorrhaging. Zantzinger, who was white, was arrested and released on bail. In August of that year he received a six months' jail sentence for manslaughter, and the story was picked up by other parts of the United States media. According to a report of the court case in *Time* magazine (1963): "The judges considerately deferred the start of the jail sentence until Sept 15, to give Zantzinger time to harvest his tobacco crop."

Fleetingly, the case was brought to national attention. Or, at least, to the attention of those paying attention, one of whom was a 22-year-old folk singer going by the name of Bob Dylan. Within days he had written *The Lonesome Death of Hattie Carroll.* "This is a true story," Dylan would tell audiences when introducing the song. "This was taken out of the newspapers. Nothing but the words have been changed" (quoted in Corcoran, 2003: 153). In what has been described as a "journalistic narrative" (Hajdu, 2001: 189), *The Lonesome Death of Hattie Carroll* introduces us to the characters, gives us the facts, fills in the background to the story, and builds layer upon layer of understanding. It has been described as "perhaps Dylan's most journalistic song" (Frazier, 2004), telling the story "with the economy of a news reporter and the imagery of a poet" (Sounes, 2002: 176). Dylan's words continue to speak to audiences down the years. Thanks to his song, countless thousands of people around the world have now heard the story of Hattie Carroll and William Zantzinger: a human interest story of two individuals that tells us something about society.

THE FIRST DUTY OF THE JOURNALIST

As with many journalists, Dylan has on occasions been accused of distorting the facts of a case to fit his own agenda (Heylin, 2001: 124–5). But Dylan is an artist, not a reporter. When a singer says that a song is true, their words are taken as meaning that the song is *based* on a true story, that the facts are *broadly* as indicated in the lyrics, and/or that the song is true to the emotion or spirit of real events. A reporter makes a very different promise; a promise that is implicit in all journalism. When a journalist says, "This is a true story," that is precisely what she or he means. That's why the very first clause of the international journalists' code – see Appendix 1 – declares: "Respect for truth and for the right of the public to truth is the first duty of the journalist." The International Federation of Journalists (IFJ) brings together journalists' organisations from more than 100 countries and, although few of their half-a-million members could recite the code in detail, most journalists understand the principle: that our job is indeed to get at the truth.

Which is not to say that journalists always report the truth, the whole truth, and nothing but the truth. Truth can be an elusive beast to hunt down, even without the help of those philosophers who tell us that it does not exist. And the truth can hurt. Consider the following three examples of truthful reporting.

After the *Derbyshire Times* reported that Brampton Rovers trounced Waltheof by 29 goals to nil in an under-nines football match, the Sheffield and District Junior Sunday League ordered clubs not to tell local newspapers the results of matches in which any team lost by more than 14 goals. This was apparently motivated by a desire to prevent the defeated children feeling humiliated (Scott, 2004). A minor example, perhaps, but it demonstrates that, for journalists, ethical considerations can arise when you least expect them, even when reporting the football scores.

In common with most local newspapers in the UK, the *Kenilworth Weekly News* routinely reports on sports days and other events at schools in its circulation area. But it was forced to stop publishing children's surnames after a bogus kidnapper caused intense distress by telephoning parents and claiming he had snatched their children. Police said the hoaxer had targeted parents whose children had been identified in newspaper coverage of primary school functions (Lagan, 2005). It is another example of a simple, everyday story having potential ethical implications.

Reporters covering the siege at Middle School Number One in the small Russian town of Beslan presumably acted in good faith when they reported the fact that relatives outside the school were receiving mobile phone calls from some of the hostages inside. But when the hijackers heard this on television they forced hostages to hand over their mobiles and shot a man for making a call (Walsh, 2004). It is a life-and-death example of the weighty responsibility borne by journalists, even when reporting accurately. But journalists do not always report accurately.

Not according to Eymen, at least. He is a Kurdish refugee who fled Saddam Hussein's regime in Iraq. Talking to a group of journalists in the UK, he told us about taking a call on his mobile one day: it was a friend, asking if he could help a new asylum seeker who had just arrived in town with nowhere to sleep, nothing to eat, and no money. The call came just as Eymen was passing a newspaper kiosk that displayed banner headlines about asylum seekers being housed in luxurious mansions. The irony was not lost on him. So obsessed are parts of the UK media with asylum seekers that, when they are absent from the front pages, he asks the shopkeeper: "What's the matter, have asylum seekers done nothing wrong today?" (quoted in Harcup, 2003a).

Such coverage is beyond a joke for Sandra Nyaira, former political editor of the *Daily News* in Zimbabwe and now a member of the Exiled Journalists Network in the UK, who explains:

> In the last year alone I have read articles, mostly in the tabloids, that blamed refugees, nay, asylum seekers … for the rapid spread of infectious diseases like TB, the dreaded HIV/Aids virus, Sars, as well as housing shortages and even terrorism … As soon as they land at Gatwick or Heathrow, they blight Britain's services. It is all sheer hypocrisy … The public trust most of the things they read in newspapers so journalists must be responsible in the way they present issues that directly affect the lives of others, especially those who are in no position to answer back.
>
> (Nyaira, 2004: 34–6)

Asylum seekers are people with histories and, therefore, with stories. But sections of the UK press too often seem intent on demonising them as a group – a label – rather than treating them as individuals with their own tales to tell. That is not just unethical journalism, it's bad journalism.

There is certainly too much stereotyping going under the banner of journalism, just as there is too much clichéd coverage, empty-headed celebrity-chasing, peering into people's bedrooms, hysterical yapping and yelping … and far, far too many columnists taking up resources that could be devoted to reporting. As the redoubtable journalist Paul Foot put it, when discussing "freedom of the press":

> Nothing wastes newspaper space more than columnists "letting off steam", especially if they are billed as "frank" or "fearless". There is nothing specially free about a courageous or fearless opinion which involves no courage or fear whatsoever.
>
> (Foot, 2000: 79)

Yet even our popular newspapers look positively highbrow in comparison to those "lads' mags" in which the height of journalistic ambition seems to be to persuade a model to pose in what one editor describes fondly as "subservient poses with her arse in the air" (quoted in Turner, 2005).

GOOD JOURNALISM

However, there is also journalism that can inform, surprise, challenge, shock, even inspire, as well as entertain. When I wake up in the morning I can turn on BBC Radio Four's *Today* programme, for example, and discover something that I didn't already know. I can even learn the "unknown unknowns" that (to paraphrase US Defense Secretary Donald Rumsfeld) I didn't know that I didn't know. It's far from perfect, and I often shout at the radio in exasperation, but listening to the *Today* programme invariably leaves me better informed, having been exposed to a mixture of reportage and discussion, interesting questions, and even the occasional straight answer. It is essential listening.

Similarly, I can never pick up a quality national newspaper without finding something to interest me. It might be the front-page splash or the hard news in the early pages, but it is just as likely to be an analytical backgrounder, a quirkily written, warts-and-all obituary, or a photograph that captures some moment of sporting ballet in all its glory. The UK "popular" papers may leave me cold with their tales about the antics of celebs, but such papers also have the ability to highlight social issues in as dramatic and powerful a manner as does any journalism anywhere on the globe. They can also make me laugh out loud. And there is something deeply pleasing about falling asleep at night listening to journalists describe a football match on the radio, then waking up and finding a newspaper on the doormat containing an account of the same game, complete with pictures. And if you don't want to wait for the morning, you can go online and get similar coverage almost instantly. It feels like magic, but in reality it's just people getting on with their jobs, often in difficult circumstances. Even the freebie *Metro* newspaper, despite its lack of investment in editorial staff, can provide enough clearly written bite-sized news items to brighten up a brief bus journey. It also has the potential to surprise, as with its description of a motorist who was fined for splashing pedestrians as a "puddle toll martyr"[1] (*Metro*, 3 November 2005).

The BBC and our national newspapers may be regarded as the regular "agenda setters" of journalism, but thousands of journalists work elsewhere in the media. There are magazines that cover virtually every subject imaginable, often with flair and imagination as well as specialist expertise. There is a minority ethnic press serving sections of the population that feel misrepresented or simply rendered invisible by much of the rest of the media. There are local and regional newspapers that – despite relentless staffing cuts – can still tell people more about what is going on where they live than they hear from their neighbours, and that can run lively campaigns on behalf of their readers. And there is *Private Eye*, which is in a must-read class of its own for most journalists.

On television there are investigative current affairs slots that – sometimes, at least – tell us things we don't already know. The powerful and challenging journalism of John Pilger can be found on ITV, albeit infrequently and usually late at night. There are 24-hour news channels that can broadcast live coverage of press conferences, parliamentary debates, and events such as a whale swimming into central London. There are broadcast journalists who do everything from distilling local events into brief bulletins on commercial radio to analysing world events at length every evening on the frequently excellent *Channel Four News*. There are journalists whose work goes straight onto the web, combining traditional elements of print, TV and radio reporting to make something new. And there are freelance reporters and news agencies who try to ensure that nobody can cough or spit on their patch without them hearing and, if possible, making a story about it. Beyond all that there are international media, mostly now available online. There also exist alternative media that make use of journalistic techniques to challenge and critique what we get from mainstream media (Harcup, 2005b; 2006).

Then there are the countless bloggers, whose online web logs include the good, bad and the ugly of the internet age, and who can inform, educate and entertain while "stretching the boundaries" of journalism (Allan, 2004: 180).

1 Anyone who doesn't understand the reference should look up the Tolpuddle Martyrs on the internet and delight in the fact that a sub on a throwaway freesheet was prepared to stretch his or her readers.

And there is the potential for citizens increasingly to get in on the act, believes broadcast journalist Jon Snow. He points to the way in which coverage of the "barbarity of American troops in Fallujah" was made possible because, although journalists were kept out of the Iraqi city, footage was taken by local people. "It has only been exposed because people have been able to take video and use the web to get it to us," says Snow. "The opportunities are fantastic. I just can't see the secret society surviving" (quoted in Kiss, 2006).

ETHOS OF THIS BOOK

There is, then, much to celebrate about journalism. But we cannot take good journalism for granted. The ethos of this book is that to be good journalists we need to be thinking journalists, or reflective practitioners. By this I mean that journalists should be encouraged to reflect critically on our job – both individually and collectively – *while* we are doing it. To date, much discussion of the ethical dimensions of journalism has been bogged down in worthy-but-abstract philosophising or sidetracked into treating ethics as a set of obstacles blocking journalists' paths. That is why this is not another book about ethics. It is a book about journalism.

Its starting point is that, as we have seen, *everything* journalists do – from reporting on a school sports day to covering international conflict – has potential ethical implications. Whether we recognise it or not, ethics are involved in every story we follow up or ignore; every interview we request; every conversation with a confidential source; every quote we use, leave out or tidy up; every bit of context we squeeze in, simplify or exclude; every decision to create (sorry, report) a "row"; every photograph we select or "improve"; every soundbite we choose to use; every approach from an advertiser trying to influence editorial copy; every headline we write; every question we ask or don't ask. For the ethical journalist, it is not enough to have a bulging contacts book or a good nose for news; being an ethical journalist also means asking questions about our own practice.

If everything that journalists do has ethical implications, it follows that no one book could possibly deal with all the ethical issues that may arise during a journalist's career. That is as true of the big issues – such as racism and sexism – as of specifics ranging from the embedding of war reporters to the selection of stick-thin models by women's magazines. So, this book will not cover every single issue ever faced by journalists, nor every type of society within which journalists operate. Although written primarily from a UK perspective, it seeks to highlight the key principles involved and to aid understanding of why and how journalism is practised. It will not attempt to lay down a series of do's and don'ts or provide a list of problems to be ticked off; still less will it attempt to provide a list of easy answers. Instead, it will explore a range of ethical considerations at a practical level, and discuss such considerations within the context of historical and contemporary ideas about what journalism is for. By discussing a range of ideas, arguments and examples – and by adopting a questioning, challenging approach – I hope it will support journalists and journalism students in thinking about the implications of what they are doing, in whatever medium and country they are doing it. The aim is to encourage critical analysis within the classroom and a more reflective practice within the newsroom, based on the idea that theory can inform practice and vice versa.

Not that we will all think alike, of course. Journalists should "become more self-reflective and less careless with their power", argues John Lloyd (2004: 141), a *Financial Times* journalist who is now a director of the Reuters Institute for the Study of Journalism at Oxford University. I agree with Lloyd on that, but the results of my reflections – on the Hutton Inquiry, for example (Harcup, 2005a) – are quite different from those in his influential lament about the state of UK journalism, *What the Media Are Doing to Our Politics*. When dealing with as messy a business as journalism, such a difference of opinion is inevitable; in fact, it is probably desirable. As John Stuart Mill put it in his famous *Essay on Liberty*:

> Truth … has to be made by the rough process of a struggle between combatants fighting under hostile banners … Only through diversity of opinion is there, in the existing state of human intellect, a chance of fair play to all sides of truth … [T]here is always hope when people are forced to listen to both sides; it is when they attend only to one that errors harden into prejudices …
>
> (Mill [1859] 1997: 26)

STRUCTURE OF THIS BOOK

This book will draw on the reflections of a range of journalists, on my own experience as both journalist and academic, on a large number of published sources, and on original research (including interviews conducted by the author in recent years). Issues and principles will be approached via specific examples and case studies, drawn from a range of media. Chapter 2 will look at why journalism matters to society and consider the implications of challenges to journalism ranging from the Hutton Report in the UK to the *New York Times* fakery case in the United States. Discussion of why journalism matters leads inevitably to the concept of journalists as a fourth estate, acting as a form of watchdog on government, and this will be addressed in Chapter 3. Fulfilling this watchdog role has led to some journalists using subterfuge, justifying their actions as being in the public interest. This public interest defence will form the basis of Chapter 4, which will explore investigative and undercover reporting. Chapters 5 and 6 will consider the implications of the choices made by journalists in selecting news stories and in their relationships with sources. All these issues will be discussed within the context of one particular genre of journalism – crime reporting – in Chapter 7. Chapters 8 and 9 will look at a range of what might be termed ethical interventions, first in the form of self-regulation and statutory regulation, then by tracing a hidden history of journalists standing up for ethical journalism. Finally, Chapter 10 will draw together the key themes of the book: that ethical journalism is good journalism and that good journalism is ethical journalism.

This book will discuss many of the pressures that, arguably, make it harder to practise good, ethical journalism; trends that, for some, came to a head at the British Press Awards in 2005, when the Scoop of the Year went to the *News of the World*'s "sensational … hugely entertaining" account of a footballer having sex with somebody who wasn't his wife (British Press Awards, 2005: 46). When the *News of the World* – aka *News of the Screws* – was also named National Newspaper of the Year, the decision dismayed those who believe that, in the words of media pundit Roy Greenslade (2005), "journalism is not about the size of a chequebook, dubious invasions of privacy and the weekly purveying of sleaze". Although the Newspaper of the Year prize was given to the redesigned *Guardian* the following year, Scoop of the Year once again went to a celebrity story, this time a tale about a model taking drugs (*Press Gazette*, 2006b). Whatever next? Final proof that bears defecate in the woods?

The idea that journalists should be content to entertain audiences with titillating tittle-tattle is an insidious one, argues Francis Williams, a thoughtful commentator on media affairs who was editor of the *Daily Herald*:

> The real danger facing a good deal of journalism today … is that it will be pressed into a pattern that denies it all purpose other than the purely commercial one of attracting the largest number of paying customers by whatever means comes most readily to hand … The defence of journalism as more than a trade and greater than an entertainment technique – although a trade it is and entertaining it must be – is properly the journalists' and no one else's.
>
> (Williams, 1959: 225)

Those words were written almost half a century ago, but – as with Bob Dylan's account of the death of Hattie Carroll – they speak to us still.

FURTHER READING

As a companion volume to *Journalism: principles and practice* (Harcup, 2004), this book is intended for those with some knowledge of the basics of journalism, gained through practice, study or both. It aims to build on such an understanding of the basics to improve the quality of journalism; at the same time, it will investigate the foundations of journalism to explore what it is all *for*. More specific suggestions for further reading will be made at the end of each chapter; full publication details for these appear in the References section. Meanwhile, you can read the lyrics of Bob Dylan's *The Lonesome Death of Hattie Carroll* at www.bobdylan.com or listen to the song on the CDs *The Times They Are A-Changin'* and *The Bootleg Series Vol 6: Bob Dylan Live 1964*.

2 WHY JOURNALISM MATTERS

It was quite a big story for a young reporter to be sent on: to go to the home town of a US soldier who was missing in action during the 2003 invasion of Iraq, to meet the family and describe their pain, with a bit of local colour thrown in. So the reporter flew from New York to San Antonio, hired a car that he would end up sleeping in, and headed south in the blazing heat. He drove down US 77 in the direction of Los Fresnos, a typical Texan town near the border with Mexico. He missed his exit, met a helpful man at a petrol station, and eventually arrived in the small, dusty town. He crossed some railroad tracks and found his way to the family home of the missing soldier. There he was shown a shrine to the missing Marine, and the family opened up to him, giving him plenty of quotes about their grief. He wrote it up, filed the copy to his newspaper, and headed back to New York with a hefty expenses claim, having fulfilled his brief.

The only trouble was, the young reporter had not spoken to the family and had never set foot in Los Fresnos. He had remained in his Brooklyn apartment all the time that he was supposed to be in Texas on behalf of the *New York Times* (Blair, 2004: 1–5; 294–5). As had become his habit, he had constructed the story by lifting quotes from news agencies and local newspapers, embellished with details drawn from a photographic archive. As the reporter in question, Jayson Blair, later explained:

> I lied and I lied – and then I lied some more. I lied about where I had been, I lied about where I had found information, I lied about how I wrote the story … It was a simple system of deception – my tools were my laptop, my cell phone, online archives and the photo database, which could be accessed from my kitchen table.
>
> (Blair, 2004: 1, 11)

BETRAYAL OF TRUST

He had been getting away with it for years but was eventually found out when a reporter on the *San Antonio Express-News* took the trouble to put in a call to the *New York Times*, pointing out similarities between her story on the missing Marine and Blair's subsequent one (Blair, 2004: 9; Mnookin, 2005: 104). After an internal investigation and some more lying, Blair resigned and on 11 May 2003 the *New York Times* published the embarrassing story on its front page. Its 13,000-word correction-from-hell began:

> A staff reporter for the *New York Times* committed frequent acts of journalistic fraud while covering significant news events in recent months … The widespread fabrication and plagiarism represent a profound betrayal of trust and a low point in the 152-year history of the newspaper … Every newspaper, like every bank and every police department, trusts its employees to uphold central principles, and the inquiry found that Mr Blair repeatedly violated the cardinal tenet of journalism, which is simply truth …
>
> (Quoted in Mnookin, 2005: 173–4)

Blair (2004: ix) conceded in his memoirs – for which he received a reported advance of $150,000 (Hanson, 2004: 399) – that his deceptions "have not only let down the employees of *The Times*, but also my family, my friends, my college professor and myself" . And, he might have added, his readers and his fellow citizens. Although Blair "had issues" – he was a black reporter in a mainly white organisation, and he also suffered from addiction and manic-depression – his is fundamentally a story about trust. Or, to be more precise, betrayal of trust.

If the Blair case is informative because it illustrates that trust is at the heart of good journalism, it is also instructive in indicating what can go wrong when fellow journalists feel their doubts are likely to be ignored. The warning signs had been apparent to some of his colleagues for some time, yet Blair was popular with those in charge of the newspaper, whose apparently dismissive attitude discouraged section editors from speaking up. As Seth Mnookin (2005: 157) observes, "a newsroom where editors are scared to voice their concerns is a disaster waiting to happen". Jayson Blair was that disaster.

Not that he was the first journalist to resort to invention. Perhaps most famously, Janet Cooke had to hand back the Pulitzer Prize she won for her heart-rending reports in the *Washington Post* about an 8-year-old heroin addict called Jimmy, when it was discovered that Jimmy existed only in her imagination (Sanders, 2003: 109). Again, as David Randall (2000: 138) notes, some of Cooke's colleagues had doubts but they "either thought it best to keep quiet, or thought the story 'too good to check'". Nor is fakery confined to the US. Granada Television in the UK, for example, was fined £2 million for a documentary, *The Connection*, in which supposed drug runners were in fact actors (Keeble, 2001a: 65). Deceit is "woven into the very nature of television", according to veteran journalist Max Hastings (2000: 92–93), who describes how some camera crews in war zones have encouraged soldiers to open fire so that they can film a dramatic episode that was missed when it actually happened.

Questions over the veracity of TV pictures were briefly and tragically brought to public attention in 2003, when other sections of the media "exposed" a Sky News item on the Iraq war that had failed to inform viewers that film of a nuclear submarine had been taken during an exercise rather than in combat. The offending item had been produced by experienced journalist James Forlong, who resigned and subsequently killed himself after failing to find another job. His death prompted his sister-in-law to write in the *Sunday Times*:

> Instead of the respect he should have been shown for his honesty, James was shunned and, worse still, ridiculed and humiliated ... Only those who have worked under the intense pressure of a war zone can really understand how mistakes can be made under such extreme conditions ... There was nothing "fake" about James Forlong. He was an honourable, decent, brave and extremely hard-working journalist who had the courage to admit he had made a mistake. I don't believe he was ashamed or had lost self-respect, as some reports have suggested. But as he paced the garden every day putting in calls to try to find work, he had moments of deep despair about how he would provide for his family. He learnt that acting decently yourself does not mean you will be treated decently in return. Perhaps his tragic death will give all those in the media pause for thought about their own courage, personal accountability and complete honesty at all times
>
> (Toomey, 2003)

Sky was later fined £50,000 by the Independent Television Commission, a forerunner of Ofcom, for breaching its rules on accuracy (Born, 2003).

It was publishing other pictures purportedly from the Iraq war that cost Piers Morgan his job as editor of the *Daily Mirror*; or, rather, it was the fact that he continued to defend their publication long after serious doubts had been raised about whether they genuinely showed British soldiers abusing Iraqi prisoners. "Sorry ... we were hoaxed", the newly Morgan-free paper declared in a front page apology after he had been frogmarched off the premises. It continued: "Our mission is to tell the truth ... If ever we fail, we are letting down the people who mean most to us. Our readers" (Allan, 2005: 1–2).

It is because journalists see our mission as getting at the truth that the Jayson Blair case – in which a journalist deliberately "fabricated history" (Mnookin, 2005: 162) – was so shocking. But it would be wrong to blame him for all of journalism's ills, argues commentator Paul McMasters (2004: 407), who says Blair is merely a symptom of a deeper malaise in which marketing the news has become more important than reporting the news. McMasters writes that the systematic shortcomings of a journalism that is "too sensational, too superficial, too immersed in celebrity, too invasive, too riddled with mistakes" are more damaging in the long run than the activities of "a gaggle of miscreants playing fast and loose with the truth".

JOURNALISM AND DEMOCRACY

The failures of journalists matter because journalism matters. And journalism matters, as Barbie Zelizer (2004: 204) puts it, "not in one prescribed way but in many ways and across many circumstances". Zelizer is a journalist-turned-professor in the US. A UK counterpart, Ian Hargreaves (2003: 25), similarly has no doubts about the importance of our craft: "I operate from the assumption that journalism matters not just to journalists, but to everyone: good journalism provides the information and opinion upon which successful democratic societies depend." This is hardly a new point. When the great English radical Tom Paine had some of his articles spiked by the *Pennsylvania Packet* in 1786, he told the editor that even privately owned newspapers had public duties, adding:

> If the freedom of the press is to be determined by the judgement of the printer of a newspaper in preference to that of the people, who when they read will judge for themselves, the[n] freedom is on a very sandy foundation.
>
> (Quoted in Keane, 1996: 261–2)

In the 1950s, Francis Williams reiterated the argument that journalism has a social obligation above and beyond the commercial considerations of the marketplace:

> The freedom of the press does not exist in order that newspaper owners should grow rich. It is not a possession of newspapers or their proprietors or editors but of the community, won by many who were not journalists, as well as many who were, during that long struggle for freedom of religion, opinion and association and for the independence of parliament, judiciary and press on which our democratic society rests.
>
> (Williams, 1959: 215)

Democracy means more than people having the right to elect representatives every few years, and journalists can play a role in facilitating more participatory and deliberative forms of democracy (Stromback, 2005). Participatory models of democracy, allowing citizens to speak for themselves, are intimately linked to the concept of social justice, writes the theorist Iris Young (2000: 17–23). She argues for a widening of "democratic inclusion … as a means of promoting more just outcomes". While the absence of a commitment to such democratic inclusion by much contemporary mainstream journalism has been noted by observers of the relationship between journalists and their sources (see Chapter 6), the idea of democratic inclusion appears to inform much of the work of alternative media (see the Indymedia mission statement in Appendix 9, for example).

A CRISIS OF TRUST?

Laments about the state of journalism go back a long way. At least as far back as 1648, when journalists were described as a "moth-eating crew of news-mongers" by *Mercurius Anti-Mercurius*, an early newsbook that bemoaned the state of affairs whereby "every Jack-sprat that hath but a pen in his ink-horn is ready to gather up the excrements of the kingdom" (quoted in Clarke, 2004: 24). Journalists have been accused of gathering up the excrements of the kingdom ever since, and journalism was described recently as "the single most depressing, misanthropic and indefensible vocation anyone can undertake" (SOTCAA, 2000). Ouch.

If the critics are to be believed, journalism has always just got worse; if it were a horse, it would be shot. "Journalism is in crisis," asserts political communication lecturer Roman Gerodimos (2004). Journalism is facing "the biggest crisis of its existence", agrees journalist Seth Mnookin (2005: 263). *Guardian* editor Alan Rusbridger (2005) has spoken of "a widespread feeling that newspapers are failing in their duty of truly representing the complexity of some of the most important issues in society", resulting in "really dreadful levels of trust". Trust, and the lack thereof, is crucial to an understanding of the role of journalism, argued philosopher Onora O'Neill in her influential series of Reith lectures:

> A free press is not an unconditional good. It is good because and insofar as it helps the public to explore and test opinions and to judge for themselves whom and what to believe. If powerful institutions are allowed to publish, circulate and promote material without indicating what is known and what is rumour; what is derived from a reputable source and what is invented, what is standard analysis and what is speculation; which sources may be knowledgeable and which are probably not, they damage our public culture and all our lives.
>
> (O'Neill, 2002)

It was to the accompaniment of this crisis chorus that John Lloyd's book *What the Media Are Doing to Our Politics* (2004) struck a chord with some of those who are sometimes dismissed as the "chattering classes" in the UK. Although Lloyd's assertion that cynical journalists are undermining democracy seems a bit rich, given the influence of political spin doctors these days (Franklin, 2004: 6), his book contributed to a wider debate that has encouraged journalists to reflect on what we do and why. For Lloyd (2004: 1, 143), as for most critical observers, journalism is too important to be left solely to market forces. That's because, although the market is good at providing entertainment, it is not so good at supporting citizenship. Yet it was the publicly funded BBC that drew much of Lloyd's wrath for broadcasting the now infamous "two-way" interview between presenter John Humphrys and reporter Andrew Gilligan on the BBC Radio Four *Today* programme.

Here is the full text of the exchange – complete with repetitions and "erms", courtesy of the official transcript – that was broadcast at 6.07am on 29 May 2003:

JH: The government is facing more questions this morning over its claims about weapons of mass destruction in Iraq. Our defence correspondent is Andrew Gilligan. This in particular, Andy, is Tony Blair saying, they'd be ready to go within 45 minutes.

AG: That's right. That was the central claim in his dossier which he published in September, the main [erm] case, if you like, against [er] against Iraq and the main statement of the British government's belief of what it thought Iraq was up to. And what we've been told by one of the senior officials in charge of drawing up that dossier was that, actually, the government probably [erm] knew that that 45 minute figure was wrong, even before it decided to put it in. What this person says, is that a week before the publication date of the dossier, it was actually rather [erm] a bland production. It didn't – the, the draft prepared for Mr Blair by the Intelligence Agencies – actually didn't say very much more than was public knowledge already and [erm] Downing Street, our source says, ordered a week before publication, ordered it to be sexed up, to be made more exciting and ordered more facts to be [er] to be discovered.

JH: When you say 'more facts to be discovered', does that suggest that they may not have been facts?

AG: Well [erm] our source says that the dossier, as it was finally published, made the Intelligence Services unhappy [erm] because, to quote [erm] the source, he said there was basically, that there was, there was, there was unhappiness because it didn't reflect the considered view they were putting forward. That's a quote from our source and essentially [erm] the 45 minute point [er] was, was probably the most important thing that was added. [Erm] and the reason it hadn't been in the original draft was that it was, it was only [erm], it only came from one source and most of the other claims were from two, and the intelligence agencies say they don't really believe it was necessarily true because they thought the person making the claim had actually made a mistake, it got, had got mixed up.

JH: Does any of this matter now, all this, all these months later? The war's been fought and won.

AG: Well the 45 minutes isn't just a detail, it did go to the heart of the government's case that Saddam was an imminent threat and it was repeated four times in the dossier, including by the Prime Minister himself, in the foreword. So I think it probably does matter. Clearly, you know, if [erm], if it, if it was, if it was wrong – things do, things are got wrong in good faith – but if they knew it was wrong before they actually made the claim, that's perhaps a bit more serious.

JH: Andrew, many thanks; more about that later.

(BBC, 2003b)

There certainly was more about that later, and we will return to the story of Tony Blair's dossier in Chapter 6.

For Lloyd (2004: 8–13), the broadcast quoted above "broke most of the proclaimed rules of journalistic inquiry" because it, in effect, accused the Blair government of lying; it was an "accident waiting to happen", caused by the cynical and politically damaging journalistic presumption that politicians are likely to be acting in bad faith (Lloyd, 2004: 10–13). The broadcast was subjected to detailed scrutiny during the Hutton Inquiry and Lord Hutton came down hard on Gilligan, who resigned shortly after the official report was published.

Three years on, by which time he had re-emerged as a staff journalist on the London *Evening Standard*, I met Andrew Gilligan and asked, among other things, what he made of the Lloyd thesis. He was clearly unimpressed:

> Journalism is under attack by a number of forces. The principal complaint seems to be that journalism is untruthful and corrupting of the political process, and I simply don't think that's factually correct. I think the political process is corrupted by *politicians*. I cannot think of a single lie told by journalists. Journalists habitually exaggerate, but I lose count of the number of times I'm lied to as a journalist. We are far more sinned against than sinning.

He accepts that a lot of citizens feel disconnected from the political process, but he blames the politicians for this rather than the journalists who report on their activities.

What about the charge that cynical and over-aggressive reporting undermines trust between journalists and politicians?

> Look, journalists and politicians on the whole shouldn't trust each other, apart from on the most basic level. I think there should be a basic level of trust that you will not betray a confidence, that you won't misquote and that kind of thing. But they shouldn't be friends. I don't think they should be at daggers drawn and hate each other and constantly undermine each other, but they shouldn't trust each other. The audience – that's who we work for, we don't work for the politicians.

The real problem with journalism these days, Gilligan argues, is not untruthfulness. Rather, it is a lack of seriousness, "by which I mean asking really hard questions about really important things".

Although there was widespread journalistic dismay at the way in which Lord Hutton's report exonerated the Blair government at the expense of the

BBC, journalists were divided on the extent to which Andrew Gilligan was the author of his own misfortune. "Gilligan got more right than he got wrong," commented *Guardian* editor Alan Rusbridger (2004: viii). Yet many others felt that Gilligan had blown what could have turned out to be a hugely significant story, if he had been able to back it up. "I am not one of those who would argue that Andrew Gilligan was 'mainly right'," said Richard Sambrook (2004), then director of BBC News, adding: "In journalism 'mainly right' is like being half pregnant – it's an unsustainable condition." Gilligan agrees that, although journalism is necessarily a rough draft, being half right is not good enough:

> But 90 per cent right, maybe even 95 per cent right which is what it was, *is* good enough. Journalists should not be obliged to behave like lawyers, because that would stifle a lot of important journalism. I think Hutton had a view that it is like the law, where you talk to somebody and you draw up a memorandum of understanding, you then have it signed and put it in a filing cabinet. And journalism is not like that. I'm not saying that's any excuse for inaccuracy, but lawyers have power to demand information, or they work for clients who freely give them information. Journalists have nothing like such powers. We are trying to open a cupboard and shine a torch around – a feeble torch in a very large cupboard – and we don't know what's in the bits of the cupboard we can't see, and some of those bits are deliberately not shown to us.

In an odd twist, Sambrook's "half pregnant" argument was rejected by Rear Admiral Nick Wilkinson, a former secretary of the Defence, Press and Broadcasting Advisory Committee, a peculiarly British invention that allows media bosses and Whitehall mandarins to meet occasionally and discuss what they don't want the rest of us to know about. Wilkinson (2004) pointed out that, if journalists always had to wait until they were certain that they were more than mainly right, "little would be revealed to the public of what was going on behind the politico-official screen, and how relieved my ex-colleagues there would be". He continued: "In this case, we now know (and many were fairly certain then) that Andrew Gilligan was more 'mainly right' than the US/UK political leadership was." Gilligan himself told the Edinburgh television festival that

> Journalism got closer to the truth, more quickly, over the dossier than politics, than the law, than parliament or anything else. The only stories I'm really ashamed of on *Today* in the run-up to war are the ones where I tamely accepted at face value what the likes of Colin Powell and Jack Straw were telling us. That kind of journalism doesn't get anyone into trouble, of course. But far more of it was inaccurate than any original story I was responsible for.
>
> (Gilligan, 2004)

In the United States, meanwhile, the *Washington Post*, the *New York Times* and *New Republic* all subsequently apologised to their readers for being too gullible or for underplaying scepticism when reporting White House claims that Iraq had weapons of mass destruction (Younge, 2004). Those newspapers, it seems, felt they had damaged the trust between journalists and citizens not by being too sceptical of their government, but by being too trusting.

A MORALLY INDEFENSIBLE TRADE?

Journalism, then, is about "something larger than a commercial relationship between a publisher and a customer" (Hargreaves, 2003: 174). If journalism wasn't about more than a commercial transaction, if it didn't really matter, if trust between journalist and audience wasn't vital, then how could we explain the serious repercussions when trust breaks down? Trust is something that should concern all journalists, not just those reporting on war and peace. Consider the case of Willie Mack, editor of the *Southern Reporter* newspaper in Scotland, for example. Mack felt compelled to resign after he accidentally published a dummy picture caption describing a group of local people as "pious little bleeders [who] should get out more often" (*Independent*, 2004). It was just a newsroom joke that was never intended for publication, but his position on the newspaper became untenable because the people in the picture were also his readers, and the bond of trust had been broken.

All such talk of trust rings hollow for Janet Malcolm, who opened her book *The Journalist and the Murderer* with the following dramatic passage:

> Every journalist who is not too stupid or too full of himself [*sic*] to notice what is going on knows that what he does is morally indefensible. He is a kind of confidence man, preying on people's vanity, ignorance, or loneliness, gaining their trust and betraying them without remorse.
>
> (Malcolm, 2004: 3)

"Can that really be?" asks Ian Jack in his introduction to the UK edition of Malcolm's book. He continues:

> Every journalist, all kinds of journalism? The foreign correspondent at the scene of the flood, the court-reporter, the fashion writer, the stock analyst? Their work may be flawed and inadequate. It may even, in the case of the share-tipper, be corrupt. But it is hard to see what they do, always and universally, as "morally indefensible".
>
> (Jack, 2004: x)

Yet Malcolm has only just started. Still on her first page, the words "treachery" and "deception" are used to describe the relationship between journalists and the people about whom they write. Her book describes a real-life relationship between journalist Joe McGinniss and convicted murderer Jeffrey MacDonald; a relationship in which, to cut a long story short, MacDonald is under the impression that the journalist believes his protestations of innocence but is then “betrayed” upon publication of the story. It all ends in tears and court cases for the two central characters, but for Malcolm (2004: 4, 20) it has a wider resonance; for her, the “deliberately induced delusion, followed by a moment of shattering revelation” inflicted upon MacDonald was actually “a grotesquely magnified version of the normal journalistic encounter”.

Malcolm (2004: 32) is struck by the fact that people keep talking to journalists – placing “crazy” and “childish” trust in their good faith – despite the near certainty of being betrayed by them. But there is another way of looking at that. Perhaps people continue to talk to journalists because, most of the time, they are *not* betrayed or stitched up. Some might argue that Dr David Kelly was “crazy” to trust Andrew Gilligan, but Kelly had spoken to him and many other journalists before, without apparently suffering any moments of “shattering revelation”. And what of the people who contacted journalist Paul Foot over many years and who asked him to investigate alleged miscarriages of justice; people who opened their hearts and often their homes to him in the hope that his journalism might be able to get at the truth? Were they betrayed? Not according to the many testimonies from sources and contacts sent in unsolicited following his death:

> Paul could be trusted with anything we told him … A brilliant journalist who never betrayed a source … He was a considerate caring person … He took the time to understand the extremely complex and arcane issues, read about them, check with other sources, supplement the facts and would double-check his facts and often his copy with us and he never left any of his sources exposed.
>
> (*Private Eye*, 2004)

Not every journalist is a Paul Foot, of course; but nor is every journalist a faker, a plagiarist, or a confidence trickster preying on people’s vanity. Someone who was interviewed many times by journalists in the months after he survived the London bombings of 7 July 2005 was John Tulloch, a media studies academic at Brunel University. Although on some occasions he felt “more or less pushed into an interview that I didn’t want to give”, on others he felt pleased with the sensitive and accurate way that journalists reported his views (Tulloch, 2006: 175–180).

I wonder if Andrew Gilligan has ever read *The Journalist and the Murderer*? Yes, he tells me:

> I think it’s preposterous. Frankly, our sources use us as much as we use them. There is a case to answer in the case of somebody unsophisticated who is entrapped by a tabloid reporter into divulging details that are not in their interests to divulge, but I don’t do that kind of journalism. People talk for a reason.

If people talk for a reason, why did he agree to my request for an interview for this book?

> Because I've got nothing to hide about what I did, I freely admitted I didn't get it all right, but I really do think that journalism and me were far more sinned against than sinning. And I do believe it's important to talk to people, because if you don't you can't blame them for not giving your side of the story.

It is because journalism is one of the key ways in which citizens are informed and misinformed that we should be prepared to wash our dirty linen in public and to engage in discussions about our work, even when to do so might be uncomfortable. The ethical codes collected in the appendices of this book have resulted from such discussions and, although no code represents the final word on any issue, reference to them can usefully inform our practice.

Journalist Gerry Brown (1995: 315) concluded his autobiographical account of tabloid investigations with the words: "Listen, pal, I don't tell you how to do your job ..." It was a neat rhetorical payoff. However, as an argument it fails to convince, because journalism has an impact on society as a whole and therefore other people *do* have a stake in how we do our jobs as journalists. Imperfect though it is, journalism is one of the key ways in which we can gain knowledge about the world in which we live. And, as will be discussed in the next chapter, knowledge is power.

FURTHER READING

Two eminently readable books written by reflective journalists, containing a wealth of relevant insight, are Randall (2000) and Marr (2005). Evidence presented to the Hutton Inquiry is available on the website – www.the-hutton-inquiry.org.uk – but for a more handy edited version, see Coates (2004), and for commentary on the Inquiry, try Rogers (2004). Lessons for BBC journalists from Hutton can be found in the Neil Report, which was endorsed by BBC Governors (Neil, 2004). Hutton is dealt with at length in chapters 1, 12, 13 and 14 of *Inside Story* by Greg Dyke (2004), who critiques the official findings in a way that the BBC declined to do following the governors' decision to sack Dyke as the corporation's Director-General.

To explore arguments about the current state of journalism, check out Lloyd (2004) and Allan (2005); see Allan (2004) too, which also includes specific chapters exploring gender and race. Chambers and others (2004) record the experiences of women working as journalists, while the Society of Editors has produced a useful guide to reporting a "multi-cultural, multi-faith" community (Elliott, 2005). For more on why journalism matters, see Hargreaves (2003) and Zelizer (2004). The concept of democracy is explored further in Young (2000), Norris (2000), Bohman (2004) and Stromback (2005).

Janet Malcolm's (2004) challenge to journalism's claims about itself, *The Journalist and the Murderer*, is rather sweeping but nonetheless thought-provoking stuff. The issue of a journalist's alleged betrayal of a subject is also the central theme of the film *Capote*, directed by Bennett Miller, which tells the story of how Truman Capote ([1965] 2000) researched his classic book, *In Cold Blood*. See Klein (2006) for a discussion of some of the ethical issues raised in the movie.

For a detailed account of the Jayson Blair affair at the *New York Times*, the best starting point is Mnookin (2005). The issue of faking also lies at the heart of the film *Shattered Glass*, directed by Billy Ray, which recounts the tale of a journalist on *New Republic* magazine whose stories were literally too good to be true.

3 KNOWLEDGE IS POWER

"Knowledge is power," as the philosopher and scientist Francis Bacon proclaimed 400 years ago (Wheen, 2004: 6). It was dangerous talk. The spreading of knowledge, or the questioning of what is commonly accepted as knowledge, has long been a risky business. As far back as the 1160s, alleged heretics were sentenced by a court in Oxford to be branded and flogged for publicly questioning Church doctrine; they were comparatively lucky, because some who came after them were burned at the stake or had their tongues bored with hot irons for similar offences (Coleman, 1997: 1–5). With the invention of the printing press in the fifteenth century, the communication of such dangerous ideas was revolutionised; and the impulse of the authorities was to restrict the growth of this potentially democratising new information technology. King Henry VIII's right-hand man, Cardinal Wolsey, put it rather melodramatically: "We must destroy the press; or the press will destroy us" (quoted in Porter, 2000: 477).

Destroying the press was not possible, however, and even restricting it was to prove far easier said than done because, if Bacon's dictum could be seen as dangerous, it was also attractive. It was attractive to the Enlightenment thinkers who came after him, for whom knowledge and reason went hand in hand; and it was attractive to those who attended public lectures on matters of scientific inquiry and frequented the new coffee houses of the late seventeenth and early eighteenth centuries (Keane, 1996: 43). The coffee house, notes Martin Conboy (2004: 50–1), was literally "the space of exchange which corresponds to Habermas' public sphere", a reference to the concept of a public sphere of rational discussion as identified by the cultural theorist Jürgen Habermas (1989). If the coffee house was a space within which news, views and gossip could be passed on and/or challenged, the printing press became "the great engine for the spread of enlightened views and values" (Porter, 2000: 91).

Two centuries after Bacon used the phrase, "knowledge is power" was adopted by the romantic poet Samuel Taylor Coleridge for the masthead of the political journal, *Watchman* (Porter, 2000: 132, 462). It was also used by the creators of a later radical press that set out to inform a broader citizenry: "knowledge is power" was the motto of the *Poor Man's Guardian* newspaper, founded in 1830 and affiliated to the National Union of the Working Classes (Williams, 1998: 37). Such publications were more likely to be read in pubs than in bourgeois coffee houses, and the practice of reading aloud multiplied their audience way beyond their sales (Rose, 2002: 84), helping to create a "plebeian public sphere" alongside the bourgeois public sphere (Habermas, 1989: xviii).

STIFLING INDEPENDENT VOICES

The idea that knowledge is power remains attractive, and dangerous, today. In 2006, for example, armed police officers raided the offices of media organisations in Kenya, closing a TV station, disabling a printing press, burning thousands of newspapers and arresting several journalists (Vasagar, 2006). Two years earlier, in the UK, web servers belonging to the alternative online news service Indymedia were seized by police (*Journalist*, 2004c). And a leaked memo even suggested that US President George Bush had considered bombing the headquarters of Arab television station Al-Jazeera (Maguire and Lines, 2005). Nothing came of that, but journalists working for Al-Jazeera have suffered raids, arrests, expulsions, beatings and even missile attacks (Miles, 2005). They are not the only ones. Every year dozens of journalists around the world pay with their lives for putting into practice the belief that knowledge is power. As the International Federation of Journalists reports:

> [J]ournalists and media employees in every corner of the globe have been targeted, brutalised and done to death by the enemies of press freedom. Some have been deliberately sought out by crooks and hired assassins. Others have been gunned down as a result of nervous, unruly and ill-disciplined soldiering. Many succumbed because they appeared to be in the wrong place at the wrong time. But it wasn't the wrong place, of course. Journalists have a duty to be on the spot when news is in the making.
>
> (IFJ, 2005a: 1)

Although many journalists are killed in international war zones, most journalist casualties die in their own countries while reporting on domestic issues such as corruption, crime and politics (Tomlin and Pike, 2005). The vast majority of journalists killed at work are not hit by crossfire but are targeted for murder because of their journalistic work, and in most cases the killers go unpunished, according to studies by the Committee to Protect Journalists (CPJ, 2005b).

Parts of twenty-first-century Africa have been described as a "serious danger zone" for journalists. Guy-Andre Kieffer, for example, was a 54-year-old freelance journalist in the Ivory Coast who disappeared without trace while working on a series of investigative stories; in the weeks leading up to his disappearance in April 2004, he received death threats because of his reporting (IFJ, 2005a: 4–5). In Latin America too, journalists have come under violent attack from both political and criminal organisations. "The reasons for the killings are always the same," says the IFJ (2005a: 6), "to stifle independent voices and punish journalists who tell the truth." Journalists such as Francisco Arratia Saldierna, 55, who was kidnapped, tortured and killed in Mexico after writing about sensitive issues including drug-trafficking, corruption and organised crime (IFJ, 2005a: 10).

In Asia, according to the International Press Institute (IPI, 2005: 114), murder is just "one of the many forms of censorship"; and China and Burma are "still holding high numbers of journalists in prison, mostly in inhumane conditions, because of their reports both in newspapers and magazines as well as on the internet". For seven years running, up to and including 2005, China was named by the Committee to Protect Journalists as the country that jails the most journalists (CPJ, 2005a). One of the 32 Chinese journalists being held in prison at the end of that year was Shi Tao, who received the committee's International Press Freedom Award. Shi, who edits a business newspaper and works as a freelance online journalist, is serving a 10-year sentence for revealing state secrets. Shi was imprisoned in November 2004 for posting online details of the Chinese government's instructions on how the country's media were to cover the fifteenth anniversary of the military crackdown in Tiananmen Square (CPJ, 2005a).

In parts of the Middle East, in addition to the large numbers of journalists killed covering the conflict in Iraq, publications are being censored or shut down and "journalists are being threatened, dismissed and imprisoned" (IPI, 2005: 265). For their part, European governments also sometimes opt to close newspapers and send journalists to prison but more often use less crude means to influence media by "manipulating coverage, taxes, and legislation" (IPI, 2005: 188). And in the United States there have been more journalists facing prison sentences and fines for refusing to reveal confidential sources of information (IPI, 2005: 92). Clearly, then, there are people around the world who feel very threatened by the work of journalists. And so they should. Because journalism *is* a threat to those who profit from ignorance, whether that be a corrupt political elite, a faceless corporation, an organised criminal gang, a legal system that takes short-cuts, or a conman who preys on vulnerable victims.

THE UNBRIDLED PEN

The concept of access to knowledge being empowering informs serious journalism; that is, the sort of journalism guided by ethical codes of practice of the kind collected in the appendices of this book. Of course, that's not the only type of journalism on offer in the marketplace these days, and a glance at more entertainment-driven products such as the *Daily Sport*, *Nuts* or *Zoo* suggests a complementary aphorism: ignorance is powerlessness. If the downside of press freedom is that people are free to produce material that treats their audience as stupid – and encourages them to be so – the upside is that freedom of the press can facilitate the participation by citizens in rational discussion of public affairs of the day. As the seventeenth-century poet John Milton ([1644] 2005: 71, 101) put it in his famous defence of the "unbridled" pen: "Give me the liberty to know, to utter, and to argue freely according to conscience, above all liberties."

Milton's views did not come from nowhere but were rooted in the social ferment of his time, when England was in the midst of civil warfare and, in the words of historian Christopher Hill (1975: 14), there was a state of "glorious flux and intellectual excitement". Just a few years earlier, King Charles I had tightened further the already strict censorship of the printed word, but the system began to fall apart in the build-up to the Civil War. Someone who was jailed before, during and after the Civil War for being "one of the notoriousest dispersers of scandalous bookes in the kingdom" was John Lilburne, leader of the radical Levellers movement (Gregg, 2000: 53). In 1638 the King's Star Chamber sentenced him to be whipped while walking behind a cart from Fleet Street to Westminster in London. Lilburne suffered around 500 strokes from the whip on the journey before being placed in a pillory, whereupon he proceeded to make a fiery speech to the people who had gathered to watch. After being gagged he pulled some pamphlets from his pocket and scattered them among the crowds, who then cheered "free-born John" back to Fleet Prison (Gregg, 2000: 64–66). Undaunted by such punishments, the Levellers and others continued to regard printing – with secret presses and distribution networks – as crucial in the effort to "undeceive the people" (Gregg, 2000: 173). Arguably, a similar desire to "undeceive" fellow citizens is felt by those who produce alternative media today, ranging from the network of Indymedia websites to the blogs of individuals such as Dahr Jamail, who reports from inside Iraq (http://dahrjamailiraq.com).

When tight control of the press unravelled, and ended for a brief period from 1641, there was an extraordinary increase in the number of pamphlets and other literature printed and circulated (Williams, 2005: 8–9). According to Henry Wickham Steed, a press historian and former editor of *The Times*:

> Regular English journalism began with the Civil War and the political strife that led up to it. From the outset it was vivacious and, on the whole, truthful ... It was not by accident that the first English newspapers took shape between 1640 and 1688 ... for at no time in English history had so many conflicting political ideas and passions filled the public mind, or had the essentials of political freedom been so fiercely debated.
>
> (Steed, 1938: 110–12)

Numerous newsbooks (prototype newspapers) appeared on both – or, rather, *all* – sides of this political and social conflict, combining the reporting of domestic news and political comment. Such journalism both reflected and fostered a period of intense democratic participation in public debate, with the Levellers among those petitioning against all restrictions on printing (Williams, 1998: 20). Indeed, Levellers within the New Model Army – which was defending parliament against the King's forces – demanded and won the right to have a printing press which they used to contribute to an extraordinary series of debates within the army itself (Foot, 1994: 64). "For a short time," notes Hill (1975: 361), "ordinary people were freer from the authority of church and social superiors than they had ever been before, or were for a long time to be again."

Having briefly felt this "breath of reason" in the air, Milton ([1644] 2005: 69) was horrified when parliament re-imposed the previous system of pre-publication censorship, so he wrote *Areopagitica: a speech for the liberty of unlicensed printing* and published it himself, as an unlicensed pamphlet in defiance of the new law. "He who destroys a good book, kills reason itself," argued Milton, utilising the imagery of a poet to bring his political message alive:

> Methinks I see in my mind a noble and puissant nation rousing herself like a strong man after sleep, and shaking her invincible locks: methinks I see her as an eagle mewing her mighty youth, and kindling her undazzled eyes at the full midday beam; purging and unsealing her long-abused sight at the fountain itself of heavenly radiance; while the whole noise of timorous and flocking birds, with those also that love the twilight, flutter about, amazed at what she means, and in their envious gabble would prognosticate a year of sects and schisms. What should ye do then, should ye suppress all this flower crop of knowledge and new light sprung up and yet springing daily in this city? Should ye set an oligarchy of twenty engrossers over it, to bring a famine upon our minds again, when we shall know nothing but what is measured to us by their bushel?
>
> ([1644] 2005: 69, 100)

Such writing knocks spots off many of today's opinion formers who like to think they have a way with words. You couldn't make it up, as tabloid columnist Richard Littlejohn might say.

Despite Milton's plea, the short-lived parliamentary regime and the restored monarchy both clung on to the power to license and censor the press for several more decades. *Areopagitica*, as Granville Williams (2005: 6) notes, received little attention when first published, but "the reputation of the work grew later in the seventeenth century, when it was abridged and cited by others in debates on censorship and the freedom of the press". This culminated in the lapse of the Licensing Act in 1695, effectively ending pre-publication censorship of printing in what was to become the UK. Milton's central argument, that "ideas should be tested and debated in the public domain rather than censored or suppressed" (Williams, 2005: 56), continues to resonate more than 300 years later. His words remind us that the relative freedoms enjoyed by journalists in some parts of the world today were not handed to us on a plate but were achieved as a result of what was "a saga of struggle against unjust laws, of assertion of the people's right to disobey them, of valour in the defence, and to a large degree, in the very creation of British democracy" (Harrison, 1974: 9). All the more galling, therefore, to see the casual way in which some journalists regard our rights and responsibilities today.

THE FOURTH ESTATE

The ending of pre-publication censorship and the further development of printing technology cleared the ground for a local, regional and national press to spring up and for journalism to develop as a skilled occupation, if never quite a profession. As with its pre-history, the subsequent growth of the press was neither uniform nor uncontested. Journalists could still be prosecuted *after* publication for a range of offences, including seditious or blasphemous libel. Government-imposed stamp duties made lawful newspapers too expensive for most people to afford, while anyone caught producing or selling the cheaper "unstamped" underground press was liable to be thrown into jail. Before, during and after such "taxes on knowledge" were abolished in the mid-nineteenth century, a commercial press devoted to profit developed alongside – and eventually helped to marginalise – a more radical press devoted to ideas.

This emergent commercial press did not share the insurgent stance of the radical press that had blossomed at times of intense political activity such as the English Civil War, the French Revolution, and the Chartist agitation. But, in its own more restrained and constrained way, it too began to train a watchful eye on what our rulers were getting up to in our name. The press came to be known as the "fourth estate" of the realm (alongside the House of Commons, the House of Lords and the clergy), playing the quasi-constitutional "watchdog" role of monitoring those in power on behalf of the people. This role was explained in a famous *Times* leader published on 6 February 1852, which declared:

> The first duty of the press is to obtain the earliest and most correct intelligence of the events of the time, and instantly, by disclosing them, make them the common property of the nation … For us, with whom publicity and truth are the air and light of existence, there can be no greater disgrace than to recoil from the frank and accurate disclosure of facts as they are. We are bound to tell the truth as we find it, without fear of consequences.
>
> (Quoted in Clarke, 2004: 231)

It is rarely quite as simple as that. The history of journalism is a contradictory one that has included journalists in the pay of corrupt politicians working alongside journalists who have gone to jail for exposing corrupt politicians; intellectually challenging publications competing with crime-ridden scandal sheets; and the power of the censor replaced by the power of the market. Yet, despite such apparent contradictions, the idea of the journalist as a watchdog remains a vibrant one; prompting recent *Times* editor Simon Jenkins (2006) to describe newspapers as the "greatest democratising force in history".

Journalism should indeed serve as "an independent monitor of power", according to the statement of principles drawn up by the Committee of Concerned Journalists in the US (see Appendix 7). One of the most celebrated examples of journalists fulfilling this role is the Watergate case, during which *Washington Post* reporters Carl Bernstein and Bob Woodward (1974) exposed the political dirty tricks and subsequent cover up by US President Richard Nixon. Nixon, aka "Tricky Dicky", resigned before he could be impeached, and the two reporters became journalistic heroes played by Dustin Hoffman and Robert Redford in the film-of-the-book-of-the-investigation, *All The President's Men*. Ben Bradlee, executive editor of the *Washington Post* during Watergate, later told a James Cameron memorial lecture in London:

> Governments prefer a press that makes their job easier, a press that allows them to proceed with minimum public accountability, a press that accepts their version of events with minimum questioning, a press that can be led to the greenest pastures by persuasion and manipulation. In moments of stress between government and the press … the government looks for ways to control the press, to eliminate or to minimise the press as an obstacle in the implementation of policy, or the solution of problems. In these moments, especially, the press must continue its mission of publishing information that it – and it alone – determines to be in the public interest, in a useful, timely and responsible manner, serving society, not government.
>
> (Bradlee [1987] 2001: 18)

A challenge to this narrative of journalists as heroic seekers of truth comes from Julian Petley, an academic who chairs the Campaign for Press and Broadcasting Freedom in the UK. He believes we need to reconsider the extent to which the commercial press has ever operated as a fourth estate, monitoring and limiting the powers of the state:

> [T]he repeal of the stamp duty and of other "taxes on knowledge" in the nineteenth century was not motivated by governmental conversion to the cause of press freedom; it stemmed, rather, from the growing realisation among politicians and other members of the establishment that if entrepreneurs and industrialists could be tempted to enter the newspaper market then this could kill off the hated radical press far more effectively than taxes had ever done … [T]he powers-that-be intended the press to be used as an agent of social control and regulation rather than as a means of popular enlightenment.
>
> (Petley, 2004a: 68–75)

A similar argument about journalism today is that it fails to live up to its self-proclaimed watchdog role because of structural problems such as a collusive relationship between media corporations and politicians, the privileging of market values over social values, an over-reliance on elite sources, and a limited ideological aperture through which events tend to be viewed. Media commentators Stephen Baker and Greg McLaughlin, for example, argue that the failure of most mainstream journalism "to ask the appropriate questions of those in power has had a corrosive effect not just upon the traditions of journalism, but upon the democratic process itself". They continue:

> Received wisdom would indicate that [journalism's] role is to serve to inform the public, to encourage public debate, and to scrutinise the actions of the powerful and hold them to account, but it has palpably failed on critical occasions to fulfil any of these important functions.
>
> (Baker and McLaughlin, 2005: 5)

Although few journalists can hope to bring down a president – let alone an entire economic or social system – there are reporters out there every day doing their best to monitor the powerful and to ask the awkward questions. In the press galleries and corridors of our parliament buildings – as in many of our courts and council chambers – there are journalists taking notes and looking for stories. There are journalists using Freedom of Information legislation as well as well-placed anonymous sources, probing everything from decisions about war to the nutritional value of school dinners. Journalists have exposed miscarriages of justice, security scandals and corruption in high places, as well as informing us about developments in education, health, business and numerous other issues large and small. At the most local level, when a National Health Service Trust refused to allow people to have a second chemist's shop in their village in the English Midlands, the Trust saw fit to take this momentous decision behind closed doors with press and public excluded. Only after journalists on the local weekly

Newark Advertiser objected "in a very forthright manner" did the Newark and Sherwood Primary Care Trust agree to hold future meetings in public (Ponsford, 2004b). Such vigilance by local media is as much a part of the fourth estate function of the press as is the monitoring of the big issues of war, peace, poverty and climate change. We are probably more likely to find out about a contentious planning application at the end of our street by seeing it mentioned in the local paper than we are by reading a notice on a lamp-post; and how many of us have met our councillor or MP in person, rather than through the eyes and ears of the local media?

Of course, these are not the only things journalists do; journalists don't always do them well; some critics dismiss the fourth estate as a myth; and some journalists hardly bother at all with the fourth estate role. Too many rights won by earlier generations of journalists are wasted today. Given the lengths to which the MP John Wilkes and his *North Briton* newspaper went to establish the freedom of the press to publish accounts of parliamentary debates from 1771 – Wilkes was locked up in the Tower of London for his pains (Harrison, 1974: 19) – it is a pity that even serious newspapers in the UK now regard gallery reporting as an anachronism, worth devoting space to only on special occasions. Similarly, lobbying by the National Union of Journalists got it enshrined in law in 1908 that journalists should be admitted to all meetings of local authorities except in exceptional circumstances, and even then the press could be excluded only after a vote in public by councillors (Bundock, 1957: 22); yet more and more newsrooms seem to rely these days on press releases rather than on the more time-consuming business of sending reporters to cover meetings and develop their contacts. Eileen Brooks, former head of communications for a local authority in South Yorkshire, observes: "Ironically, the only media presence in the council chamber at Rotherham these days are students from the journalism degree course at Sheffield University. But will they be there when they're out in the real world?" (quoted in Humphries, 2005). If journalists are to be watchdogs rather than lapdogs, then we must hope so.

SOCIAL RESPONSIBILITY

Despite editorial cost-cutting, and an apparent shift to less serious news (see Chapter 5), good journalists do continue to act as the eyes and ears of the public, putting into practice the belief that knowledge is power. One such is Kevin Peachey, consumer affairs correspondent of the *Nottingham Evening Post*, who has won a series of awards for campaigning journalism on behalf of his readers. I asked him to talk me through one of his typical stories:

> There was a couple who had a guy knock on their door and he offered to do their guttering for them, then he went round the back and said "I'll build a conservatory for you". They agreed and paid him £5,000. He built a two-foot high brick wall and then disappeared. They didn't know who he was, he had a mobile phone number that was always off, he never returned any calls, they'd given him five grand and all they'd got literally was a two-foot high wall.
>
> It's an incredible story because everybody could appreciate what the situation was. It related to doorstep sellers – which was something that we then campaigned for, banning all cold-calling by property repairs salesmen – and the wider issues of the law. We took a dossier of stories down to MPs in London, making it an active campaign where we could go and lobby for something to happen. The great thing about that story was that we then got inundated with calls from legitimate builders who were also pretty miffed that their industry was being tarnished, and a company offered to come in and finish off the job. So the couple got their conservatory, and it was a nice bit of publicity for the legitimate company.

Such campaigning is a vital link between the public and journalists, particularly those on local and regional newspapers, believes Peachey. "You can get your news from so many different places now that you've got to campaign to survive as a local paper," he says. At any one time, a newspaper such as the *Nottingham Evening Post* is likely to have around a dozen campaigns on the go, ranging from fundraising for local charities to lobbying for a change in the law. Most are prompted by readers' concerns as expressed in letters or telephone calls. Does this mean he feels a sense of social responsibility?

> Yes, you're there to some degree to represent your readers, in a stronger way than they'd be able to do on their own. They see the power of the local paper as much greater than them individually. And it is, because if you ring up a company on behalf of 10 people, then they tend to take some action. Doing this job makes you feel as if you are doing your bit for the community really, and most of that is just education, raising awareness.

Warning readers about bogus builders and dodgy dealers is all well and good, but it hardly tackles the big issues that have a greater impact on society; structural issues such as economic inequality and exploitation. How does Peachey respond to the suggestion that he is merely taking on the small fry rather than the bigger fish?

> You've got a guy who is going door-to-door and ripping off old ladies by doing terrible driveway jobs or by not doing the job at all, just taking the money and disappearing. To me, somebody who does that isn't small fry, because they've taken someone's life savings and they're then going to do it to a load more other people. If they had stopped a lady coming out of the Post Office and taken her entire life savings off her, and then done it outside the same Post Office to scores of other pensioners, then that would always be a front-page story. They're taking huge amounts of money off people who are the most vulnerable in our society, and therefore by definition they are not small fry. If you've got the chance to expose them then it's a social responsibility to do so, or a newspaper's responsibility to do so, no doubt about it.

Victims of such scams are often deeply embarrassed by their own gullibility, yet they frequently overcome this to tell their stories to journalists as a warning to their fellow citizens. To demonstrate this point, Kevin Peachey tells me that his quickest outline in shorthand is, "We don't want this to happen to anybody else," because that's what so many of his interviewees say. As Bacon said, knowledge is power.

FURTHER READING

The relationship between printing and the Enlightenment is explored further in Porter (2000), particularly Chapter 4, which deals with print culture. The history of the English Civil War, aka the English Revolution, is told in *The World Turned Upside Down* by Christopher Hill (1975, also available in more recent editions). John Milton's *Areopagitica* (1644) has recently been republished and accompanied by a Granville Williams (2005) essay placing it in historical context and discussing its relevance to today's media. Rose (2002) tells the hidden story of the intellectual life of working-class people and challenges many preconceptions about who reads what, why and how.

For more specifically on the history of journalism in the UK, see Conboy (2004), Williams (1998), Curran and Seaton (2003) and Marr (2005). Also try to lay your hands on a second-hand copy of *Poor Men's Guardians* by Stanley Harrison (1974), a journalist on the *Daily Worker/Morning Star* who traces the history of the radical press from 1763 to 1973. Atton (2002) brings the alternative press story into the twenty-first century, while Miles (2005) discusses the growth of Al-Jazeera.

Up-to-date information on threats to press freedom is available on the websites of the International Federation of Journalists (www.ifj.org), the Committee to Protect Journalists (www.cpj.org), and the Campaign for Press and Broadcasting Freedom (www.cpbf.org.uk).

Finally, for a classic account of the fourth estate in action, see Bernstein and Woodward (1974) and the film *All The President's Men*, directed by Alan J Pakula.

4 IN THE PUBLIC INTEREST

Coffee was being served in Buckingham Palace and the Queen was making small talk with her guest of honour, the President of the United States. Servants were busying themselves catering to the needs of George W Bush who, at the time, was probably the most powerful man on earth. Palace servants are expected to pretend to be invisible, to avoid unnecessary eye contact with anyone above their own rank, even to walk along the edges of corridors so that their royal highnesses can enjoy the luxury of a carpet that has not been worn down by inferior feet. On the occasion of the President's visit, one footman was so good at making himself invisible that nobody spotted him standing behind a net curtain, from where he observed proceedings and sent text messages on his mobile phone.

There was said to be a temporary telecommunications block in that part of London to prevent anyone setting off a bomb by phone, but the young footman had no difficulty using his mobile before resuming his duties, calmly helping to clear up the coffee cups. When his shift was over, he returned to the footmen's living quarters within the palace itself and gathered up his few possessions from the tiny room that had been his home for the previous eight weeks. He put them into a holdall and walked off into the night. Across town, meanwhile, tension had been mounting at the offices of the *Daily Mirror*, where his text messages had been received with growing excitement. The paper's print-run had been increased by around 100,000 copies in anticipation of record sales when the following morning's edition hit the streets. A nasty surprise was awaiting the royal family.

THE INTRUDER

Those extra copies were not wasted, because the story caused a sensation. Labelled "world exclusive", the front page of the *Daily Mirror* on 19 November 2003 featured a photograph of Ryan Parry standing on the balcony of Buckingham Palace, and the headline: INTRUDER – AS BUSH ARRIVES, WE REVEAL MIRRORMAN HAS BEEN A PALACE FOOTMAN FOR TWO MONTHS IN THE BIGGEST ROYAL SECURITY SCANDAL EVER. The story continued on pages 2, 3, 4, 5, 6, 7, 8, 9, 10, 11, 12, 13, 14 and 15. It was indeed sensational stuff, revealing how Ryan Parry had applied for the job using his own name but a combination of real and bogus references. Nobody at the palace suspected that he already had a job: as a reporter. Had they typed his name into *Google* it would have taken them less than two seconds to discover not only that he was a reporter, but that just weeks earlier he had hit the headlines with a similar undercover investigation into security lapses at the Wimbledon tennis championships. Game, set and match to a reporter who had displayed the very qualities that Nicholas Tomalin ([1969] 1997: 174) once described in the *Sunday Times* as the essentials for a successful journalist: "ratlike cunning, a plausible manner and a little literary ability".

Parry left *Mirror* readers in no doubt about the "right royal fiasco" he had found in the security operation surrounding not one, but two heads of state:

> For the past eight weeks, I have enjoyed unfettered access throughout Buckingham Palace as one of the royal family's key aides. Had I been a terrorist intent on assassinating the Queen or American President George Bush, I could have done so with absolute ease. Indeed, this morning I would have been serving breakfast to key members of his government, including National Security Adviser Condoleezza Rice and US Secretary of State Colin Powell. Such is the shocking incompetence at the heart of the biggest security operation ever in Britain. Not once, from the moment I applied for my job as a footman to my walking out of the palace at midnight last night, did anyone ever perform anything close to a rigorous security check on my background. Not once during the entire three month operation did anyone ever search me or my bags as I came and went at Buckingham Palace. On my first day I was given a full all-areas security pass and the traditional uniform of the Queen's trusted aides that allowed me unquestioned access to every member of the royal family. And within days of starting my job, I was even shown the secret hiding places for skeleton keys that will open every door in the building. From my small bedroom on the palace's second floor, directly above the famous Picture Gallery and just yards from the Queen's bedroom, plotting a devastating terrorist attack would have been simple.
>
> (Parry, 2003)

He went on to explain how easily he could have poisoned the Queen or planted a bomb in the President's bed. He demonstrated this with photographs he had taken of the royal breakfast table – complete with cereals in Tupperware containers – and the Belgian Suite in which the Bushes were to spend the night.

Within hours, home secretary David Blunkett was on his feet in the House of Commons announcing that a thorough review of procedures would be undertaken by the Security Commission, a previously little-known arm of the Cabinet Office. Parry, meanwhile, was on his way to winning an armful of Scoop of the Year awards. Much later, he told me how the story had come about:

> The idea came from Jane Kerr, our royal reporter. I did Wimbledon and she said, "You know what you should do next? You should go on the Buckingham Palace website because there are always jobs advertised there." So I did and I saw the footman job and that's what I applied for. I thought I'd give it a try. I never thought in my wildest dreams that I'd end up serving the head of state. I had suggested it at an ideas meeting but it wasn't until I got the interview that anyone took it seriously. One of my editors said, "Yeah, like you're going to do that," at which point I pulled out a letter with the royal crest inviting me to interview.

And what was the point of the exercise?

> We set out to test security. It was about testing security at the palace at a time of terrorist threat. Post 9/11 there is always a terrorist threat and there is clearly a fear in the royal household. All we did was test out their recruitment system, which should be airtight and which should have checked my friends, my family and my finances.

In reality, the system failed on all three counts. If they had checked with his friends they would have been told that he worked as a journalist; if they had checked with his family they would have found out that his claim to have been employed by his father's painting company was untrue; and if they had checked his finances they would have seen that his salary was in fact being paid by Trinity Mirror. Instead, in addition to genuine academic references, the palace accepted a verbal reassurance from a bloke in a pub where Parry used to collect glasses – "Yeah, I know him," said the customer when a barmaid shouted out if anyone had heard of him – and a fax from a fictitious foreman at his father's firm:

> I was on a press trip on the Isle of Man when I got a call from the palace personnel office because they hadn't had a reference from my dad. I made something up about a family feud so they wouldn't ring my dad, and the personnel woman was really sympathetic. I came up with a plan to get someone on a pay-as-you-go mobile phone to pretend to be the foreman at my dad's firm. I was at my sister's and the palace faxed over a form for a reference, and I filled it in and faxed it back.

So he lied, even to somebody who was being sympathetic towards him. How can he justify that?

> At the end of the day it was a security issue. Any terrorist wanting to plant a bomb in the palace wouldn't think twice about lying to a personnel officer. It was a security issue, so it was hugely in the public interest.

If deception could be in the public interest, where would he draw the line? "You don't do anything hugely illegal," Parry assures me.

DOING THE QUEEN A FAVOUR

The public interest is an interesting phrase. It has long been used by the *News of the World* to justify the actions of its controversial undercover specialist Mazher Mahmood, who has tricked countless people with his infamous "fake sheikh" disguise. He once described his methods as: "You befriend them, you spend a lot of time with them, you have dinner with them – and then you betray them" (quoted in Marr, 2005: 47). However, the public interest is not the preserve of journalists who are engaged in undercover work, and is often cited by reporters involved in other forms of exposure – or intrusion – as opposed to straightforward reportage. But what does it mean? That rather depends on who is talking. The Press Complaints Commission (PCC, see Appendix 4) defines the public interest as including:

(i) Detecting or exposing crime or a serious misdemeanour.
(ii) Protecting public health and safety.
(iii) Preventing the public from being misled by some statement or action of an individual or organisation.

But what is a "serious misdemeanour", what is meant by "public health", and what sort of "misleading" statements or actions might be included? Does it include exposing the bedroom and bathroom behaviour of celebs? Yes, according to the popular newspapers that pay good money for such stories. No, counter those who argue that what interests the public is not necessarily in the public interest.

Few people have seriously argued that the *Mirror*'s exposure of security flaws at Buckingham Palace would fail the public interest test – not least because it is the public that pays for security there – but what about some of the material on the rest of that day's 15 pages, not to mention 12 more the following day? Was it really in the public interest to know what the Queen had for breakfast, to see pictures of her family's private rooms, or to read which royal called another footman a "fucking incompetent twat"? Yes, says Parry, because it demonstrates just how close he got; besides, the *Mirror* operates in a competitive market and makes no apology for trying to boost circulation:

> Once you've told the gist of the story about duping the personnel office to get the job, there is the juicy tittle-tattle about the Tupperware, and at the end of the day we're a tabloid newspaper. We had to justify it with all those references [to being close enough to poison the Queen] but the fact that I found out they put their cornflakes into Tupperware containers showed the intimacy of my job and the access I had. All that juicy information showed we had got amazingly close to the head of state. And the pictures were very interesting. People are interested in seeing the Queen's rooms, but I wouldn't have been able to take them if I hadn't got that access.

Could the paper not have told readers it had such pictures – and possibly handed a dossier of evidence to the authorities – rather than publish them? Not in the real world:

> We're a tabloid paper and a commercial entity so we're going to go big on it. You can be a cynic and say that it was sensationalism and all about getting headlines, but there was a serious motive behind it, to test security at Buckingham Palace. It could have gone monumentally wrong if I'd been arrested and the paper could have ended up with egg on its face.

In fact, for the newspaper, the whole exercise went far better than it had hoped. When Parry applied for the job, the visit of George Bush had not even been announced:

> That was a bonus. We initially thought I'd stay for maybe three or four weeks but when we found out the President was coming we decided I should stay for that. There was a £14 million security operation to protect the President and cordon off the area around Buckingham Palace, with concrete blocks and Special Branch search stations, and yet I was coming backwards and forwards carrying holdalls in and out and nobody searched me or asked me what I was doing. It's a lot harder to get into my office [at the *Mirror*] in the morning than it was to get into the palace. There was a naïve assumption that all terrorists have a criminal record. I could have been in Afghanistan for the previous four years, for all they knew.
>
> After the story they appointed a new director of security at the palace, which spoke volumes, and they got police to make the checks in future rather than the personnel office. We did the royal family a favour. If a terrorist had got in there and attacked the Queen, imagine the fallout from that. As a result of our story they've completely shaken up the security there, so it would be harder for a terrorist to get in there now than it would have been before our story. If it had just been a tabloid attempt at getting the headlines then all that action wouldn't have been taken. It couldn't have been a better operation, it was a sensational story and it got the desired result.

The success of the operation depended not just on Parry's now legendary coolness under pressure, but also on the ability of a small group of *Mirror* journalists to keep schtum:

> We had to be extremely secretive, and only about half a dozen people knew. It was like James Bond style meetings in the office. They set up a room on a different floor where all the copy was laid out and where the royal reporter went to check things like where the Queen had been visiting on particular days. The lawyers were all over it [the copy].

On the final evening of the operation, Parry was receiving panicky text messages from the *Mirror* telling him to leave the palace immediately, as they feared that at any moment he might be rumbled and arrested. But he stayed put until he had finished clearing up the coffee cups. "I was quite laid back," he recalls. "I thought if I just suddenly leave now they'd get suspicious, so I just finished my shift." Had his true identity been discovered at that time, lawyers for the palace would undoubtedly have woken up a judge to obtain a late-night injunction preventing publication. As it was, the injunction came two days later, after the *Mirror* had already published virtually all of its revelations and tittle-tattle alike.

THE SECRET POLICEMAN

One undercover reporter who did have his collar felt was Mark Daly, who was arrested after spending several months working as a trainee police officer to expose racism in the ranks. He was released on bail after a night in the cells and went on to be regarded by many as something of a hero after the transmission of his film *The Secret Policeman* (BBC1, 21 October 2003). His covertly filmed report revealed a minority of police recruits routinely using racist terms, including "nigger" and "paki", while socialising among themselves, despite being instructed that such language could lead to dismissal. One officer was filmed boasting of how he would give white people preferential treatment on the streets. He said that black teenager Stephen Lawrence, whose unsolved murder by racist thugs had led to changes in police policy, had "deserved" to die. In one bizarre episode, this officer was filmed putting on a Ku Klux Klan-style hood made out of a pillowcase and joking about wearing it to frighten a fellow recruit who was Asian.

Daly had set out to investigate whether the police's public commitment to countering racist attitudes was reflected among officers on the ground. As he explains:

> In 1999 the Macpherson Report branded London's Metropolitan Police institutionally racist. The report, which followed the Met's failure to successfully prosecute a gang of white youths for the murder of Stephen Lawrence, found ethnic minorities in Britain felt under-protected as victims and over-policed as suspects … We wanted to see what steps were being taken to eradicate this. But more importantly, we needed to see if they were working. The only way we could find out what was really happening was to become a police officer – asking questions openly as a journalist would not have uncovered the truth.
>
> (Daly, 2003)

So he applied to become a police officer and, once accepted, used hi-tech surveillance equipment to record secretly the views of his fellow young recruits at a police training centre in Cheshire. As with Parry, this involved deception:

> I had become a friend to these men. They trusted me with their views. And they believed I was one of them. I operated under strict guidelines. I was not allowed to make racist comments or incite anyone to do or say anything which they wouldn't have otherwise said or done. But I had to laugh at their jokes and behave like a dumb apprentice.
>
> (Daly, 2003)

Prime minister Tony Blair said he was shocked and appalled at the racism revealed in the film, and home secretary David Blunkett agreed that the revelations were "horrendous" (Carter, 2003a). This was something of a turnaround, because before transmission the programme had been condemned by Blunkett – who was responsible for the police – as a stunt designed to *create* rather than report the news. The film contained such shocking evidence of deep-seated racial prejudice among police recruits that it forced the home secretary to admit: "It was a mistake on my part to call it a stunt. The revelations themselves justify, in this case, the way in which they came to light" (quoted in Travis, 2003). In other words, Daly's methods were deemed to be in the public interest. An official police investigation was prompted by the revelations and within days of the broadcast a number of police officers had either resigned or been suspended from duty. The Crown Prosecution Service quickly decided that Daly – who was still on bail on suspicion of obtaining money by deception (his police salary) and of damaging police property (by inserting a pinhole camera into his bullet-proof vest) – would not be charged with any offence (Carter, 2003b). When Cheshire police announced that recruits were to be shown *The Secret Policeman* as part of their anti-racist training, the story had travelled full circle (Ward, 2004).

THE UNDERCOVER TRADITION

Daly and Parry are just two of the latest exponents of a tradition of undercover journalism that, in the UK, dates back to 1885. That was when William Stead, editor of the *Pall Mall Gazette*, exposed the scandal of child prostitution in Victorian England. Posing as a punter, he "bought" a 13-year-old virgin girl for £5, ostensibly for his own sexual gratification. His subsequent articles on this trade in human misery, which ran for several days under the heading THE MAIDEN TRIBUTE OF MODERN BABYLON, boosted the newspaper's sales from 8,360 to 12,250 (Snoddy, 1992: 46–9).

But the reports were denounced by the rival *Standard* newspaper for containing "the most offensive, highly-coloured and disgusting details … which appeals to the lascivious curiosity of every casual passer-by, and excites the latent pruriency of a half-educated crowd" (quoted in Clarke, 2004: 261). Stead was arrested and served two months in prison for the offence of procuring the girl, but he achieved his aims of shocking parliament into raising the age of heterosexual consent from 13 to 16 years and of increasing the circulation of his newspaper (Clarke, 2004: 259). In the process, he established the template for many subsequent exposés, as Hugo de Burgh points out:

> Stead changed the style of reporting by conjoining high moral tone with sensational description, the favoured style of many newspapers in Britain today. Stead got attention not only by prurience, but also by revelation. That this kind of trade existed was almost certainly news to most of his readers. His undercover, investigative style was premonitory … Investigative journalism had been invented.
>
> (de Burgh, 2000: 39–40)

Journalists are rarely remembered by posterity – unless they branch out into more respectable pursuits such as fiction – so it was a pleasant surprise when, walking along the Thames Embankment in London one day, I came across a bronze memorial plaque to Stead. It was erected in 1920 "by journalists of many lands in recognition of his brilliant gifts, fervent spirit, and untiring devotion to the service of his fellow-men". Homage of a different sort was also paid when the *Sun* exposed a "sex slave racket" involving women from Eastern Europe in 2006; an undercover reporter "bought" a Romanian woman for £450 (Harvey, 2006).

William Stead is remembered not only for his undercover exploits but also for his belief in the power of journalism to change things. As he wrote in the *Contemporary Review* in 1886:

> I am but a comparatively young journalist, but I have seen Cabinets upset, Ministers driven into retirement, laws repealed, great social reforms initiated, Bills transformed, estimates remodelled, Acts passed, generals nominated, governors appointed, armies sent hither and thither, war proclaimed and war averted, by the agency of newspapers.
>
> (Quoted in Clarke, 2004: 266)

Sadly, Stead went down with the *Titanic* while en route to New York in 1912; it is said that he helped women and children onto the few lifeboats, and even declined to take one of the scarce lifejackets himself (Snoddy, 1992: 49). As the *Daily Mirror* (1912) reported at the time: "The greatest tragedy of Mr WT Stead's life was that, being present at the most disastrous shipwreck in the world's history, he was unable to send off a full and vivid description of what really happened."

Across the Atlantic a wannabe reporter by the name of Nellie Bly had been committed to an asylum for the insane. She had not been driven mad by the intensity of her desire to be a journalist and she was, in fact, perfectly sane. She was pretending to be mentally ill so that she could expose the shocking conditions within the asylum. Her undercover stint in 1887 worked a treat: the story caused a sensation, the city of New York invested an extra $1 million in care for the mentally ill, and young Nellie got the job she was after as a staff reporter on the *New York World* (Randall, 2005: 99–103). Over the next few years she went undercover countless times:

> She also got inside a paper box factory to write about the conditions of virtual slavery in which its young women workers toiled; learnt to fence, swim and cycle; joined a chorus line, covered graduation at West Point, spent a night in an opium den; exposed a mesmerist, an unlicensed money lender, gimcrack washing machine sellers; and she made a laughing stock of seven of the most prominent doctors in New York by presenting all of them with the same symptoms and getting from them seven different diagnoses, ranging from malaria to "shattered nerves" ... [S]he had an incurable curiosity and an unshakeable faith in the power of reporting. If only the true facts could be uncovered, she believed, then people and authorities could be roused to act and make improvements.
>
> (Randall, 2005: 103–13)

A similar mixture of curiosity and ingenuity has been displayed throughout the unorthodox career of Günter Wallraff, a German journalist who has assumed a range of identities to report – usually at length in book form – on life as it is lived at the bottom of the heap in modern Europe. After revealing the racism, brutality and unsafe working conditions suffered by many Turkish workers in Germany, for example, Wallraff ([1985]2004: 160) wrote: "Of course I wasn't really a Turk. But you have to disguise yourself in order to unmask your society, you have to deceive and playact to get at the truth." In other words, there are times when a journalist must deceive to avoid being deceived (Schuffels, 1979: 2). Similarly, in Italy, journalist Fabrizio Gatti went to great lengths to investigate the treatment meted out to immigrants lacking the necessary documentation: he jumped into the Mediterranean sea and floated to shore on a raft, before being picked up by a motorist and handed to the police. Gatti spent seven days in a detention centre, which allowed him to witness – and experience – physical and verbal abuse at first-hand (Hooper, 2005). As in the cases of Daly and Stead discussed above, such undercover operations can land journalists in trouble with the law. When accused of going too far, Wallraff has defended his methods as "only slightly illegal" in comparison with some of the scandals he has exposed (quoted in Schuffels, 1979: 8). In short, he argues that what he does is in the public interest.

TRUMPED-UP NONSENSE?

The trouble is, they all say that, don't they? "Don't complain to me about invasion of privacy," writes veteran tabloid investigator Gerry Brown (1995: 315). "If it's in the public interest, I prefer to call it invasion of secrecy." That is all well and good when what is being revealed is corruption, racism, dodgy estate agents, corporate greed, airport security bungles or how easy it is to buy lethal weapons; but where is the public interest in revealing politicians' bedroom behaviour, exposing couples who host parties for "swingers", photographing celebrities on holiday with their children, or prying into the lives of individuals who have the misfortune to become embroiled in a story not of their own making? It was hard to detect much public interest when the *Sun* sent a female reporter to pose as someone who had taken a fancy to a middle-aged male MP who was between relationships at the time. A day of deception resulted in a double-page spread telling us … that the MP bought his young "admirer" a box of House of Commons mints (Iggulden, 2006). William Stead would be turning in his grave, if only he had one. Even those "newspapers" that print "upskirt" photographs of z-list celebs falling out of nightclubs might be able to think up something that resembles a public interest defence: exposing the hypocritical behaviour of people who should be role models for the young, blah blah blah. It would be a feeble defence, to be sure, but perhaps not much more flimsy than the excuses trotted out by some of the more prurient elements of the UK national press.

With the honesty of an ex-editor, Piers Morgan said of his time in charge of the *News of the World*:

> I was … lacking in any real humanity for the mayhem we were causing, which is probably the right way to be on the *News of the World*, because the humanity aspect just compromises you. There's no point in pretending what you're doing is good for the human spirit. Most of the time, the public interest defence was trumped-up nonsense. The reason we were doing it was to sell papers and amuse and titillate people.
>
> (Quoted in Hattenstone, 2005)

Which, of course, is exactly what Stead had been accused of doing more than 100 years earlier.

Sometimes, for all of us except the editors and proprietors involved, there is a clear distinction between something that is in the public interest and something that will merely interest or titillate the public. But there are plenty of grey areas. Take, for example, the tapes of Princess Diana's intimate mobile telephone conversations, which were recorded – apparently by chance – by two members of the public. As the Princess of Wales was referred to in the conversations as "Squidgy", the story became known as "Squidgygate", in the time-honoured tradition of adding the word "gate" to every supposed scandal since Watergate in the early 1970s. Or consider the revelation of Prince Charles's equally intimate conversations with his then "secret" lover Camilla Parker-Bowles, inevitably known as "Camillagate". On one hand, publication of the tape transcripts was a clear invasion of privacy designed to titillate the public and boost newspaper sales. On the other hand, Charles and Diana were not you or me. At the time, the early 1990s, they were the UK's rulers-in-waiting, whose "fairytale" romance had been sold to the public – who picked up the bill – via the media. Therefore, argues Gerry Brown, the *Sun* was clearly acting in the public interest by publishing details of the Squidgygate conversations:

> [I]t wouldn't have been right for the sham royal marriage to continue and the rest of us to watch misty-eyed as they ascended the throne as King and Queen with only a handful of *Sun* executives, a retired bank manager and a secretary [who made the tapes] knowing Diana had been secretly rogered by a used car dealer and her Army riding instructor. It was a stunning victory for technology in the service of mankind and tabloid journalism.
>
> (Brown, 1995: 313)

Perhaps it was; on balance, I would rather err on the side of revelation than go along with the sort of cover-up that occurred in the 1930s, when undue deference prevented editors from telling the public about the impending abdication crisis. I couldn't help feeling, however, that there was something distasteful about reading the transcripts of such excruciatingly private conversations. Still, they were very funny.

Arguably, this tension between that which is in the public interest and that which people merely find interesting was demonstrated by the way journalists covered the Profumo affair[1] in the early 1960s, when – for neither the first nor the last time – a male government minister slept with someone who was not his wife. Because the young woman concerned had also hung out with someone from the Russian Embassy, it was portrayed as a Cold War

1 Younger readers might like to conduct a public interest test at this point. Ask your grandparents about the Profumo affair. They will probably remember that a bald, middle-aged politician slept with a woman called Christine Keeler, who was less than half his age. They might also remember that Keeler posed for what turned out to be one of the most iconic photographs of the 1960s, sitting naked on a back-to-front chair. The chances are that they won't be able to tell you too much about supposed Russian spies.

security scandal. But Roy Greenslade argues that the supposed security angle was blown up out of all proportion to justify the press revealing – and revelling in – the sex life of a supposedly upstanding politician:

> If papers had stuck to a rigid formulation of public interest in the Profumo affair, they would have dealt only with the security danger, which was quickly found to have been bogus. By concentrating on sex, they were appealing to baser appetites among their readers, and they knew it. The public interest was a figleaf for a sales-winning exercise.
>
> (Greenslade, 2003: 191)

John Profumo had the misfortune to live in a country that equated sex with scandal and, although he was in a position of political power, he was not allowed to get away with defying what were held up as the moral norms of society. Yet his political downfall came about not because of the affair itself, but because he lied to parliament about it. Therein lies the real public interest test, argue many journalists: if someone is prepared to lie about their private life, how can we trust their word on public matters? That is merely self-justifying rhetoric, counter the critics, who point out that he would have had no occasion to lie to parliament had the press not been sniffing around his sex life in the first place. A charge of hypocrisy is levelled at editors who have the power to decide whose peccadilloes will be exposed to the public glare and whose will be ignored (or kept on file for possible future use). And, heaven forfend, journalists themselves may even be guilty of the same offences of which they are accusing others. This was the point made by the singer Robbie Williams, when he said of some journalists who attacked model Kate Moss: "Some people in various media groups who I have personally taken cocaine with are now talking about her, saying she shouldn't do it" (quoted in Butt, 2005).

SERVING THE INTERESTS OF CITIZENS

Implicit in Robbie Williams' allegation of hypocrisy, and in Greenslade's comments on Profumo, is the question: Who the hell are journalists to decide what is or is not in the public interest? It is a good question. Fortunately, as with all the ethical issues discussed in this book, individual journalists are not left entirely to their own devices to consider it. We can be guided by the work of other journalists, contemporary and historical; we can be guided by the work of philosophers, commentators and other thinkers; and we can be guided by the people whom we serve and by ideas of citizenship. We may come up with different answers. The most important thing is that we are asking the question, both of ourselves and of other journalists.

Journalists can also be guided by ethical codes such as those reproduced in the appendices of this book. To help its journalists decide what is in the public interest, within the context of justifying deception, the BBC has issued the following guidance, which goes beyond the PCC definition cited earlier:

> There is no single definition of public interest, it includes but is not confined to:
>
> - exposing or detecting crime;
> - exposing significantly anti-social behaviour;
> - exposing corruption or injustice;
> - disclosing significant incompetence or negligence;
> - protecting people's health and safety;
> - preventing people from being misled by some statement or action of an individual or organisation;
> - disclosing information that allows people to make a significantly more informed decision about matters of public importance.
>
> There is also a public interest in freedom of expression itself. When considering what is in the public interest we also need to take account of information already in the public domain or about to become available to the public.
>
> In news and factual programmes where there is a clear public interest and when dealing with serious illegal or anti-social behaviour it may occasionally be acceptable for us not to reveal the full purpose of the programme to a contributor. The deception should be the minimum necessary in proportion to the subject matter. Any proposal to use deception must be referred to a senior editorial figure … and in the most serious cases to Controller Editorial Policy.
>
> (BBC, 2005)

Any guidelines that contain words such as "significant", "clear", "serious" and "in proportion" must be open to interpretation, but their message is plain enough to explain why, even if they wanted to, BBC staff would be unable to uncover many of the stories that are splashed across the Sunday redtops.

Not that intrusion is restricted to such newspapers, to undercover reporting, or to the activities of prominent people. Consider the way that the provincial press routinely reports inquest hearings into the deaths of local people, for example. Editors of most such newspapers take it for granted that these hearings should be reported because they are both newsworthy (by definition, inquests involve tragedy) and cost-effective (hearings typically last only around an hour or so yet provide good copy). However, at least one editor has questioned this policy and now requires there to be some form of "public interest" element to justify intruding on what is a personal tragedy:

> For instance, if a schoolboy was found hanged, then there were possible issues relating to the pressure of exams and bullying. However, if a man committed suicide because he was depressed over marriage difficulties, then there was no clear public interest and so we didn't cover it.
>
> (*Press Gazette*, 2003b)

This editorial decision, taken within the offices of a small regional newspaper in the middle of England – the *Scunthorpe Evening Telegraph* – suggests that public interest considerations do not come into play only when journalists engage in what is commonly known as investigative journalism. Investigative journalism, as defined by John Ullmann and Steve Honeyman, involves:

> [T]he reporting, through one's own work product and initiative, matters of importance which some persons or organisations wish to keep secret. The three basic elements are that the investigation be the work of the reporter, not a report of an investigation made by someone else; that the subject of the story involves something of reasonable importance to the reader or viewer; and that others are attempting to hide these matters from the public.
>
> (Quoted in Keeble, 2001b: 188–9)

Such investigative journalism has been described as "the first rough draft of legislation", which makes explicit the link between the revelation of a wrong and action to put it right (de Burgh, 2000: 3). However, if we conceive of journalism as existing fundamentally to serve the interests of citizens, then the concept of the public interest can inform more than just specifically investigative reporting. James Ettema and Theodore Glasser (1998: 61, 181) argue that investigative journalism offers a different model from what they term "daily journalism" because it makes claims that certain facts are verifiably true and is not afraid of making moral judgements, for example about the performance of public institutions. But, rather than a wholly different model, can that not be seen as an intensification of what *all* serious journalism seeks to do? That was certainly the view of veteran investigator Paul Foot, who told me:

> It's a complete fraud, the idea that there is a race apart called investigative journalists. An ordinary reporter doing a perfectly ordinary story carries out these functions, the difference would be the enthusiasm and the scepticism with which you approach something.

Such a view is also the starting point of many whose journalism has been practised within alternative, rather than mainstream, media. When I began my journalistic career on an alternative newspaper, we had open editorial meetings in which any of the contributors and readers who took part might suddenly declare: "I don't see the point of this story. What's it *for*?"

It is a question worth asking, as is Karen Sanders' one about whether the concept of the public interest could be better expressed as the *public good*:

> Undoubtedly the notion of public interest serves a useful normative role: it is the yardstick by which editors, publishers and broadcasters determine the boundaries of ethical behaviour. However, it is also unclear and abstract … The notion would repay closer scrutiny and perhaps recasting in the form of public or common good rather than that of "interest" which smacks of economism. Invading privacy for the public good expresses the truth that justice sometimes requires a private good to be subordinated to a public one.
>
> (Sanders, 2003: 90)

Asking questions is, arguably, what journalists do best. We may sometimes get things wrong, but we are usually better at asking questions than, say, were the Buckingham Palace officials who employed Ryan Parry as a footman. Or the government's Security Commission (2004: 2) which, during its six month-long investigation did not bother to ask any questions either of Parry or his referees; by the end of it all the Commission still seemed to be under the false impression that he had actually worked for his father's company. "The official report was laughable," says Parry. It did seem to vindicate his investigation, though, concluding that he had uncovered flaws in the system that "could be exploited by terrorists or others to endanger the Queen, her family and official guests and thus to endanger national security". In other words, as the paper had claimed all along, it had done the Queen a favour. That some security lessons were learned was indicated when, early in 2006, two undercover reporters who tried to get jobs at Buckingham Palace were arrested on suspicion of "attempting to obtain pecuniary advantage" (Gibson, 2006). However, former *Mirror* editor Roy Greenslade (2006) was unimpressed by the public interest claims of such journalism, dismissing the palace stories as childish stunts "without merit or purpose".

Following Ryan Parry's palace escapades, other journalists began sending off bogus CVs left, right and centre, getting jobs everywhere from airports to parliament, planting fake "bombs" and taking sneak pictures – all in the name of the public interest. "It's getting a bit boring now," says Parry. "It has to have a valid point, don't do it for the sake of it. Sometimes these days it's just the tabloids having fun." It certainly wasn't much fun when he had to pull out of another undercover job as a security officer – because the rival *Sun* newspaper also had an undercover reporter in the same company and published the story first. Oh well, Ryan, you can't win them all.

FURTHER READING

The concept of the public interest is addressed explicitly in books on journalistic ethics by Frost (2000) and Sanders (2003), who both locate the discussion within broader philosophical and moral arguments. For an introduction to investigative journalism, including more from an interview with Paul Foot, see Chapter 6 of Harcup (2004). A personal, and entertaining, account of investigative reporting can be found in Foot (1999). Spark (1999) introduces some of the techniques involved, Brown (1995) reveals some of the tricks of the tabloid trade, and contributors to de Burgh (2000) discuss investigative journalism within a wider context. John Pilger (2004: xiv), in his edited collection of public interest journalism by Martha Gellhorn, Seymour Hersh, Gunter Wallraff, Robert Fisk, Anna Politkovskaya and others – including Pilger himself – looks beyond investigative "detective work" and includes "journalism that bears witness and investigates ideas". A more upbeat volume to read alongside Pilger is Randall (2005), which tells the story of Nellie Bly and another dozen great reporters who used their cunning, their plausible manner and their literary ability to good effect in the public interest. For more on the exploits of William Stead, see the WT Stead Resource website at: www.attackingthedevil.co.uk.

5 DANGER: NEWS VALUES AT WORK

Just a few months before a small group of suicide bombers brought terror to its public transport system, London hosted one of the largest debates about war, peace and global justice ever held. For three days somewhere between 20,000 and 30,000 people, most of them young, from more than 60 countries took part in a series of lively discussions at the European Social Forum; they even managed to find a use for the Millennium Dome, as 5,000 participants slept on the floor of the much-mocked monument. But anyone relying on mainstream UK media for news would have been hard-pressed to know that the forum was taking place. This non-coverage prompted a senior BBC journalist to bemoan the news values that prevailed during the event:

> As I write the fate of Dino the Dog is in the running order of the main news bulletins. But it seems to be of no interest to BBC News, or the many current affairs outlets, that the biggest political conference of the year in Europe is taking place in London. Major political thinkers and campaigners, whom it would cost thousands of pounds to interview via satellite, are on our doorstep. Ditto articulate young people engaged in politics in a way everybody thinks they are not. Decisions are taken by a frightened bunch of editors who believe that politics begins and ends within 200 metres of Millbank, and that "world affairs" equals the war on terror. The war on poverty, injustice, corruption and environmental destruction – being waged by millions of people – is of little interest to them, even though it is setting the agenda of the World Bank and the International Monetary Fund, much of the corporate world, and many governments in the global South. Of course if there is a riot, a full complement of cameras and crash-helmeted reporters will be deployed.
>
> (*Journalist*, 2004b)

There was no riot so, except for the *Guardian* newspaper, the forum was largely ignored. The same cannot be said for Dino the German shepherd dog, whose experience gave the lie to the maxim that "dog bites man isn't news, man bites dog is". Actually, Dino had bitten a woman and had previously been sentenced to death by magistrates. When Dino's owner successfully challenged the destruction order – with a media-savvy judge remarking that "a dog will have his day" (BBC, 2004) – the story attracted copious amounts of coverage in print and broadcast media. Saving the life of one dog was, it seemed, of more significance than trying to save the planet.

A SPECTACLE OF BANALITY

Animals such as Dino put in frequent appearances in news output, where they are portrayed variously as villains, victims or simply as objects of amusement. Regional television news in the UK is particularly keen on such stories, often provoking the cry among discerning viewers: "Why is *that* news?" It's a very good question. Although I have not yet spotted any skateboarding ducks or dogs that can say "sausages" – archetypal inconsequential stories that have passed into TV legend – a moving menagerie of fluffy animals is daily paraded before our eyes accompanied by reporters feigning enthusiasm while secretly wondering if it was for this that they entered journalism. But killer beasts and cute pets are by no means the only journalistic clichés in the news, and they frequently find themselves in the company of other stereotypes such as the brave cancer victim, the heartless thief, and the have-a-go-hero; all stock characters in stories that, we are told, write themselves.

This sounds like a job for … Reverend Utah Snakewater. The self-styled Reverend and his Newsbreakers offer a radical critique of television news in the United States by staging "parody and non-traditional media transformations", it says here (Newsbreakers, 2005). Put more bluntly: they take the piss. Their speciality is disrupting live two-way outside broadcasts in protest at the trivialisation of local TV news. As a hapless reporter tries to answer questions from a presenter in the studio, the Newsbreakers prance around in fancy dress and Rev Snakewater performs on-air exorcisms (Shaw, 2005). It's all the idea of former television journalist Chris Landon, from New York, who is campaigning for real news to replace the "voyeur's fantasy" that he says has "shifted from the role of challenging those in power to exploiting the weak" (quoted in Luscombe, 2005). A study by the Washington-based Project for Excellence in Journalism lends credence to such criticism by pointing to the three-stage "hook-and-hold" approach favoured by local TV news, in which the lead item may be a weak story with strong pictures (a fire in which nobody is hurt, for example), harder news stories about politics or industry are squeezed in the middle, and the final stories are largely inconsequential human interest items. "TV defines reality for a lot of people," according to Landon. "We just want to startle them enough to disrupt that view of reality" (quoted in Luscombe, 2005).

Such stunts may be a bit of fun – for viewers, if not for the poor reporters caught up in them – but they highlight the serious point that much TV news in the US has become a spectacle of banality. Not just in the US, and not just on television. Journalists have long attracted criticism for their selection of news, and even at the birth of printing there was concern about a disproportionate interest in "lewd and naughty matters", ie sex and violence (Williams, 1998: 16–17). UK tabloid journalist Harry Procter (1958: 58) recalled that, when he joined the *Daily Mirror* as a reporter before the Second World War, the paper's key ingredient was sex: "Sex, the *Mirror* discovered, sold papers – papers by the million. Hard news was merely the third course." He later moved to the *Sunday Pictorial*, where the recipe for building circulation was similar: "Sex, scandal, surprise, sensation, exposure, murder. And as many pictures of half-dressed, big-bosomed damsels in distress as possible" (Procter, 1958: 141). Such fare remains the staple diet of the UK's biggest selling newspapers today.

HOW HIGH ARE THE FLAMES?

But it is not only "downmarket" tabloid newspapers that have a distorted sense of news values, argued the Labour party politician and radical campaigner Tony Benn at a James Cameron Memorial Lecture in London:

> Every hour we're told what's happened to the Dow Jones Industrial Average and the Footsie [Financial Times Share Index] and the value of the pound against the dollar and the value of the pound against the euro, though I've no idea how many people are hanging on every hour to hear this news … The news media continue to be obsessed by business, yet the statistics which really might be interesting you get perhaps once a year if there's a relevant report. One of the local London radio stations the other day reported that 74% of the children in the borough of Tower Hamlets live in poverty. Why isn't that statistic deemed worthy of being broadcast every hour? … I've always believed that if the number of accidents on building sites were broadcast on a daily basis for a couple of weeks there would be legislation immediately to deal with the problem … I was with [pensioners' leader] Jack Jones in Blackpool this year at a rally of 2,000 pensioners, and I pointed out to Jack that the meeting would not be reported in the media at all – unless he were to throw a brick through the window of McDonald's: then there would be two bishops on *Newsnight* talking about the rising tide of violence among older people. But Jack didn't throw the brick, and there was no report of the meeting.
>
> (Benn, 2001: 334–5)

Such news values apply not just to pensioners on parade in Blackpool but also to campaigners at G8 summits of world leaders, such as the one held in Scotland in July 2005. A 250,000-strong peaceful march through Edinburgh to "Make Poverty History" received considerably less media coverage than did fighting between police and a small number of protesters in the days that followed, prompting *Herald* columnist Iain MacWhirter to lament: "I'm afraid the lesson of these demonstrations is that violence works. The Battle of Princes Street was a minor public disorder, but it was magnified out of all proportion" (quoted in Mackay and Pike, 2005). Again, this is not a new phenomenon. Roy Greenslade (2003: 238) recalls a time when, to decide whether a riot in Northern Ireland was worth reporting, UK newsdesks would ask: "How high are the flames?" For Greenslade, such a query reflected a flawed news agenda, concerned only with "results rather than causes".

A symptom of this concern with the latest consequence rather than the deeper cause is the tendency for journalists – especially editors and news editors – to lose interest in stories after a short while. Many perceive their audience as having an even shorter attention span. Many significant issues of the day are seen as worthy but dull, made of interest to a wider public only occasionally by a dramatic event or a celebrity photo-call, before the media circus moves on. Many long-term issues that affect large numbers of citizens are likely to be squeezed out by more immediate and individual stories, complains Robert McChesney (2000: 49–50), an academic and media campaigner in the US who argues that "the historical and ideological context necessary to bring public issues to life" is too often absent. In a similar vein, journalist and media commentator Danny Schechter ([1994] 2001: 263) complains, in the midst of a discussion of how black communities in the US are represented, that too much journalism marginalises history and collective memory: "Yet journalists, especially those who report on sensitive issues of race – often buried as they are, in minefields of nuance – can only make these issues intelligible if they locate a historical context and larger meaning."

Within mainstream UK journalism, the funding of local authority Social Services departments is seen as boring; until, that is, a social worker is blamed for letting a child be abused or killed by its parents. Protecting health and safety at work is dismissed as a dull subject, until there is an explosion, preferably with dramatic pictures. And the homeless are a story just for Christmas, not for life. Even natural disasters are relative, judging by how quickly most of the UK news media lost interest in the 2005 earthquake that devastated parts of Pakistan and Kashmir. As one news executive explained: "Lots of poor people far away get killed. Nothing more to be said" (quoted in Cole, 2005). The poor may always be with us, but they appear to be of little interest to most news editors most of the time. Although we had a week of coverage of poverty in Africa around the time of the G8 summit in July 2005 – aided and abetted by the presence of rock stars doing their bit for the cause and their careers – we get comparatively little coverage of poverty the rest of the time. Poverty is still out there even when the cameras are gone but, as Richard Keeble (2001a: 34) notes, "the experiences of the poor are marginalized" in most news.

"People tend to suppose journalists are where the news is," observes former BBC journalist Martin Bell. "This is not so. The news is where journalists are" (quoted in Marr, 2005: 292). Where too many senior metropolitan journalists appear to be is a curious place: a world of rich lists and celebrity parties, where it is taken for granted that rising house prices are a good thing, speed cameras are a bad thing, and that individual wants should come before social needs. Such "aspirational" journalists may not leave their desks very often to mingle personally with the rich and famous, but it is upon them that their gaze is fixed; the poor and the powerless rarely seem to come into their field of vision at all, at home or abroad.

NEWS VALUES

News, then, happens where journalists are – or, at least, where they are looking – and news is that which editors decide to publish. Studies of news values suggest that decisions about what makes a news story are informed by ground rules that, although they may not be codified in a formal sense, govern daily newsroom practice. Notwithstanding differences between media and within different sectors of the market, research suggests that, when assessing potential news, journalists look for one or more of the following elements:

- *The power elite*: stories concerning powerful individuals, organisations or institutions;
- *Celebrity*: stories concerning people who are already famous;
- *Entertainment:* stories concerning sex, showbusiness, human interest, animals, an unfolding drama, or offering opportunities for humorous treatment, entertaining photographs or witty headlines;
- *Surprise*: stories with an element of the unexpected and/or contrast;
- *Bad news*: stories with negative overtones such as conflict or tragedy;
- *Good news*: stories with positive overtones such as rescues and cures;
- *Magnitude*: stories perceived as sufficiently significant either in the numbers of people involved or in potential impact;
- *Relevance*: stories about issues, groups and nations perceived to be relevant to the audience;
- *Follow-ups*: stories about subjects already in the news;
- *Media agenda*: stories that set or fit the news organisation's own agenda. (Harcup and O'Neill, 2001: 279)

The existence of such news values means that stories are not selected according to their social significance or to their prevalence in society; indeed, they often seem to be selected in inverse proportion to those qualities. Coverage of crime, for example, is skewed by the operation of news values that privilege the unusual, the dramatic and the tragic (see Chapter 7) but crime is not the only area of such concern.

Research into the way that health issues are covered in the UK reveals unhappiness among public health experts that news media give undue prominence to short-term "scare" stories while failing to explain more complex or long-term developments (Harrabin and others, 2003: 2). A study for the King's Fund think tank found that news media prefer stories about new health risks and "crises" in the NHS to ostensibly less dramatic ones about things that might affect far more people, such as measures to improve health, prevent illness or reduce health inequalities (Harrabin and others, 2003: 1). In an earlier study of media coverage of health issues, sociologist Clive Seale (2002: 187) even claimed that there were a disproportionate number of news stories about breast cancer compared with other illnesses, "because of the presumed appeal of such 'soft' news to a female readership, as well as because it provides male readers and news editors with the opportunity to contemplate breasts".

When asked why there might be such disparity between the scale of public health risks in the real world and the reporting of health risks in the media world, editors and reporters all gave the same answer: news values. This is hardly surprising – after all, as *Times* science correspondent Mark Henderson (2003) comments: "News, by definition, involves the unexpected and dramatic, not the run-of-the-mill" – but it does raise concern about potential effects on public behaviour and public policy. Does it really matter? Yes, according to the King's Fund, because news coverage can influence the decisions of policy-makers and the behaviour of the public (Harrabin and others, 2003: 1). Yes, according to Professor Seale (2002: 213), who says that too much health reporting amounts to a sensational "fairy story" of bad bugs and good people, resulting in audiences changing their behaviour in response to scare stories rather than to "more realistic dangers that have not been covered in the media".

The world is not always made up of the unambiguous blacks and whites of such journalism, but of "many shades of grey", argues Seale (2002: 40). To illustrate the point, he gives the example of a road bridge in New York, which collapsed and caused 10 deaths. Suddenly, bridges were news and "for a while every reporter in the state was alert to possible bridge stories so that every crack, groan or sign of dilapidation became evidence of a pattern, which was now the story". Bridge stories captured the journalistic imagination for a period, but in such a way as to simplify what were complex realities involving different types of bridge, different types of location, and different types of problem:

> Typically, monocausal, simple explanations were preferred by news media, since complex multicausal explanations made it harder to allocate blame completely and threatened readers with the prospect of "good" people sharing responsibility for the bad event … Phenomena that were previously disregarded and unconnected were, through the alchemy of the media, noticed, their significance heightened, and ultimately classed as instances of a pattern.
>
> (Seale, 2002: 33–4)

In their classic study of news values, Galtung and Ruge (1965) argued that the more clearly an event could be understood and interpreted unambiguously, without multiple meanings, the more likely it was to be selected as a news story. However, it is not necessarily the event itself that is unambiguous; a lack of ambiguity might be due to the way an event has been perceived and/or described by the journalist. A study of news values operating in the UK press found "many news stories that were written unambiguously about events and issues that were likely to have been highly ambiguous", such as military interventions or government announcements (Harcup and O'Neill, 2001: 270).

Increased news coverage of an issue may in fact be a response to political rhetoric, argues the academic researcher Justin Lewis, who points out that international terrorism has been the subject of many more news stories since 2001 than it was in the 1980s, when more terrorist incidents actually took place. As with the health stories cited above, Lewis argues that "this kind of coverage distorts our perception of risk", adding: "So, despite the government's chief scientific adviser's warning that global warming is a much greater threat to life than global terrorism, terrorism ranks high on the public's list of concerns, while climate change scarcely registers." (Lewis, 2004). It is interesting to note that, even in the short time since Lewis wrote those words, the issue of climate change seems to have moved higher up the media agenda; however, the bulk of such coverage has erred on the side of simplistic explanations.

It is this lack of perspective and context within much reporting – an absence of shades of grey – that has prompted academic commentators Stephen Baker and Greg McLaughlin to wonder aloud about the usefulness of news itself:

> News is an institutional and professional selection of contemporary events that produces nothing more than an inventory of proceedings. Curtailed by time and space, it has no opportunity to expand upon or explain the events and issues it presents each day. In short, news just isn't up to the job of making the world intelligible. So here is a radical proposal: let's abolish it! And in its place let's invent a new media genre that can be relied upon to investigate, contextualise, inform and scrutinise.
>
> (Baker and McLaughlin, 2005: 5)

I would not go all the way with their claim that "watching or reading the news can impair your ability to understand what's going on in the world". People I know who regularly consume news generally seem to have a better handle on the world around them than those who don't. This anecdotal evidence is backed up by research, according to academic Pippa Norris (2000: 11, 17, 311), who refers to a "virtuous circle" in which "attention to the news media gradually reinforces civic engagement, just as civic engagement prompts attention to the news". With this in mind, although we may not wish to abolish news as Baker and McLaughlin suggest, we may usefully ask questions about what news is, for whom it is intended, and about whether mainstream news values serve the democratic participation and civic engagement of citizens as well as they might.

CAMPAIGN FOR REAL NEWS

Challenging conventional ideas of news in this way has been one of the motivating factors behind the production of a range of alternative media, from local newspapers to international websites. A local radical newspaper called the *Liverpool Free Press*, for example, operated with an alternative concept of news as being "useful information" (Whitaker, 1981: 105). That may be so wide a definition as to be of limited use, but it has the virtue of beginning from the starting point that news should have more than novelty value. The alternative local press that grew in the UK from the late 1960s into the 1980s prioritised the news and views of otherwise marginalised groups: people living on low incomes, people in social housing, people involved in community groups, trade union activists, the unemployed, and people active within the women's and gay movements and the black communities, among others. Such newspapers were an alternative to a mainstream press whose prevailing attitude was summed up by a former editor of the *Birmingham Evening Mail*, when he recalled: "At my first meeting with members of the black community I was told, 'The *Mail* has lots of black faces – they are all on the Crimestoppers page'" (quoted in Elliott, 2005: 14). Despite limited resources, the alternative press attempted to provide such otherwise marginalised groups with useful information, and with a voice.

A sympathetic reporter from a mainstream newspaper once told a gathering of alternative journalists that they could usefully "fill in the gaps the straight press leaves" by setting stories in a broader context (National Conference of Alternative Papers, 1984: 2). Another newspaper that tried to do just that was *Leeds Other Paper* (*LOP*), which had a news agenda constructed in opposition to what it regarded as the shallow approach of too much journalism (Harcup, 1994; 2006). Whereas mainstream journalists too often seemed content to get an "angle" on a story before moving on to the next one, contributors to *LOP* – of whom I was one for a while – were expected to think about the meaning of stories and to cover them in both depth and breadth, as another of the paper's journalists explained in an internal discussion document:

> [P]olitically, a good story for me is one that reinforces the ability of the mass of people to do things for themselves and decreases their reliance on others (especially in work and in the community) … We are committed to doing justice to the subjects we cover. This means well-researched, in-depth articles often and *LOP* stories are longer on average than those in the commercial press … We should be conscious of the need to slow down our readers – to reverse the in-one-ear-out-the-other process – and create lasting impressions.
>
> (Leeds Alternative Publications, undated: 1–3)

If that sounds like a highly political approach to news values, that's because it is, transparently and unapologetically so. It can be argued that the news values that favour Dino the dog over the European Social Forum are no less political, while less transparent. For the cultural theorist Stuart Hall (1973: 235), although the news values of mainstream journalism may appear to be "a set of neutral, routine practices", they are part of an "ideological structure" privileging the perspectives of the most powerful groups within society by allowing them greater access to the media and greater influence over social attitudes. The creation of alternative journalistic practices and outlets is one way of countering this, as another journalist who has worked in both alternative and mainstream media told me:

> There's always a need for alternative viewpoints and diversity if any change is to be made to current conditions. One example might be: in the 1970s feminist journals raised issues which were taken up by trade unions in the 1980s and became copy for (a part of) the mainstream in the 1990s – issues like domestic violence or sexual harassment at work, which were "unsayable" till said by the alternative media … Taking a longer view, there are numerous other issues (over the centuries) which were first aired in contemporary "alternative media" before becoming part of the mainstream, like the struggle for universal adult suffrage.
>
> (Quoted in Harcup, 2005b: 368)

Journalism produced by alternative media today features heavily in the *Project Censored* compilation of significant stories that have been either ignored or under-played in mainstream media in the United States. Compiled every year by staff and students in the School of Social Sciences at Sonoma State University, a typical selection of the "top 25 censored stories" includes evidence of government manipulation of scientific information to support a pro-business agenda; high levels of uranium found in civilians and soldiers in Afghanistan and Iraq after the US use of uranium weapons; US destabilisation of the government of Haiti; and a legal ruling that apparently gave Fox News the right to distort its news reports (Phillips, 2004). None of these stories was actually censored in the sense of the police kicking down doors and removing presses or computers, of course. They were just deemed too boring, too contentious or too expensive to warrant much attention from news organisations that were too busy following each other and watching their own backs. As investigative journalist Greg Palast writes in an introduction to *Censored 2005* (Phillips, 2004: 31–2), important stories have been "blocked, ignored, crushed, buried while the Fox in the news henhouse lingers on the investigative revelations in the latest *Sports Illustrated* swimwear issue".

Journalism need not be as shallow as that, believes Peter Phillips, director of Project Censored. Echoing the old *Liverpool Free Press* ethos of news as useful information, he asks us to envisage what "real news" might look and sound like:

> Imagine "real news" as media information that contributes to the lives and socio-political understandings of working people. Such real news informs, balances, and awakens the less powerful in society. Real news speaks truth to power and challenges the hegemonic top-down corporate entertainment news systems. Real news empowers and keeps key segments of working people … tuned in, informed, and active.
>
> (Phillips, 2004: 229)

The Committee of Concerned Journalists came up with a similar idea after holding 21 public meetings across the United States to discuss what journalism was for. They concluded that its first principle was "to provide people with the information they need to be free and self-governing" (Kovach and Rosenstiel, 2003: 12).

If that sounds as if it might be a little on the dull side, it needn't be. Consider the following examples.

During the G8 summit in July 2005, BBC television's *Newsnight* had all the usual heavyweight political coverage you would expect on such an occasion, but they also sent correspondent Paul Mason out into the fields to spend the week embedded with groups of protesters. Mason's illuminating despatches from behind the demonstrators' lines helped inform us about what was going on and why, and gave a contrasting perspective to the mainstream media view from behind police lines. This was enhanced by the imaginative decision to have him writing a blog on the *Newsnight* website in addition to filming reports for the programme itself (Mason, 2005).

A similar shift in perspective was used to good effect in BBC Wales' coverage of the aftermath of a recent flood that hit a village. A journalist took a lightweight video camera and spent several days with a local family, recording how the flood had affected them. When a government minister paid the village a visit, the event was filmed not by the usual crew accompanying the politician on his whistlestop tour, but by the journalist in the house. In a reversal of the conventional approach to such an event, the action is seen from the villagers' point of view as they open their front door and find the minister on their doorstep (Kinsey and others, 2006).

The alternative news-sheet *SchNEWS*, published in Brighton since 1994, has a popular "Crap arrest of the week" column that details and ridicules examples of over-zealous policing from around the world. This idea found a powerful echo in the mainstream media when the *Independent* newspaper devoted its front page to a juxtaposition of three separate court cases that happened to take place on the same day:

> WAR CRIMINALS
> *Maya Evans*, 25, convicted for reading out names of 97 British soldiers killed in Iraq at unauthorised protest
>
> *Douglas Barker*, 72, threatened with jail for withholding part of his tax payment in protest at the Iraq conflict
>
> *Malcolm Kendall-Smith*, a 37-year-old RAF medical officer, facing court-martial for refusing to serve in Iraq
>
> (*Independent*, 8 December 2005)

On another occasion, the same newspaper gave over its front page to a story so simple and effective it is a wonder that nobody had thought to do it earlier. Faced with the US and UK governments' refusal to do "body counts" of civilian casualties in occupied Iraq, Robert Fisk (2005) did what good reporters do in such circumstances: he went to see for himself. The people described in his resulting story about the mortuary in Baghdad were the "ordinary" victims of conflict, people who rarely get much coverage in mainstream journalism when they are foreign and far away:

> The Baghdad morgue is a fearful place of heat and stench and mourning, the cries of relatives echoing down the narrow, foetid laneway behind the pale-yellow brick medical centre where the authorities keep their computerised records. So many corpses are being brought to the mortuary that human remains are stacked on top of each other. Unidentified bodies must be buried within days for lack of space… In just 36 hours – from dawn on Sunday to midday on Monday – 62 Baghdad civilians had been killed. No Western official, no Iraqi government minister, no civil servant, no press release from the authorities, no newspaper, mentioned this terrible statistic. The dead of Iraq – as they have from the beginning of our illegal invasion – were simply written out of the script. Officially they do not exist.
>
> (Fisk, 2005)

That's the worthy *Independent*, of course, which has also challenged the prevailing discourse about immigration, with headlines such as: REVEALED: HOW IMMIGRANTS HELP THE ECONOMY (14 May 2005). But the more popular papers are also capable of revelation and insight when they remember that news need not begin and end with sex and celebs. *Metro*, for example, chose to step aside from the habitual news agenda when it splashed on: 15,000 CHILDREN A DAY KILLED BY HUNGER (3 May 2006). Of course, one day's shock headline is unlikely to change dominant news values – and, arguably, the scale of world hunger would be expressed only if there were to be a similar splash every day – but *Metro's* selection demonstrates that there are choices to be made.

In an echo of its "shock issues" of the 1960s, the *Daily Mirror* devoted several pages in 2003 to challenging some of the prejudices against asylum seekers:

> MIRROR SPECIAL ON THE ISSUE TEARING BRITAIN APART: ASYLUM – THE TRUTH
> It is the most hotly debated issue of our time, a debate driven by fear, myth and the hysteria of the right-wing press. Asylum seekers – scroungers sponging off our over-stretched state or global victims who need help? ... [A]ccording to a Home Office study, migrants – including asylum seekers – actually contributed around £2.5 billion in taxes in 1999–2000. A recent Mori poll showed that people in the UK believe that Britain takes in 23 per cent of the world's refugees. But in reality, we take in less than 2 per cent. Although seen as a soft touch, Britain is actually only ranked tenth in the EC in asylum applications in relation to overall population ...
>
> (Donnelly, 2003)

Even the *Daily Express* – which, as we shall see in Chapter 9, has been accused by its own journalists of pandering to racism – can resist its knee-jerk impulse on occasions, as when it reported on a London school where pupils speak 58 languages as a success story rather than as the end of civilisation as we know it (Willey, 2005).

One Thursday in the middle of August every year the A-Level results are published, accompanied on that day's TV news and the following day's newspapers with the predictable row about falling standards and the even more predictable pictures of teenage girls in crop tops hugging each other. But, while doing its duty in this manner, the *Sun* also had an original thought in 2005, which was to go to the family of black teenager Anthony Walker who had been killed in a racist attack three weeks earlier. Sure enough, the family had just received the news that Anthony had achieved straight As in his exams and the *Sun* got a front page splash: WHAT A WASTE: TOP GRADES FOR ANTHONY (19 August 2005). Of course, a racist attack on somebody who is good at school is no better or worse than a racist attack on somebody who fails their exams, but the story did remind readers of the murderous results of racism.

The *Sun* put its enormous influence to good use again when it decided that domestic violence had for too long been a hidden crime:

> EVERY WEEK TWO WOMEN ARE KILLED BY THEIR PARTNERS
> By the end of this week two more women will be dead – victims of their abusive partners. More British women aged 19 to 44 are killed as a result of domestic violence than anything else …
>
> (Hunter and Bolouri, 2005)

The paper's editor Rebekah Wade inadvertently raised the profile of domestic violence even further when, shortly after launching the *Sun* campaign, she hit the headlines for allegedly hitting her husband, much to the amusement of other journalists throughout the land (Edwards, 2005). Apparently it was "just a silly row which got out of hand," Wade told her own newspaper (*Sun*, 2005). In the normal course of events, however, domestic violence attracts much less news coverage than does violence by strangers.

Recounting the hidden story of those at the bottom of the social heap is the speciality of Nick Davies, a journalist who has frequently been given large amounts of space in the *Guardian* newspaper, as with a series on poverty that began:

> Ryzard studied banking and finance in Warsaw. He has ended up in a bank in London – sleeping in its doorway … It is half past six in the morning. Ryzard rolls up his sleeping bag and sets off for a day of survival. He calls it "walking for food", tramping miles in search of the soup kitchens where he can eat, and of the hidden refuges where he can find the others who, like him, have fallen off the edge and tumbled back to the days of Dickensian London. A day with Ryzard is a journey through a secret city.
>
> (Davies, 2005a)

Personal stories of individuals such as Ryzard are not just recounted with empathy but are placed in a wider context. Such reporting seems to be an example of what the academic Simon Cottle argues that we need a lot more of:

> [R]eportage … which seeks to go beyond "thin" news reports, headlines and news values, to reveal something of the deep structures, contending perspectives and lived experiences that often underpin if not propel news stories forward and which grant them meaning – both for the participants and protagonists involved as well as potentially for us, the audience.
>
> (Cottle, 2005a: 109)

Cottle (2005a: 116–17) cites the example of a report on BBC television's *Panorama* (5 October 2003) that sought to give a "human face" to the "terrorism suspects" being held without trial by US forces in Guantanamo Bay – people who are rendered "speechless" in most coverage.

Although such contextualised reporting is too often absent from the news, it does get in sometimes, according to an academic study that highlights several further examples, including:

- A report on BBC News 24 concerning global warming, which focused on the Greenland ice caps and explained the ways that this could impact everywhere on the globe.
- A Sky News report on congestion charging, which explored the way in which it could work, the impact on the average motorist, and experience from where it had been tried.
- A report on BBC One's *Ten O'Clock News* that covered the refugee crisis in Sudan by looking back at British Commonwealth involvement in the country and at how the crisis had developed.

(Lewis and others, 2005: 471–2)

By stepping back to gain perspective in this way, journalists attempt to give the audience a bigger picture of what is going on in the world.

And there are many other examples. Such as when ITV News combined reports from those parts of the world most affected by climate change with details of the impact made by individuals' decisions in the UK (*Press Gazette*, 2006a). Or when local newspapers told some of the real-life horror stories lived by refugees who had moved to their areas (Grant, 2005). Or when, to the accompaniment of noises in the US about a possible attack on Iran, *Channel Four News* (6 March 2006) went back to the 1953 US-backed coup to put the story in context for viewers today. These are just a few of the ways in which journalists are reporting the news in a thoughtful way – not in some supposed golden age 20, 50, or however many years ago, but here and now in the twenty-first century – and giving the lie to the cynical view that ethics and journalism have to be opposites. I could have selected other stories to illustrate this point, from journalists working in a range of media in a range of locations, and readers of this book may well be aware of further examples. It cannot be denied, however, that such examples are too often the exception rather than the rule.

BEYOND THE DIARY

Anyone who despairs of the unethical excesses, the debased news values and the lack of proportion of some journalism should perhaps go to the website of

BBC Radio Four's long-running *From Our Own Correspondent* and listen to the recent despatches archived there. This is a programme in which reporters are freed from the constraints of news values and the diary, freed from the necessity of providing audio soundbites, and freed from the requirement to sum up a complex situation in a few seconds. Instead, their stories can live and breathe, with the best examples blending the personal and the political, painting a small picture in sufficient detail to illustrate a bigger picture.

Not everyone is a fan. *Panorama*'s Tom Mangold (2006) dismisses *From Our Own Correspondent* as "anodyne". Certainly, some items are too twee, the audience is assumed to be middle class and middle aged, and even unorthodox reporting can develop its own clichés; but mostly the programme leaves its listeners better informed about the world and its contributors less frustrated about their craft. BBC world affairs editor John Simpson says that it is the favourite programme among BBC foreign correspondents because it allows them to tell stories in more depth than they are usually allowed on broadcast news:

> We still have endless battles with editors who think a minute and a half (about 270 words) is long enough for a complicated story, but … the detail is what matters. If a report is too brief, people can't understand what is happening; so why bother to broadcast it? Explaining things is the basic purpose of reporting … You don't lose the detail in *From Our Own Correspondent*: it luxuriates there in full, florid complexity. Long may it survive.
>
> (Simpson, 2005)

Indeed. But rather than restricting such an approach to the ghetto of a specialised programme that covers only overseas events, could the windows of more newsrooms not be opened similarly to let a bit of fresh air blow across other stories?

MATTERS OF LIFE AND DEATH

Not that everyone would welcome such a departure from reporting conventions, judging by reaction to the following description on *From Our Own Correspondent* by Barbara Plett of events surrounding Palestinian leader Yasser Arafat:

> The world watches the unfolding drama as the man who has become the symbol for Palestinian nationalism seems to hover between life and death … To be honest, the coverage of Yasser Arafat's illness and departure from Palestine was a real grind. I churned out one report after the other, without any sense of drama. Foreign journalists

> seemed much more excited about Mr Arafat's fate than anyone in Ramallah … where were the people, I wondered, the mass demonstrations of solidarity, the frantic expressions of concern? Was this another story we Western journalists were getting wrong, bombarding the world with news of what we think is an historic event, while the locals get on with their lives? Yet when the helicopter carrying the frail old man rose above his ruined compound, I started to cry – without warning. In quieter moments since I have asked myself, why the sudden surge of emotion?
>
> (Plett, 2004)

In a calm and measured manner, Plett went on to analyse both her own reaction and those of the Palestinian people. But it was all too much for the BBC Board of Governors (2005) which, following a complaint by a listener, ruled that "the reference to the reporter starting to cry did breach the requirements of due impartiality". It was not clear if the objection was to the act of crying itself, or to mentioning the fact. However, we did not hear the governors speaking out when the BBC repeatedly reported that "the whole nation" was mourning the death of Princess Diana or the Queen Mother, when the reality was that most people seemed to be getting on with their lives as normal … much as the people of Ramallah were apparently doing as Arafat lay dying.

It ought to go without saying that the reporting of death is a sensitive business, perhaps never more so than in the case of suicide. How, then, did *The Times* come to publish a graphic photograph of a woman falling through the air, having just jumped from a hotel window ledge? The decision to publish the photograph over most of a page was apparently taken after lengthy discussions involving senior editorial figures. But it left many commentators, including Peter Cole (2006), unhappy about the use of such a picture for "ghoulish entertainment". Mike Jempson (2006), director of the media ethics charity Mediawise, condemned the decision to publish by *The Times* and a minority of other national newspapers as irresponsible, because of the additional distress caused to friends and relatives, and also because research suggests there is a risk of copycat behaviour when such coverage occurs. In rejecting a complaint by a friend of the dead woman, the Press Complaints Commission (PCC) (2006) said it was wary of restricting "the right of newspapers to report newsworthy events that take place in public". However, upon reflection the PCC later amended its code of practice and now urges editors to avoid printing "excessive detail" about suicide methods.

There are occasions when journalists have been accused of prompting suicide. The headteacher of a school apparently killed himself after appearing in court on a child abuse charge, having gone missing the day before the case was due to be reported in his local newspaper. The National Association of Headteachers blamed his death on the publicity the case had attracted, but the newspaper's editor defended publication:

> I didn't think twice about naming him. He appeared in open court and was charged. We carried two or three pars of straightforward, factual reporting; we didn't dress it up in any way. No representation was made to me to keep his name out of the paper, but I wouldn't have done anyway … [T]here is a public interest in reporting that a headmaster has appeared on charges like that. The moment you start making moral judgements about which cases to include and which to leave out, you are on a slippery slope.
>
> (Quoted in Pape and Featherstone, 2005: 182–3)

Death can bring out the worst in journalism – "How would you describe Diana's greatness?" I seem to recall one distinguished TV hack asking another distinguished TV hack on that cringeworthy Sunday morning back in August 1997 – but it can also bring out the best. When Rosa Parks died, the *Guardian*'s Gary Younge wrote a piece that treated her with the dignity she had seized for herself and other black citizens of the United States 50 years earlier, while also placing her individual story within a wider geographical and historical context:

> "Y'all better make it light on yourself and let me have those seats," the bus driver, James Blake, told three black passengers on the fifth row of his bus when it stopped outside Montgomery, Alabama's Empire Theatre. Two gave up their places so a white man could sit down. Rosa Parks stayed put.
>
> "If you don't stand up, I'm going to have to call the police and have you arrested," said Mr Blake. "You may do that," said Ms Parks.
>
> And so with a passive aggressive act of political rebellion against the racism of the deep south, Ms Parks, who died yesterday aged 92, took her stand by keeping her seat …
>
> At a time when apartheid was the international rule – enforced by all colonial powers including the British – rather than the exception, her challenge was to the established order of the global south as well as the deep south. Within the next 10 years 20 African countries would gain independence from white minority rule …
>
> From the position where she was ushered off the bus on Dexter Avenue she could see the point where Jefferson Davis had stamped his foot and declared an independent Confederacy to defend slavery less than a century before, and where the former governor George Wallace would promise "segregation now, segregation tomorrow, segregation for ever" less than 10 years later …
>
> As an icon Ms Parks entered not just history but mythology, constantly misportrayed as an accidental heroine … The truth was that she was a lifelong anti-racism activist and feminist who had often been expelled from the local buses for refusing to comply, including once by the same Mr Blake some 12 years previously …
>
> (Younge, 2005)

That article was on the news pages, but it is in the Obituaries sections of papers such as the *Daily Telegraph*, *Independent* and *Guardian* – full of extraordinary people in ordinary circumstances and ordinary people in extraordinary circumstances – that you are more likely to find such a good read. Australian academic Nigel Starck (2005: 281), a connoisseur of obituaries in UK newspapers, has noted a shift in their tone and style over the past two decades: "The reverential voice and faithful recitation of curriculum vitae have been replaced by inventive phrase, shafted observation, and understated humour … Quite simply, the best obituaries of today are sublime to read." True. But must we always wait for people to die before we can write about their lives with insight and shafts of observation?

Speaking of waiting to die, what of Dino the dog? There is something to be said for reporting his fate and that of others like him, just as long as we don't squeeze out more consequential stories while doing it. It might help if more of us paused occasionally to ask the question: "Why is *that* news?" And if we looked beyond the end of our "nose for news" to find the answer.

FURTHER READING

See Chapter 3 of Harcup (2004) for further discussion of news values in mainstream journalism, Harcup and O'Neill (2001) for an introduction to relevant research and theoretical concepts, and Harrison (2006) for a readable account of the academic study of news. Chapter 7 of Lynch and McGoldrick (2005) unpicks the whole idea of news values and uses the work of Derrida and other critical theorists to analyse what the authors see as journalism's structural bias in favour of event over process, effect over cause, and dominant discourse over critical reflection.

The news values of alternative media are contrasted with the mainstream approach in Whitaker (1981), and Phillips (2004) gives plenty of examples of stories that have been ignored or downplayed by mainstream journalism. Cottle (2005a) explains his concept of "thick" – as in depth – journalism and gives further examples from television news and current affairs. For examples of reports on *From Our Own Correspondent*, see the programme's website at http://news.bbc.co.uk/1/hi/programmes/from_our_own_correspondent/ default.stm or Grant (2005) for a collection of transcripts. Chapter 5 of Chambers and others (2004) explores the extent to which the increase in the proportion of women journalists has impacted upon news values and newsroom culture. Finally, useful guidelines and advice on sensitive reporting of suicide are available from the National Union of Journalists (NUJ, 2005) and Mediawise (2003); a report on improving the reporting of mental health issues has been produced by Shift (2006); guidelines on the reporting of race are reproduced in Appendix 3; and Elliott (2005) offers further advice on the reporting of people of different races and religions.

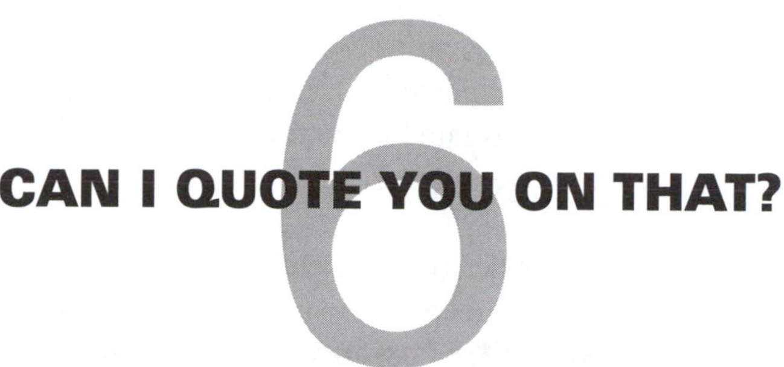

6 CAN I QUOTE YOU ON THAT?

Journalists and their Sources

John Simpson still recalls his first assignment as a BBC reporter. That's hardly surprising: it ended up with him being punched … by the prime minister of the day. It was 1970 and Simpson was a fresh-faced young radio journalist. The news editor told him that the Prime Minister's Office had organised a photocall for London's Euston station, from where Harold Wilson would be catching a train to his parliamentary constituency of Huyton. This was considered potentially newsworthy because of speculation that Wilson might call a general election at any moment. When the prime minister arrived, surrounded by the usual posse of security men and flunkeys, none of the more experienced reporters tried to ask him anything. So the BBC's newest recruit stepped from the hack pack into Mr Wilson's path and, thrusting a microphone towards him, said: "Excuse me, prime minister ..." Simpson describes what happened next:

> My entire world exploded. Wilson grabbed the shaft of the microphone with his left hand and tried to break it out of my grasp. With his right he punched me hard in the stomach. He was saying things to me, but I couldn't give them my undivided attention because I was too busy bending over and gasping … Then he let go of my microphone and swept past … The journalists gathered round laughing. "You can't just doorstep the PM like that, sonny," said one of the older reporters, patting me comfortingly on the shoulder … It was only five past eleven on my first working day, and I had been physically assaulted by the prime minister. My career was finished before it had begun.
>
> (1999: 93–4)

Not quite. Wilson didn't carry out his threat of making an official complaint, and Simpson went on to become the BBC's world affairs editor, no less. But the episode hints at the shift in the relationship between journalists and sources over the decades, with questions such as, "Is there anything else you would like to tell the grateful nation, prime minister?" giving way to a rather less deferential style of journalism. And a good thing too. Back in 1970, despite the presence of numerous photographers and TV crews, nothing was broadcast or printed about the incident at Euston station; if the same thing happened today we would be treated to action replays for days afterwards, and then everyone would have a good laugh about it on *Have I Got News For You?*

John Simpson was neither the first nor the last journalist to be thumped in the line of duty, of course. Gerry Brown (1995: xiv) recalled turning up on the doorstep of a 17-year-old boy who was due to marry his 26-year-old teacher. As soon as Brown announced himself as being from the *News of the World*, the teenager shouted "Yaaaa baaastard", punched him on the nose, and slammed the door on the hack, who by this time had blood pouring down his face. Even for a foot-in-the-door man from the tabloids, however, this was not an everyday occurrence. Thankfully, not every relationship between a journalist and a source is as fraught as John Simpson's meeting with Harold Wilson or Gerry Brown's clash with the young bridegroom.

THE JOURNALIST AND THE WEAPONS EXPERT

Probably no encounter between journalist and source has been scrutinised more closely than was Andrew Gilligan's meeting with Dr David Kelly in a London hotel on 22 May 2003. As would soon become all too well known, Dr Kelly was the UK's top scientific adviser on so-called weapons of mass destruction (WMD), and he worked as a weapons inspector and a consultant to the Ministry of Defence; Andrew Gilligan was the defence correspondent for BBC Radio Four's flagship *Today* programme. The subject of their meeting was a dossier published by the UK government on 24 September 2002 entitled *Iraq's Weapons of Mass Destruction: the assessment of the British Government*. That was the dossier in which prime minister Tony Blair wrote a foreword that stated:

> In recent months, I have been increasingly alarmed by the evidence from inside Iraq that ... Saddam Hussein is continuing to develop WMD ... What I believe the assessed intelligence has established beyond doubt is that Saddam has continued to produce chemical and biological weapons, that he continues in his efforts to develop nuclear weapons, and that he has been able to extend the range of his ballistic missile programme ... I am in no doubt that the threat is serious and current, that he has made progress on WMD, and that he has to be stopped ... And the document discloses that his military planning allows for some of the WMD to be ready within 45 minutes of an order to use them.
>
> (HM Government, 2002: 3–4)

The 45-minute claim was referred to several times in the dossier. The executive summary emphasised that Iraq had "military plans for the use of chemical and biological weapons" and that "some of these weapons are deployable within 45 minutes of an order to use them" (HM Government, 2002: 5–7). Because of evidence to both the Hutton and Butler Inquiries, we would later learn that the dossier was revised in the days before publication. During this process, Downing Street chief of staff Jonathan Powell was asking: "What will be the headline in the *Standard* on day of publication? What do we want it to be?" (quoted in Norton-Taylor, 2004: 4). Entirely predictably, given the seemingly specific nature of the deadly threat outlined by Tony Blair, that day's London *Evening Standard* carried the headline 45 MINUTES FROM ATTACK, a theme adopted by the bulk of the UK media over the following 24 hours. As the *Guardian*'s security affairs editor Richard Norton-Taylor (2004: 5) notes, Downing Street seemed "only too delighted at headlines in the press at the time warning of a 45-minute threat to Britain".

Eight months later, Andrew Gilligan met his source in the Charing Cross Hotel for a background conversation about how things were going in Iraq. By this time, the country had been invaded, US President George Bush had declared hostilities over – although the killing had only just started – and awkward questions were being asked about why WMD had been neither fired nor found. "This was an informal and off-the-record meeting that I wasn't expecting to become a story at all, let alone the big deal that it did," recalls Andrew Gilligan when I ask him about it in another hotel bar three years later.

Big deal it certainly became, when conversation between Gilligan and Kelly turned to the September 2002 dossier that had helped pave the way for the UK's involvement in the Iraq war. According to notes typed into an electronic organiser by Gilligan, Dr Kelly told him:

> Transformed week before publication to make it sexier. The classic was the 45 minutes. Most things in dossier were double source but that was single source. One source said it took 45 minutes to set up a missile assembly, that was misinterpreted. Most people in intelligence weren't happy with it because it didn't reflect the considered view they were putting across. Campbell: real information but unreliable, included against our wishes. Not in original draft – dull, he asked if anything else could go in …
>
> (BBC, 2003a)

The Campbell referred to was Alastair, the former Fleet Street journalist who had become Tony Blair's confidant and spin-doctor-in-chief. A week after this conversation, Andrew Gilligan reported on the *Today* programme with reference to the prime minister's 45-minute claim:

> Now that claim has come back to haunt Mr Blair because if the weapons had been that readily to hand, they probably would have been found by now. But you know, it could have been an honest mistake, but what I have been told is that the government

> knew that claim was questionable, even before the war, even before they wrote it in their dossier. I have spoken to a British official who was involved in the preparation of the dossier, and he told me that until the week before it was published, the draft dossier produced by the Intelligence Services added little to what was already publicly known. He said, "It was transformed in the week before it was published, to make it sexier. The classic example was the statement that weapons of mass destruction were ready for use within 45 minutes. That information was not in the original draft. It was included in the dossier against our wishes, because it wasn't reliable. Most things in the dossier were double source, but that was single source, and we believed that the source was wrong." Now this official told us that the transformation of the dossier took place at the behest of Downing Street, and he added, "Most people in Intelligence weren't happy with the dossier, because it didn't reflect the considered view they were putting forward."
>
> (BBC, 2003b)

Those words had been scripted by Gilligan on the basis of his conversation with Dr Kelly, whose identity he did not reveal. They were first broadcast just after 7.30 am on 29 May 2003 and were repeated in edited form on BBC news bulletins throughout the day. However, little noticed at the time, the reporter had used rather looser language in a two-way interview broadcast on *Today* at 6.07 am (see Chapter 2). In this earlier item, he had reported being told by his source that the government "probably knew" that the 45-minute claim "was wrong, even before it decided to put it in" (BBC, 2003b). Those words were not exactly what Dr Kelly told Andrew Gilligan, according to the latter's electronic notes. The BBC man would eventually concede this point, telling the Hutton Inquiry that it had been a slip of the tongue to say that he had been told the government probably knew the 45 minutes claim to be wrong. His imprecise wording was not the focus of much attention around the time of the broadcast because the government's aggressive response concentrated on denying the more general charge that it had "sexed up" the dossier to strengthen the case for war.

Looking back on the whole affair, Andrew Gilligan says it was a mistake to run the initial report as a two-way broadcast, because that had made it easier for such a slip of the tongue to occur:

> We shouldn't have done a story like that as a live, frankly, but we didn't know it was a big story. It was quite wrong to get that one sentence in that one very early morning two-way wrong. *I* could have said it, but the key words were "I've been told" when I hadn't been told. Even though it does turn out to be in fact right, it's not quite what I was told. Actually, I would have been perfectly justified in saying it on my own. Quite clearly, the government did know it [the 45 minutes claim] was wrong, and I don't mean they knew it was a lie or that they'd made it up, but that they knew it was exaggerated. They didn't make a fuss about that at the beginning, then they realised it was the chink in our armour.

The conversation between Kelly and Gilligan is an example of what is termed a journalist–source relationship. The journalist–source relationship has been described by academics such as Herbert Gans (1980: 116–17) as part dance and part tug-of-war, while Jerry Palmer (2000: 17) calls it a transaction in which "both journalists and sources have motives which lead them to interpret events in particular ways". Dr Kelly was not a novice as a source, and he frequently provided reporters with background information on his areas of expertise, but he was certainly a stranger to the kind of media storm that erupted around him after the UK government took exception to Andrew Gilligan's reporting. Downing Street, in the person of Alastair Campbell, demanded that the BBC apologise; the BBC, not unused to attacks from that quarter, stood by its story. As this battle of wills continued for several weeks, Dr Kelly volunteered the information to his employers that he had met Andrew Gilligan but did not recognise himself as the source of the controversial story. Events moved fast: Downing Street made Dr Kelly's name public and he was questioned by two committees of MPs before, apparently, going for a walk alone and killing himself, thereby setting in train the Hutton Inquiry (Hutton, 2004; Coates, 2004; Rogers, 2004).

The final report by Lord Hutton was dismissed by many commentators as an Establishment "whitewash". However, the process of the inquiry itself exposed to scrutiny not just the innards of the normally secret state, but also the workings of journalism in general and the journalist–source relationship in particular. Aspiring journalists – indeed, *all* journalists – would do well to study the evidence collected on the inquiry website, to reflect on issues such as a journalist's responsibility to a source, a journalist's responsibility to the audience, the importance of taking and keeping good notes, the importance of precise wording in journalism and dossiers alike; and to imagine themselves in the position of journalists Andrew Gilligan, Susan Watts or Gavin Hewitt, who were all called before the inquiry to be questioned in public about their working methods. As their BBC colleague Andrew Marr (2005: xv) later observed: "Many of the reporters slouched at the back of the courtroom … wondered how their own practices would stand up to that kind of examination."

Although Dr Kelly was the source for the Gilligan story, he attempted to distance himself from it, telling the Foreign Affairs Select Committee of the House of Commons: "From the conversation I had with him [Gilligan], I do not see how he could make the authoritative statement he was making from the comments that I made … It does not sound like my expression of words. It does not sound like a quote from me" (FAC, 2003). The next day Dr Kelly told the Intelligence and Security Committee: "I actually very rarely meet journalists although I do talk to them on the telephone and on this occasion,

I must admit, I'd regarded it more as being more a private conversation than I had a briefing or in any way a disclosure at all" (quoted in Coates, 2004: 133). Yet we know that Dr Kelly had said some similar things to another journalist: Susan Watts, science editor of BBC Two's *Newsnight*. We know that because Susan Watts had a written note – in a mixture of shorthand and longhand – and a tape recording of separate conversations with Dr Kelly. The whole world can now read her notes as well as a transcript of the taped telephone conversation on the inquiry website (BBC, 2003c; 2003d). You might like to pause and think of that fact the next time you are about to interview somebody: how would your notes stand up to such scrutiny?

We know that, a fortnight before he met Andrew Gilligan, Dr Kelly told Susan Watts that it had been a mistake to include the 45-minute claim in the government dossier. He said it had been included because Alastair Campbell had seen it and thought it had sounded good, even though the information had not been corroborated. Unlike Andrew Gilligan, Susan Watts did not make a story out of this, seeing it as a "gossipy aside comment" rather than a real revelation (quoted in Rogers, 2004: 104). The day after the *Today* programme had run Gilligan's story, Susan Watts told Dr Kelly: "I may have missed a trick on that one" (BBC, 2003d). Following the *Today* broadcast, Dr Kelly had also been contacted by Gavin Hewitt, a special correspondent for BBC One's *10 O'Clock News*. Gavin Hewitt's note of what Dr Kelly told him on the telephone includes at the top of the first page, clearly legible in longhand, the words: "Dossier. No. 10 spin came into play" (BBC, 2003e), and that was the phrase Hewitt used on the television news. So, although Dr Kelly apparently said similar things to these journalists, all three ran slightly different stories. If the journalist–source relationship is indeed a dance, then clearly it takes two to tango (Gans, 1980: 116).

Academic commentator Steven Barnett (2005: 333–6) notes that Gilligan, Watts and Hewitt had all discovered "a legitimate story of huge public significance" from "a senior and reliable source": the story being that changes were made to the September 2002 dossier at the behest of Downing Street. Each of the three journalists had spoken to the same source independently and used the information slightly differently. Barnett argues that Gilligan was the one who broke the dossier story, but without the scrupulous care that was required. Intelligence experts Anthony Glees and Philip Davies (2004: 65) write that "virtually the only BBC journalist to come out of the Kelly affair with an enhanced reputation" was Susan Watts, who had treated Dr Kelly's comments about the 45-minute warning as gossip rather than the basis for a story.

In the final days of his life, Dr Kelly told his daughter Rachel that he did not understand how Gilligan could have made "such forceful claims" based on their conversation (quoted in Dodd, 2004: 77). He would not be the first person to talk to a journalist and then be surprised at the resulting story, as we saw in the very different case of Joe McGinniss and Jeffrey McDonald discussed in Chapter 2. And, if Dr Kelly felt that what he told Gilligan in the Charing Cross hotel had been more of "a private conversation" than a disclosure, then he would not have been the first source to speak to a journalist who had a different understanding of the "transaction". We also know that he was not the last, because another Kelly – Tom, an official spokesman for Tony Blair at the time – appeared to suffer from just such a misunderstanding. Two weeks after the death of Dr Kelly, the *Independent*'s deputy political editor Paul Waugh (2003) quoted an un-named "senior Whitehall source" as describing the deceased scientist as a "Walter Mitty" fantasist who had exaggerated his own role in the dossier saga. After the Walter Mitty story appeared, an official spokeswoman was asked about it at the daily Downing Street press briefing; if the resulting exchange as written up on the Downing Street website was any kind of dance, it appears to have been a dance around the subject as far as the Prime Minister's Spokeswoman (PMS) was concerned:

> Asked for a reaction to a report in today's *Independent* newspaper in which a "source" had suggested that the government considered Dr Kelly to be a "Walter Mitty" character, the PMS said that she did not know where the comment had come from, but we wanted to make it absolutely clear that no one would say such a thing with the approval of the prime minister – or indeed anyone else within Downing Street ... Asked if she was saying that those in Downing Street who spoke to the press did not do so with the prime minister's approval, the PMS said that she was making the point that no one would say such a thing with the approval of the prime minister. Asked by the *Independent* correspondent to explain in what capacity those who had spoken to him had been acting, the PMS said that she couldn't say because she did not know where the comment had come from. Put to her that it must have come from someone in authority in Downing Street, the PMS repeated that she did not know where the comment had come from. Put to her by the *Independent* that it was clearly a government "line to take" given other people had been saying similar things last week, the PMS repeated that she did not know where the comment had come from and underlined once again that it had not been made with the approval of the prime minister or anyone else in Downing Street. Asked the prime minister's view of the comment, the PMS said that she hadn't spoken to the prime minister this morning.
>
> (Number Ten, 2003)

Dr Kelly's grieving widow Janice would later tell the Hutton Inquiry that the fantasist claim had left her feeling even more "devastated" because it was so far from the truth (Rogers, 2004: 204). The story rumbled on, and Downing Street eventually admitted that the offending briefing had been given by Tom Kelly (Hall, 2003) who, for his part, expressed regret that "what I thought was a private conversation with a journalist ... has led to further public controversy" (quoted in Rogers, 2004: 143).

As we saw in Chapter 2, sources sometimes feel themselves to have been betrayed by journalists. What an examination of the David Kelly case shows is that things are rarely that simple, and for Richard Norton-Taylor (2004: 7) the evidence suggests that "almost everyone" involved was to blame in some way for "the whole ugly and, in the end, tragic episode".

Reflecting on this episode with the benefit of hindsight, Andrew Gilligan is prepared to accept his share of the blame – but only his share. That is, in the initial live two-way (which he points out was not his idea), he should not have said his source told him something that may well have been true, but which his source did not actually tell him. He feels BBC management was also at fault for not subsequently examining every word that was broadcast to see what could be defended and what should be corrected. And he feels that David Kelly himself was less than frank when questioned by his employers and MPs:

> He is not exempt from blame. He probably should have come out and said, "Yes I did say that", but he was worried that he would lose his job. Had he but known it, he couldn't possibly have been sacked, because he'd have been a national hero. The political climate became much more aggressive, because clearly the war in Iraq was not going well, and David realised that he might have been getting into more trouble than he anticipated, I suppose.

But the bulk of whatever blame there is belongs on the government side, insists Andrew Gilligan:

> The complaint from the government was that the entire story was wrong. Had we corrected the 6.07 broadcast during the row, it wouldn't have made any difference. The government would have settled for nothing less than a complete retraction of the story, which was not something that I or the BBC could ever truthfully have given, because it *was* true. It was totally absurd that the Hutton Inquiry became about me and my story as it did, rather than about Tony Blair and his dossier. My story, even if it had been completely wrong, it's a news story, whereas the dossier sent the entire country to war and was responsible for something like 30,000 deaths. The trouble is that a lot of the understanding of my story has been in the light of what happened afterwards, and because it resulted in the resignations of the chairman and director general of the BBC, then it must have been a terribly bad story. But actually, if you go back and look at it, it's a terribly limp little thing, it's awfully measured and equivocal.

So why does he feel that Dr Kelly was willing to talk to him and other journalists? Specifically, because he was concerned about the credibility of the dossier. Generally, because "he was naturally chatty and enjoyed talking to journalists and displaying his knowledge". After a political storm erupted over the dossier story, Andrew Gilligan again tried to contact Dr Kelly, but this time without success:

> I was worried about compromising him. I was fairly sure that the numbers I called were being logged and I thought it entirely possible that somebody was listening to my calls.

> I did call him from a pay phone, but I couldn't get through, and I didn't want to leave a message, I didn't want to do anything which would compromise him because it was very, very frightening.
>
> I had a great deal of unpleasant stuff written about me but I coped because I knew that most of it wasn't meant personally, it was political rhetoric. The trouble is, I think David didn't realise that, he thought it was real, and he thought it was all terribly serious. And it was terribly serious in one way, but in another way it was a political game that was being played, one of those Westminster games, and he didn't realise that, he took it all very much to heart. For all that I've said about the political game, it was extremely frightening, and it must have been absolutely terrifying for him. I was an experienced practitioner, I'd seen it happen before to other people, I'd done it to other people, I'd been part of it. I've doorstepped people. But God knows how frightening it was for him, to have that kind of thing orchestrated against oneself by the government.

A KIND OF JOURNALISTIC DUTY

In the context of political reporting, Andrew Marr writes that there are times when a journalist "must behave like a shit – must build up close sources and then, quite often, betray them". Betray them, that is, by revealing what the journalist sees as the truth, if and when the public interest in revelation is judged to outweigh the personal loss of a source; a source who may also have become a friend, or almost a friend. This complex and delicate situation is illustrated by Marr's description of his relationship with a politician:

> As a rising Tory minister he was an excellent and frank source, loyal to the prime minister but also outspoken about the dilemmas ripping through Whitehall. I thoroughly enjoyed his company, and his wife's, and we lunched together regularly. I visited him at home; he was a wonderful host, and generous with stories. Then came the time when, as education secretary, he was visibly struggling and his policies were unravelling. Instead of writing supportively and understandingly, I joined the critical pack. It seemed to me to be the correct objective judgment of his performance, and therefore a kind of journalistic duty. It seemed to him a personal betrayal and he never forgave me, cutting me dead for years … This pattern … is common across Westminster. The cynical but professional answer is to have a range of good sources, with more always under cultivation. … But we all go easy on pals occasionally – the decent among us, at least. In return, we hope, the public gets a better feeling about what's really happening behind closed doors.
>
> (Marr, 2005: 184)

Some journalists manage to avoid the feeling that they are behaving like a "shit" by avoiding personal contact with those in their firing line. Former *Private Eye* editor Richard Ingrams (2005: 95) recalls that Paul Foot, for example, "was often loath to meet any of his potential victims because he was afraid he might like them too much". Not all reporters at the sharp end enjoy that luxury. One for whom it eventually became too distasteful was

Harry Procter, a Fleet Street veteran who was accused of betrayal by the father of a 16-year-old boy who had shot dead a policeman. Procter (1958: 187–8) covered the story and befriended the boy's family, keeping them away from rival reporters in the process. When the Old Bailey trial was over, his newsdesk wanted a dramatic conclusion in which the father would condemn his own son, as a warning to other parents. The reporter "ghosted" a piece based on the many expressions of regret that the father had uttered during their friendship. Procter asked him to sign it if it was true; the father agreed it was a truthful account and reluctantly signed on the understanding that the newspaper would not treat it sensationally. The next day's paper had a splash headline – MY FAILURE: BY CRAIG'S FATHER – and Procter recalled: "Some months later, when we met again, he refused to shake my hand; he told me our friendship was at an end." Within a few years the reporter's Fleet Street career was also at an end, when he left his job because he had had "more than my fill" of such stories (Procter, 1958: 218).

ACCORDING TO A RELIABLE SOURCE

Before he told his employers about his meeting with Andrew Gilligan – and before his employers "outed" him in public – Dr David Kelly had been what is known as a confidential source: that is, somebody who gives information to a journalist on the understanding that they will not be identified as the source. Such people are highly valued by journalists, which is why a common thread running through most of the ethical codes collected in the appendices of this book is that confidential sources of information should – indeed, must – be protected. If that means a journalist faces prison for refusing to reveal their source, then so be it. In fact, the last time a journalist was jailed in the UK for protecting a source was as long ago as 1975, when Gordon Airs (2003) of the *Scottish Daily Record* was locked up for one night before being fined £500 for contempt. The last UK journalists to be jailed for substantial periods for protecting their sources were Reginald Foster of the *Daily Sketch* and Brendan Mulholland of the *Daily Mail*, who were both sentenced to six months' imprisonment in 1963 (Airs, 2003). However, the risk of being sent to prison has not gone away, and several journalists have appeared in court in recent years having been warned by their barrister to put a toothbrush in their pocket just in case.

There is broad agreement among journalists that it is preferable to be able to attribute information to an identifiable source, but there are occasions when this is not possible. A source may wish to place information in the public domain but be unwilling to be identified for a number of reasons: they may lose their job because they are revealing their employer's secrets; they could be breaching the Official Secrets Act; they may be prosecuted if they have been involved in criminal activity; they may be embarrassed politically or personally if they are seen to be "leaking" information; they may fear physical or other reprisals for spilling the beans. The journalistic justification for agreeing to confidentiality is that citizens need access to such information even without a named source, if it is in the public interest. This was the argument put forward by Robin Ackroyd, a freelance journalist who spent more than six years fighting off legal attempts by Merseyside National Health Service Trust to force him to reveal the identity of a confidential source who had supplied him with information. His story, published in the *Daily Mirror*, revealed that Moors murderer Ian Brady was on hunger strike and was being force-fed in a high security mental hospital. Ackroyd risked the possibility of being jailed for contempt of court; instead, a High Court judge ruled that he was "a responsible journalist whose purpose was to act in the public interest" (quoted in Ponsford, 2006a).

Another journalist who has risked jail to protect a source is Steve Panter, a crime reporter who fell out big time with the police. Based on information supplied to him confidentially, he revealed in the *Manchester Evening News* that the prime suspect for a huge bombing was not to be arrested or prosecuted. Detectives had identified a man they alleged was behind an IRA attack on Manchester in 1996, which injured around 300 people and caused damage estimated at up to £300 million; but Crown lawyers decided that there was insufficient evidence to secure a realistic chance of conviction. Until Panter's article three years after the bombing, the citizens of Manchester had no knowledge of the decision not to proceed; a decision that some observers suspected was taken for political rather than policing reasons. Publication of the story prompted the police hierarchy to go after Panter, who was arrested and questioned about where he obtained his information. "If you upset authority, they're going to hammer you," he explained when I asked him about the case several years later. When he refused to reveal his source, the police went through his phone bills and bank accounts in an unsuccessful effort to find the mole, and "they even drew a three-mile radius around my house and identified every phone box, and got British Telecom to back-check phone calls made from the kiosks to see if they could find a pattern".

A police officer was arrested and charged with leaking the information. He was cleared after Steve Panter went to court to testify that the officer was *not* his source. In court, the reporter risked being jailed for contempt of court by again refusing to reveal the identity of his confidential source, despite an instruction to do so by a High Court judge presiding over the case. As with

Robin Ackroyd, Panter managed to avoid being sent to prison thanks largely to legal support supplied by the National Union of Journalists, and a later decision by the attorney general not to prosecute for contempt of court. Although Panter won in the end, the case had involved several years of worry about what would happen, and it effectively ruined his chances of continuing as a crime reporter because sources would assume he was a marked man; he discovered that some detectives had been asked why they had telephoned his office in the past. Why had he taken such a stand?

> It's both personal and professional. On a personal level, you don't bayonet those people who actually stick their neck out for you and help you. Professionally, if you go down that road of betraying sources, you are letting down the profession, you're letting down your employer, your own professional integrity, and you're making it more difficult for any journalist in the future to maintain sources. You're doing it for the public because, if you're not going to protect your sources, then eventually the public are the losers because whistleblowers will not come forward any more, they won't trust journalists, and journalists won't be able to inform the public. Even though I was genuinely scared at the time, I was convinced I was doing the right thing for all those reasons. Between 1991 and 1996, Irish terrorists attacked Manchester on four separate occasions, and the police have only made two arrests – a reporter and a policeman. The story was in the public interest, overwhelmingly. But the NUJ helped save my skin, and I was grateful for that.

As we have seen, we can find out more by occasionally agreeing to keep the identity of our sources secret; and any journalist who "betrays" a confidential source makes it less likely that such sources will come forward in the future. Simple. But real life has a habit of being more messy than that, as indicated by the case of Judith Miller, a *New York Times* journalist who served 85 days in prison in 2005 to protect the identity of a government official whose identity had already been reported (Borger, 2005). Argument over the rights and wrongs of the Miller case is likely to continue for years to come. One journalist who did not end up in jail – but whose source did – is Peter Preston. Foreign Office clerk Sarah Tisdall delivered to the *Guardian* newspaper's London office a photocopy of a confidential Ministry of Defence document, concerning the controversial siting of US cruise missiles in the UK. She did so anonymously. Preston, then editor, did not know her identity, and had no way of communicating with her, so in a sense his newspaper had no obligation towards her. However, once it was decided to publish a story based on the leaked document, the newspaper could be seen as assuming responsibility for protecting the anonymity of its confidential source. It was a responsibility that the newspaper failed to fulfil. The newspaper fought and lost in the courts; then, after much agonising, the *Guardian* complied with a court order to hand over the photocopy. Markings on the document identified Sarah Tisdall as the source, and she was duly jailed under the Official Secrets Act.

As Welsh and others (2005: 303) comment in their legal "bible", *Essential Law for Journalists*: "Journalists should note that had the *Guardian* destroyed the document after it was used to prepare the article but before its handing over was ordered, the paper would have escaped the painful necessity of having to reveal the identity of its source." But journalists, trained to support their stories with documentary evidence, are notoriously reluctant to shred material. Looking back on the sorry saga from a distance of more than two decades during which he has been haunted – even taunted – by the case, Preston (2005: 52) concludes that running the story based on the leaked document was "the bargain moment", and not destroying the document as soon as the story was written had been his stupidest move because "we need to honour our bargains". Journalist Paul Foot (2000: 85) went further and declared the *Guardian*'s actions "an outrage", adding that "no one will ever know how many future whistleblowers decided to keep quiet for fear that they might end up behind bars".

Somebody who makes no apology for failing to honour a bargain with a source is Nick Martin-Clark, a freelance journalist based in Northern Ireland who went to court not to protect the identity of a confidential source but to help convict that source of murder. Martin-Clark (2003: 35–39) describes how, when he was visiting a loyalist prisoner who was inside for armed robbery, the man swore him to secrecy before boasting about taking part in a paramilitary killing. The journalist continued to visit the prisoner who, he says, came to trust him. That trust was shattered when Martin-Clark revealed the story in a *Sunday Times* article and agreed to give evidence in the subsequent murder trial. He explains why:

> [D]espite the difficulty of going against a source, this was a promise I eventually felt, after some agonising, that I could not keep ... There was a clear public interest in solving a murder ... The answer is not to take a black and white view, but to face up to the difficult balances we have to strike as journalists with values, and be prepared to defend those values. In exceptional cases, and this was one, striking the right balance can involve overriding the principle of extending confidentiality to sources ... [S]omeone who might well have killed again will now almost certainly never have the chance to do so ... How can I not be glad I helped put him in jail?
>
> (Martin-Clark, 2003: 35–9)

However, Martin-Clark's actions won him few friends among the journalistic community in Northern Ireland; a community that has lived through a series of ethical battles since the outbreak of the "troubles" in the late 1960s. John Coulter of the *Irish Daily Star* typified the reaction of most of Martin-Clark's fellow journalists when he argued:

> For me, the fundamental ethical principle of journalism is that we have a moral imperative to give a guarantee of anonymity to genuine confidential sources providing bona fide

> information ... If we sacrifice that trust, we betray our credibility as reporters of the truth ... [I]f you can't keep your word, don't do the story.
>
> (Coulter, 2005: 66–7)

So, although journalistic codes of conduct tend to agree that confidential sources should be protected, there are different views on whether this principle should be considered as absolute. If it is absolute, does that mean that a journalist should not pass on potentially life-saving information – "X told me he is intending to plant a bomb," for example – yet, if it is not absolute, can it be regarded as a principle at all?

A problem with the more "absolutist" position is that it seems to require journalists to follow codes of ethical conduct out of a sense of duty to a set of rules rather than out of consideration of the consequences of their actions, argues journalist and academic Michael Foley. He suggests an alternative position:

> Maybe it is now time for journalists to adopt a new imperative to judge and guide their actions, trustworthiness. Are my actions or decisions likely to increase the trust between me and my readers, viewers or listeners? Such an approach would have journalists seriously question the use of anonymous sources and ensure that they are used rarely and when a full explanation is given as to why. With trust placed central to journalist practice fewer anonymous sources would be used and so the problem of anonymity would arise less often.
>
> (Foley, 2004a: 19)

In any event, adds Foley, anonymous sources are just as likely to be manipulative spin doctors as courageous whistleblowers; and how is the public interest served by a journalist's willingness to go to prison to protect the identity of somebody who is spinning a yarn on behalf of the rich and powerful?

MAKE A NOTE OF THAT

Few journalists are going to come within punching distance of a prime minister, have their actions scrutinised by a public inquiry, or face jail to protect a source. Although one of the joys of journalism is that you never know what the next story will bring, most journalist–source relationships are more straightforward than those described in this chapter so far. Yet, even in routine encounters, many of the same issues will arise: trust, responsibility, reliability, accuracy. That is why, in the wake of the Hutton Inquiry, the BBC issued new editorial guidelines to cover all the Corporation's journalists, not just those burrowing away trying to uncover state secrets. The guidelines include the following sections, which have been informed by the Gilligan–Kelly encounter:

GATHERING MATERIAL

> We should try to witness events and gather information first hand. Where this is not possible, we should talk to first hand sources and, where necessary, corroborate their evidence.
>
> We should be reluctant to rely on a single source. If we do rely on a single source, a named on the record source is always preferable …
>
> We should record our interviews with sources wherever possible. In circumstances where recording might inhibit the source, full notes should be made, preferably at the time, or if not, then as soon as possible afterwards.

NOTE TAKING

> We must take accurate, reliable and contemporaneous notes of all significant research conversations and other relevant information.
>
> We must keep records of research including written and electronic correspondence, background notes and documents. It should be kept in a way that allows double checking, particularly at the scripting stage, and if necessary by another member of the team.
>
> We must keep accurate notes of conversations with sources and contributors about anonymity. A recording is preferable where possible.
>
> When we broadcast serious allegations made by an anonymous source, full notes of interviews, conversations and information which provide the basis for the story must be kept.
>
> (BBC, 2005)

Many journalists point to Andrew Gilligan's lack of shorthand as a crucial weakness in his dossier story. But he regards the issue as a "red herring":

> Clearly my employers did not think it necessary for me to have shorthand. I doubt very much if any shorthand note I could have produced would have been greatly more comprehensive. Lawyers like things on paper. They were worried about something in an [electronic] organiser, they didn't understand it. But a shorthand note would have made no difference whatsoever. It didn't come down to a dispute about what was and was not in my notes because Hutton ruled that the dossier was not sexed up, not embellished in any way, despite having heard weeks of evidence that it was. A shorthand note might have made our lives a bit easier at the Inquiry, but it wouldn't have saved David Kelly's life.

Following his experience at the Hutton Inquiry, Andrew Gilligan now tapes all his interviews as a matter of routine. He actually had a BBC tape recorder with him when he met Dr Kelly, but he did not use it. Why? Because it was intended to be an informal meeting:

> I had my tape recorder in my bag, but it has a great big microphone with it and I thought that would have scared him off. Frankly, people aren't always quite so keen to be full and frank if they think that their every word is going to be taken down for use against them. This conversation was never intended to be something that would be quoted under David Kelly's name, it was intended to be a background conversation that would be reported as the words of an off-the-record source. And that's what it was.

Post-Hutton, there has certainly been renewed emphasis on the importance of journalists recording accurately what they are told by sources, but it has long been a central part of journalism as *reporting*. Newspaper historian Bob Clarke argues that the role of the reporter – as opposed to the recycler of second-hand information – developed in the UK during the eighteenth century:

> Instead of being solely dependent on reports from soldiers and sailors and other third parties, the papers paid reporters to attend trials, interview felons in the condemned cell and provide eyewitness accounts of executions ... The growing use of shorthand gave the newspaper a special air of authority and increased the status of the reporter as the possessor of a specialized skill. Through the shorthand reporter, the newspaper became the accepted channel by which a speaker, whether politician, churchman, scientist or teacher, could speak from a platform and reach thousands of people all over the country the next day.
>
> (Clarke, 2004: 255)

Indeed, argues Michael Foley (2004b: 376): "The journalist inscribing his notebook with a shorthand note at a public meeting was, in effect, facilitating the development of a public sphere within which political debates took place."

Not that every reporter who brandishes a notebook necessarily has facilitating the public sphere uppermost in his or her mind. Andrew Marr (2005: 74) notes how the growth of shorthand among court reporters allowed Victorian newspapers to run lengthy and voyeuristic verbatim accounts of the cross-examination of witnesses in juicy trials and divorce cases. And, in the wake of the July 2005 London bombings, St Mary's hospital complained about a number of Australian journalists who walked into wards to interview survivors and relatives. One hospital press officer complained that a reporter had obtained an "interview" with an injured Australian academic, who was suffering vertigo and feeling nauseous, after arriving with a pot plant and allowing the disoriented patient to think she was one of his students (Tulloch, 2006: 34–6). The press officer said: "In the 13 years I've worked in PR I have never once come across such outrageous reporting practices" (quoted in Michael and Fixter, 2005). If those journalists had been working for UK print media, their alleged behaviour would have been in breach of item eight in the Press Complaints Commission (PCC) code:

> *Hospitals
>
> (i) Journalists must identify themselves and obtain permission from a responsible executive before entering non-public areas of hospitals or similar institutions to pursue enquiries.
>
> (ii) The restrictions on intruding into privacy are particularly relevant to enquiries about individuals in hospitals or similar institutions.
>
> (PCC code: see Appendix 4)

Anyone wondering why hospitals have their own special place in the PCC code has, presumably, not heard about the day that a reporter and photographer pretended to be medical staff and turned up in the hospital room where TV actor Gordon Kaye was seriously ill with a severe brain injury. They photographed and even tried to extract some quotes from the semi-conscious star of *Allo Allo*. They were not the first journalists to have invaded someone's privacy in hospital, but their high-profile intrusion embarrassed the press as a whole. The "newspaper" involved, the *Sunday Sport*, was ticked off by the Press Council (Frost, 2000: 190); hence the sensitivity to hospital intrusions when the PCC replaced the Press Council shortly afterwards. However, you may have noticed the little asterisk next to the word "hospitals", signifying that "there may be exceptions … where they can be demonstrated to be in the public interest". The public interest no longer seems to include asking an actor, who is at death's door, "How does it feel?"

The *Sunday Sport* staff's unwelcome appearance at Gordon Kaye's hospital bedside – "a landmark in atrocious intrusiveness" (Shannon, 2001: 26) – is one of many low points in the relationship between journalists and their sources. However, it would be wrong to think it typical. We do not necessarily hear much about them, but many journalists are scrupulous in their relationships with sources, particularly with people who are telling sensitive stories or who have little experience of how the media operates. One journalist told me how he tries to put this into practice:

> I think I tend to care quite a lot that my work is "honest" journalism – that's using the word honest in a fundamental sense, to mean among other things not simplifying issues in a lazy way, or exploiting the people I'm interviewing or reporting. Unusually

> for many journalists I will often check quotes back or explain to people how I intend to use their contributions. Not business or PR professionals who know the score, but ordinary people who can be mesmerised by a media inquiry and not realise the importance of choosing their words carefully.
>
> (Quoted in Harcup, 2005b: 367)

Many journalists insist on not showing copy to people before publication, and the idea of "copy approval" is generally frowned upon. However, on sensitive or technical stories – and when deadlines permit – some are willing on occasion to let interviewees see what they are going to be quoted as saying, and to point out any errors or misunderstandings. Even when this happens, control of – and therefore responsibility for – what is submitted for publication remains in the hands of the journalist.

ROUND UP THE USUAL SOURCES

Just as important as the relationship between journalists and sources is the question of who becomes a source in the first place. Academic studies of news sources and the routines of news production suggest there is a tendency for those with the most economic and political power within society to enjoy the most access to journalists, resulting in the interpretive frameworks of the powerful tending to be accepted as the norm, and the consequent "marginalisation of resource-poor social groups and interests" (Cottle, 2000: 433). News tends to be dominated by sources drawn from "a limited set of professions: specifically politics, business, law and order, and the news media", according to a study by Lewis and others (2005: 463). This is bad news for democratic societies, argues academic Paul Manning (2001: 227), because it means "the market in which news is commodified works against diversity in coverage and perspective".

Paradoxically, people whose stash of social capital gives them access to the media when they want it also seem to be more capable of – or more interested in – protecting their privacy against what they see as media intrusion. Journalists invariably find it hard to get people to talk when they are sent to knock on doors in well-to-do areas, whereas reporters calling on working-class housing estates are more likely to be followed around by excited locals eager to tell you their neighbours' business. That is a dreadful caricature, of course, but in my experience there is more than an element of truth in it. Having journalists descend on a locality when some tragic event occurs, asking people to provide local reaction and colour, does not alter the everyday power relationships that appear to be reflected within much mainstream journalism. If some sources have the power to set a media agenda, others are restricted to making the occasional comment while bringing around the tea trolley. Few journalists seemed to be interested in asking about the opinions or experiences of people living in the Beeston area of Leeds, for example, before the area hit the international headlines as the place where several of the London "suicide bombers" had lived. For a few days afterwards, any local venturing onto the streets was likely to be asked for a comment. Then the world media's satellite trucks disappeared, and, apart from anniversaries, only the local media have shown much interest in the area since then.

Yet journalism does not have to restrict itself to the traditional sources that dominate so much of the news: courts, police, central government, local councils, big business, political parties, universities, think tanks, showbiz and the public relations industry. Proof that journalism can engage with a wider range of people and perspectives lies in the existence of a range of alternative media that, from the working-class press of the industrial revolution to the anti-capitalist websites of today, privilege the opinions and experiences of an altogether different cast of sources (Harcup, 2003b). One journalist who has worked in both alternative and mainstream media describes her journalism as stemming from "a commitment to helping give a voice to people who aren't usually otherwise heard"; for example, by going directly to the people directly affected by an issue, such as homeless people on the streets, rather than to those who may speak *about* them, such as housing professionals (quoted in Harcup, 2005b: 367). Many journalists working within mainstream media also go out of their way to consult a wide range of sources, including those directly affected by issues, but the news agenda tends to be dominated by the established sources of information. This routine dominance needs to be challenged if citizens are to be adequately informed, argues Manning:

> News audiences are active and sceptical but the political economy of news reminds us that audiences can only begin their critical decoding with the available tools, or information, to hand. The obstacles faced by subordinate news sources in the struggle to supply a wider range of sharper tools are rather more perplexing than is good for democracy.
>
> (Manning, 2001: 227)

Maybe not as perplexing as a punch from a prime minister, but still worth thinking about before we pick up the phone to make another round of calls to the usual suspects.

FURTHER READING

See Manning (2001), Palmer (2000) and Chapter 4 of Harcup (2004) for further discussion of the sources used in mainstream journalism, while Atton (2002), Harcup (2003b; 2005b) and Whitaker (1981) all deal with the ways in which alternative media have blurred the lines between journalists and sources. Franklin (2004) and Marr (2005) both discuss relations between journalists and politicians, from the perspective of an academic and a journalist respectively.

A fascinating account of being on the other side of the relationship between journalists and sources can be found in *One Day in July* by John Tulloch (2006), the media studies professor who survived the suicide bomb attack on an underground train at London's Edgware Road station. In addition to describing what happened to him and discussing the wider implications of the 7 July bombings, he analyses how his story was told in UK and international media. He also explores the way that an iconic photograph of him covered in blood and bandages was used "to signify things that I could not control, and which by and large attributed to me motives and moods that I didn't necessarily share" (Tulloch, 2006: 41).

For a critique of the various ways in which governments and the armed forces try to control the flow of information at times of war, see McLaughlin (2002) and Knightley (2000). For research into the role of reporters embedded with the military during the Iraq war, see Lewis and others (2004). You can read the evidence presented to the Hutton Inquiry on the website – www.the-hutton-inquiry.org.uk – or in an edited book version (Coates, 2004). Finally, the relationship between journalist and source is the central thread of the film *The Insider*, directed by Michael Mann, which is based on the true story of a tobacco executive who became a whistleblower.

7

ROUND UP THE USUAL SUSPECTS

How Crime is Reported in the Media

I once spent a night in the company of the police, but I wasn't helping them with their inquiries. In fact, they were helping me. They took me on patrol in an inner-city area, beginning with a briefing on local villains whose mugshots decorated the walls of the operations room, and ending back at the police station, with all of us diving into some Chinese food that had been provided free by a restaurant apparently keen to impress the forces of law and order. The takeaway was the highlight of the night, because nothing much else happened. Some motorists were questioned before being allowed to proceed, some burglars ran away when disturbed by a resident, and in between our genial copper took a photographer and me on a guided tour of the remains of cars that had been twocked (taken without consent) and burned out. The nearest we came to some action was when a message came over the police radio that a man had reacted to the clamping of his car by threatening the clampers with a Samurai sword. By the time we got to the scene he and his sword were safely locked into the police van that had got there before us; hardly surprising, given that our lone police officer seemed reluctant to put his foot down on the accelerator of his patrol car when faced with the prospect of tackling a Samurai warrior on his own.

I wrote up an account of my night on the town with the police, squeezing in every conceivable bit of colour and anecdote to make up for the lack of thrills and spills. But the article was spiked by the newspaper editor who commissioned it, because I couldn't hide the fact that nothing much happened, and "nothing much happened" is not much of a story. There may be a million stories in the naked city, but that wasn't one of them. Running it would have required a conscious decision by the editor to defy the conventions of news values, which is something that may be commonplace in alternative media but rarely happens in the mainstream.

What if pot luck had been different and my jaunt with the police had coincided with a few juicy crimes? It would have been just as much a random snapshot as was my "quiet night, nobody hurt" story, but it would not have been spiked. It may have been splashed with a headline such as WELCOME TO LAWLESS BRITAIN. And it might even have prompted a leader along the lines of the following, in which the *Daily Mail* laments the latest crime wave:

> Hardly a day passes without the report of some atrocious act of violence. Murders of children and women after assault, attacks on old people, hold-ups by gunmen, and the shooting of policemen, have become almost commonplace.

Those words could have been written today, but they were published on 8 July 1949. They are quoted in a history of the press by Roy Greenslade (2003: 38–9), who notes that the UK popular papers of the 1940s were "full of gruesome murders, petty assaults, robbery and racketeering", with headlines such as WORST MONTH OF CRIME YARD HAS KNOWN (*Daily Herald*, 11 December 1945) appearing with alarming frequency.

There was nothing new about any of this, even in the 1940s. A hundred years earlier there were newspapers running headlines such as BRUTAL MURDER AT PRESTON, MURDEROUS BURGLARY, and A DEATH-BED CONFESSION OF A MURDER (Clarke, 2004: 244). Indeed, nineteenth-century newspapers were said by one contemporary observer to be almost entirely filled with "murders and robberies, and rapes and incest, and bestiality and sodomy … and executions and duels, and suicides" (quoted in Marr, 2005: 68). Similarly, anybody picking up a newspaper or tuning into broadcast news today is likely to be bombarded with headlines about stabbings, shootings, muggings and sexual assaults. The incidents might not be in our street, neighbourhood or even town – and we probably won't know anybody involved – but we are left with the knowledge that the other side of our front door is a very dangerous place. The experts tell us that this "knowledge" is quite out of proportion to the chance of any one of us becoming a victim of serious crime in real life; but their voices tend to be drowned out by screaming headlines. As reporter Richard Harbinger says in the spoof TV news broadcast *Broken News*: "One thing's for certain, things will get a lot worse before they get worse still" (quoted in Armstrong, 2005).

A BEDROCK OF DEMOCRACY?

Crime stories have been described as "the lifeblood of British newspapers", offering tales of bravery, stupidity, viciousness, greed, justice and injustice

(Hanna, 2006: 192–3). Not only does crime provide some cracking human interest stories, but reporting the resulting court cases is "one of the bedrocks of our democracy", argue Susan Pape and Sue Featherstone:

> Essentially, the court reporter is acting as the eyes and ears of the public, ensuring not only that justice is done, but also that it is seen to be done. It is an important function and one that journalists should feel privileged to fulfil. On the other hand, let's be realistic, court reporting remains a staple of newspaper coverage because, as Mark Bradley, editor of the *Wakefield Express* observes, readers lap it up: "Everybody loves it," he says … "people like to look at the list and see their mates, their enemies, their neighbours."
>
> (Pape and Featherstone, 2005: 64)

Although all but the smallest newsrooms will have specialist crime and court reporters, *all* journalists involved in news will find themselves working on crime stories at times, as will many journalists who work in features and even sports. Given its central importance to everyday journalistic practice – not to mention the claim that it is part of our democratic duty – it is surprising that the ethical considerations of crime reporting seem to prompt so little critical reflection among journalists. There is no shortage of books by and about war correspondents, for example, but there are far fewer about the rather more common task of reporting from the frontline of crime.

This state of affairs is to be regretted because a serious examination of the ways in which crime is represented in the media can be, as Philip Schlesinger and Howard Tumber (1994: 11) argue, a useful way of exploring "the workings of the flawed, contemporary public sphere". And what such an examination reveals is that, although crime stories are prevalent in much of our news media, there is little attempt at putting them in context. There are occasional backgrounders or specials, usually at the more serious end of the news market. An example of contextualised reporting was the item on *Channel Four News* (2002) at the height of the investigation into the murder of two schoolgirls in the village of Soham, which placed the dangers to children in perspective: "Today the chance of a child being killed by a stranger is one in 185,000 – about the same risk as being hit by lightning." But on a daily basis we hear relatively little of such statistics, of wider trends, of "hidden" crimes such as domestic violence, or of the social, economic, psychological, educational and political factors that may influence the prevalence of criminal behaviour. As ex-crime reporter David Krajicek (1998) complains, too many crime stories "begin and end with who did what to whom, embellished with the moans of a murder victim's mother," rather than seeking to enhance our understanding.

In the real world, it seems, the risk of being a victim of crime is generally falling; in 2004–5 it was at the lowest since the British Crime Survey was launched in 1981 (Nicholas and others, 2005: 1). The survey, based on interviewing around 45,000 adults, is generally regarded as more accurate than the recorded crime figures, which require crimes to be formally reported to the police and which can be distorted by changes in how the police record certain incidents. However, because some serious offences are excluded from the British Crime Survey, any definite claim that crime is up, down or stable should be greeted with scepticism, as all the statistics offer "only a partial view of the reality", as BBC home affairs correspondent Danny Shaw (2004) points out. If the figures tell one story – or, rather, stories – the headlines tend to tell other stories, which may help to explain why the British Crime Survey also shows that more than six out of ten people believe the crime rate is actually increasing (Nicholas and others, 2005: 21). The headlines drip-feed us an unrelenting diet of random and terrifying acts of violence; of things getting worse, and then worse still. Of course, selective reporting of crime, as of any other phenomenon, is inevitable; otherwise newspapers would be the size of Mount Everest. Such selection is based on news values rather than on any conscious intention to deceive; and those news values may change over time as once-novel crimes become commonplace, thereby ratcheting up the threshold another notch. However, just because journalists are never going to be able to report every crime that is committed – nor are we going to be able to append a contextualising essay to every piece of crime news – this does not absolve us of responsibility for the fact that citizens may be getting a distorted picture of society because of the way we do our jobs. The least we could do is to think about what we are doing.

The fact that each of us is statistically unlikely to become a victim of a horrific crime will be of little comfort to anyone who *does* become a victim of serious crime; nor will it overly impress people living in high-crime areas, where their neighbours are unlikely to include many senior journalists, criminologists or chief constables. Social inequality is one of the factors that is reflected in patterns of offending but finds little expression in journalistic accounts, argues Danny Dorling, a professor in human geography at the University of Sheffield. Writing in the alternative magazine *Red Pepper*, he points to evidence that an increasing number of murders in recent years have been concentrated among men of working age living in our poorest areas:

> Despite regular panics in the mainstream media, the evidence shows that for the majority of the population the chances of being murdered have fallen, in some cases considerably. For males aged over 60 and under 5, and for females of all ages, the chances of being murdered have either fallen or remained constant over the past 20 years ... Women are now far less likely to be murder victims because they are in a better position than they were two decades ago to escape violent relationships before those relationships become deadly. By contrast, the chances of being murdered have

> increased significantly for most men – with those between 20 and 24 facing twice the risk now compared with 20 years ago ... Most murders of men by men occur within relationships of friendship turned bad – situations in which the murders and victims know each other well ...There is a common myth that gun crime is behind high murder rates in poor areas. In fact, a higher proportion of rich people are killed by guns than [are] poor people. The most common way of being murdered in poor areas is through being cut with a knife or broken glass. Most murders are shockingly banal – such as a fight after a night out drinking in which a threat was made and someone died. Such murders do not make the headlines.
>
> (Dorling, 2006)

Nor do such banal murders usually lead to what is known among sociologists as a "moral panic"; that is, when an issue comes seemingly from nowhere to dominate the headlines and the thoughts of politicians, church leaders and others concerned about the latest threat to civilisation. In recent years the UK has seen such panics over everything from road rage, air rage, and so-called "happy slapping" to the presence of paedophiles and asylum seekers in our midst. In the process, the atypical is presented as typical, and the question, "How could it happen in a place like this?" is transformed into the statement, "It could happen anyplace" (Cohen, 2002: x–xii).

One of the periodic moral panics that occur over the criminality of young people took place in the mid-1990s and focused on an 11-year-old child who became known as "Balaclava Boy". A television news crew filmed him and his mates wearing ski masks and cavorting around a crashed stolen car on a Hartlepool housing estate, putting two fingers up at the authorities both literally and metaphorically. The images briefly dominated TV and the tabloids, and Balaclava Boy was born. His televised show of bravado was condemned by Tony Blair – who, as shadow home secretary, used it to attack the Conservative government of the day – as "behaviour that scars the very fabric of our society". The boy at the centre of all this attention died just a few years later, while still a teenager, by which time he had 40 convictions to his name. One of his neighbours felt the media attention had encouraged his law-breaking: "Before he became Balaclava Boy, he was just a naughty kid. Afterwards, he was a criminal with something to live up to" (Brockes, 2000).

It is not only individuals who get labelled in this way. Groups of people, ways of life, particular activities and geographical areas can all become labelled by sections of the media as deviant, lowlife, "other" – as *them* rather than *us*. It is as if the UK's popular tabloids try to establish a "community" of their own readers by creating moral outrage against "evil outsiders" (Conboy, 2006: 104). The rest of the media may not adopt the more extreme prejudices of some of our redtop newspapers, but the tabloid agenda can still influence the priorities of other journalists, often to the detriment of background and context. The process of simplification inherent in journalism that deals in the "binary oppositions" of good versus evil – and normal versus sick – deprives citizens of exposure to more complex realities and more subtle shades of grey (Jewkes, 2004: 45).

Also absent from most media discussion of crime are those crimes that slip under the radar of mainstream journalism: the misappropriation of public funds by profiteering corporations, perhaps, or fraud and corruption in high places. Maybe they do not look like crimes because those responsible do not look like our image of criminals. There are certainly plenty of victims, though. Take the hundreds of people who die each year in workplace accidents, many of which are caused by employers breaching health and safety legislation. Or the 5,000 people every year that the International Labour Office estimates are still dying in the UK as a result of work-related exposure to asbestos – along with 21,000 people in the United States and 110,000 people in China – more than a century after it was discovered that asbestos was a killer (*Hazards*, 2006: 14; Tweedale, 2001). If they are reported at all, such deaths tend not to be reported as crime stories, and the perpetrators tend not to be "monstered" in the way that more easily recognised villains are. That seems to be common sense. But, in crime reporting as in other areas of reporting, it is surely part of the job of good journalists to question the very concept of common sense (Harcup, 2004: 65).

REFLECTIONS OF A CRIME REPORTER

You will not normally pick up stories of corporate manslaughter on police calls. Nor will you be handed details of governments breaking international law on issues such as torture and war (Sands, 2006). Such things are not part of the beat of a crime reporter. Although I have never been a specialist crime reporter, I have done my fair share of sitting in grim police stations picking up stories, making the routine calls to all the emergency services, and going door-knocking after murders. I know from experience the adrenalin rush that a journalist gets when working on a big crime story; and I know that newsrooms will continue to rely on a steady supply of crime stories to fill their pages and bulletins. Much everyday crime news is a form of "churnalism", a word coined by BBC journalist Waseem Zakir to describe the way in which too many newsrooms rely on journalists simply processing – churning out – copy that arrives from news agencies and press releases (Harcup, 2004: 3–4). Recorded telephone newslines, frequently updated by police, provide a stream of leads and nibs (new in brief items) that can be gathered even by inexperienced reporters who need never leave the office.

But the best crime stories are not necessarily those handed out in press releases or put on recorded voicebanks, argues Steve Panter, who spent 25 years covering such tales, more than 10 of them as crime reporter for the *Manchester Evening News*. He told me about his modus operandi:

> I'd try to find out what's behind the press release from the police; what are they not telling us? And very often I'd find something behind the scenes that was quirky and would make a better story. If you are a crime specialist – and it's the same with education, health, whatever – you cultivate your own contacts so that hopefully one day they come to you and say, "I'll tell you this off-the-record; use it, but it's not from me."

Why does he think people are prepared to speak to journalists on a confidential basis? A variety of reasons, it seems, of which the public interest is just one:

> I think very often because they feel the hierarchy are covering things up. Some are disillusioned with their organisation or have an axe to grind; some like to wind-up a colleague by revealing their big secret; and sometimes I think it is for the thrill of it. I never paid a policeman. Hospitality maybe, but I never paid a policeman. No policeman could ever say that I betrayed a confidence or a source, and I am proud of that. I could be accused by very senior police officers of being anti-police, which I wasn't, but the people who used to work with me knew I would never, ever betray them and that's why they would trust me.

He would be told about all sorts of things that had not been made public by the police press office, but he still had to weigh up whether they were worth pursuing:

> You have to decide whether or not what you've been told is a story, has it got potential, and whether there are any ethical issues involved. As a crime specialist, if you have a quiet spell the newsdesk think you're skiving, they want to know why you're not bringing in stories any more. The pressure is always there, so probably the desire or need to get stories in the paper outweighs the ethical considerations.

He tells me that news values have changed during his career in journalism, and he points to the example of an armed robbery. A few years ago such a "blag" would have made a front-page splash but today it would not get much of a show in a busy city evening newspaper. There are just too many such robberies to have much shock value unless there are other factors, such as it being the largest amount of money ever stolen.

What stories are most likely to get picked up, then?

> I'd be looking for more interesting crime stories, more offbeat ones, with a general appeal. I was looking around for more human interest, really. Certainly, if they find the body of a schoolgirl and the parents will talk to you, then that's the sort of story that will have a wide appeal compared to a guy out in the street, 35, who's involved in a fracas and he dies, which is more common.

A spotlight was briefly shone on this process of journalistic selection in 2006, when Metropolitan police chief Sir Ian Blair accused the news media of "institutional racism" in the way that deaths of people of different races were covered. "With one or two exceptions," said Blair, "the reporting of murder in minority communities appears not to interest the mainstream media" (BBC, 2006). Steve Panter was one of many journalists who took exception to Blair's remarks, which seemed to simplify the factors involved in the selection of stories, but he recalls a time when the UK media certainly did distinguish between victims from different communities:

> I'll give you an example. Twenty-odd years ago I witnessed a situation in a newspaper office on a Saturday morning. We'd no splash and then a reporter said to the newsdesk that we had a story from early morning calls of a car that turned over, killing six people in the early hours of the morning. The news editor said, "Great, that's our splash." The reporter did a few more calls and turned round 10 minutes later and shouted across the office, "The victims are all Asian." And he got the reply, "Four pars." Now, he wasn't being overtly racist. His mindset was that Asian people at that time didn't read newspapers, and that was the selection process.

People are more likely to be treated on an equal basis now, he believes, but that does not mean that issues of race do not arise:

> When I used to cover murders in the Moss Side area of Manchester, there were black gangs shooting at each other. You had kids of 10 or 12 years using machine guns, killing each other, and I was accused of being racist by some people in the community for covering it too much rather than ignoring it. They were using machine guns, it was new, it was novel, it was unique in this country at the time. That drove the news interest, and if it had been white guys it would have been the same coverage, because it was so unusual and so dramatic.

In contrast, drama was oddly lacking in the case of Dr Harold Shipman, who turned out to be the UK's biggest serial killer. Panter was not alone in finding the story of the family doctor quietly murdering his patients less exciting than many of the smaller cases he has covered:

> It was a strange story. The attitude among certain journalists – me included, really – was this was a terrible, terrible thing that had happened, but there was no sex, no rock 'n' roll, no secret bank account. It lacked a degree of salaciousness, really. There was no drama: we were looking for it and it wasn't there. Maybe it was the age profile of the victims. Had they all been young women, it would have been an even more massive story, but they were older women. And it was the method of execution as well: needles, rather than a savage, violent act.

That absence of spice did not prevent another journalist – Brian Whittle of the Cavendish Press agency – from spotting the implications of the Shipman case early on and breaking a series of stories about so-called "Dr Death" (Harcup, 2004: 79). "Brian, to his credit, taught me a lesson because he saw it as being a massive story and I was fairly cold about it," says Panter as he looks back on the case today.

Panter has been doing a lot of such looking back since leaving the typeface for the chalkface and becoming a journalism lecturer in 2003. "I've become more reflective now," he says, before describing a story he covered a few years ago about which he has more ethical qualms now than he did at the time. One of his contacts told him that police had been called to investigate a break-in at a posh boys' school, and that they found gay pornography in the headmaster's study. The source said the whole thing had been hushed up, as Panter recalls:

> Now, it wasn't illegal to have them, it wasn't paedophilia, it was simply adult gay pornography. The police looked at it and decided no action should be taken. The chair of the governors was aware of it, the headmaster was aware of it, I was aware of it, and one or two police were aware of it. The chair of the governors wasn't going to tell the rest of the governors. I had to decide whether or not that was a story. I look back on this now and think that maybe it wasn't in the public interest, but at the time I just wanted to get a splash out of it, simple as that. I told the newsdesk, they had no qualms about it. You've got to think about the operational side and the ethical side. Operationally, you've got to make sure you don't lose your exclusivity. Obviously you've got ethical considerations as well, but looking back I didn't consider those, it was purely operational for me.

So he pursued the story and confronted the headmaster and chair of governors with what he knew:

> Operationally, you were always trying to go to these people saying you know it's happened rather than asking, "Has it happened?" That would put them on the back foot. In this case, they tried to put me off. The chair of governors was saying it was not in the public interest and the headmaster's family had to be considered. The headmaster said his family didn't know – "If you publish this story you might wreck my family life." I knew he had a family but, looking back, I didn't even consider them. Maybe I should have done. That's what disturbs me a little now, really. At the time, to be honest with you, I had no sympathy at all, I just wanted the story. I went back and reported all this to the office, and we published it. One editorial manager on that day has told me since that, as the story was being put to bed, one of the more respected sub editors approached him and said, "Congratulations, you've just destroyed a good man's life."

At the time, the editor justified running the story on the grounds that it was in the public interest because the parents and governors had not been informed. Panter is no longer totally convinced:

> Looking back, I think even though the parents hadn't been told, the public interest argument there was a bit thin, but the editor decided it was right. Personally, I just wanted an exclusive story on page one, which was what I got. That was the adrenalin flowing.

Confronting people who may have been accused of wrongdoing is just one part of a journalist's job. Another is to approach victims or their relatives for information, quotes and pictures. Some people are happy to talk to reporters in such circumstances, others are not; either way, the reporter wants the story. Panter looks back with a sense of embarrassment on some of the "tricks of the trade" that he used to obtain such stories, particularly in the years before the Press Complaints Commission's code of practice began to be taken seriously in newsrooms (see next chapter):

> When you go to a door now you have to say who you are, be upfront. If they say, "I don't want to talk," you say, "OK" and you go away. But going back before the code, at the time of the Hillsborough disaster, for example, I was sent out to interview relatives. I remember going into one guy's house, at that time I had dark hair and a moustache and a tie, and invariably they thought I was in the CID. I never said I was a policeman, but I used to go into houses many a time when they thought I was a policeman. I'd knock on the door and say, "Excuse me, can I talk to you about whatever?" I'd never show a press card, conversely I never said I was a policeman. If they thought I was, I'd regard that as fair game. I'd go into a house, Hillsborough is one example, where the guy made me a cup of tea, we sat in his living room and he said to me, "OK officer, how can I help you?" At that point I said, "Actually I'm a reporter." The psychology was that if you were actually in the house they were more reluctant to say to you, "Go away."

And such psychology usually worked. As did using what he describes as "emotional blackmail" on the doorstep of a bereaved relative, to persuade them to talk:

> You would go to a house and they'd say they don't want to talk about it and I would say, "OK, well if you don't talk about it, and if I get it wrong in tonight's paper, then you're partly to blame." It was disgraceful behaviour, looking back. That's why the code is a good thing because, on reflection, I'm ashamed of that. But I was doing a job, my only instruction was to get the story. Ethics was a county down south, as far as I was concerned in those days.

Sometimes it was a question of getting a picture as well as a story, and he recalls that early morning visits often paid dividends:

> I'd go along to a house at about half past seven in the morning – these might be totally innocent people who had lost a child in a road accident – and I'd go along there with a photographer and we'd work out how we were going to get the picture of the victim's mother on her doorstep without her knowing it, in case they turned down a polite request. I'd take the milk bottle off their step and put it halfway down the driveway or pathway and I'd knock on the door and stand to one side. The photographer would be in place behind a hedge or in a car. They come to the door unaware, see the bottle, walk down the pathway and pick it up. Then they'd see their picture in the paper that night. It was scurrilous really. Again the code says you can't do that, and quite right. This was the culture, it was the way things were done. Victims were regarded as being fair game. You'd be sympathetic, you knew you weren't going to a villain, but then again you had to get the picture and the words, so it was par for the course, just one of the tricks of the trade.

Today Steve Panter recounts such experiences in the hope of encouraging the journalists of tomorrow to think more about the ethical implications of what they are doing, and to keep in mind that they are dealing with human beings. "I want my students to go on to be incisive, inquisitive reporters," he explains, "but at the same time to respect people's human rights."

ON THE RECEIVING END

To find out what it might feel like to be on the other side of a crime story, I turned to Janet McKenzie, whose family suddenly found itself the focus of journalists' attentions when her sister Liz Sherlock was murdered in 2001. The behaviour of reporters covering the case was not particularly appalling, and the facts were mostly reported fairly accurately; yet her account of being on the receiving end of our trade should make uncomfortable reading for journalists, because it highlights the ways in which we sometimes trample over people's feelings even when we are simply doing our jobs.

Most deaths – most murders, even – do not make the national news. As we have seen, journalists apply news values to select those that are most newsworthy. The manner of Liz's death was both dramatic and unusual: she chased a woman who had stolen her handbag at a crowded London railway station, she ended up on the bonnet of a getaway car, and she was killed by being thrown off the moving car that was then driven over her by its male driver. Journalists immediately labelled her a "have-a-go heroine" (Coles and Sullivan, 2001). So, at the same time as the family were trying to absorb the shocking news of Liz's death, journalists were informing the rest of the world what had happened. To the family, however, the person referred to in national headlines bore little resemblance to the real woman, as Janet explains:

> The day after Liz was killed she was described as an unknown woman, which was a kind of label. Then she was described as a wife, which is another label – a crass one, because there was more to her than that. In the later cuttings she was described as a BBC costume designer, which was a new form of labelling to make her more interesting because she had worked with celebrities, but again there was more to her than that. It was as though the media was selling a commodity, packaging her to sell newspapers or TV airtime. She was labelled and sold like a tin of beans, and we weren't in control of the labelling. There was a feeling of horror that our personal misery was other people's entertainment. That's hard – that feeling of a lack of control and of being used. The circumstances were that two drug addicts were stealing to feed their habit – they scavenged off her, she was a thing to be used by them, and then she was used by the media as a tin of beans to be sold.

During this period, police had warned the grieving family against speaking to journalists, to avoid the possibility of them saying anything that might prejudice a fair trial for the accused. In any event, in the days immediately following Liz's death, her distraught parents were in no condition to talk to reporters. That didn't stop the press trying, as Janet recalls:

> After my parents got home from viewing Liz's body – she had been run over and dragged, and there had been an autopsy, so it was very traumatic – a journalist from a national newspaper turned up and asked how they felt. She was very polite and very nice, but she was persistent and didn't go away. Neither of them were in a fit state to talk to her. The upshot was that I got a phone call saying, "She won't go away". She was just sat outside the house on a wall. So I phoned the police in London and they told the local police, and as a result a policeman went round and told her to, "Fuck off". She got the message. My mother was very shocked at a police officer saying that, but it did the trick.

After a trial at the Old Bailey, the man who drove the getaway car was sentenced to life imprisonment for murder, and the woman who had stolen the bag got three years for theft. The court heard that both were drug addicts who funded their £300-a-day habits by shoplifting or stealing people's bags (Clough, 2001). After the trial, the family wanted to talk to the media. They spoke at a press conference because they were keen to correct what they saw as misconceptions about Liz's actions on the day she was killed; they wanted to pay tribute to the real person they knew and loved; and they wanted to challenge those who celebrate the use of drugs, by pointing to the connection between drug habits and the sort of crime that Liz had fallen victim to. But they found that this was deemed too complex for the press and broadcast news, who wanted simple, snappy quotes. Janet describes some of the reporting that upset the family:

> The image that was created was that Liz had leapt onto the bonnet of a car, but the evidence that came out in the trial was that she was standing to the side, leaning over the bonnet and banging on the windscreen. She was trying to stop them driving off but they did drive off and she ended up on the bonnet. She didn't *leap* onto the bonnet. She was gung-ho, but not that gung-ho.
>
> What offended us in the press reports was the implication that people shouldn't fight back, that people should just accept being vulnerable and hand over their possessions. It was also reported that her handbag didn't have much money in it, implying that she shouldn't have tried to get it back. But she was a self-employed costume designer and the bag had her contacts and her keys and so on. The bag also had sentimental value and she had splashed out on it – it was symbolic. Although we had a press conference immediately after the trial, only soundbites and brief quotes were used, and none of what I said about drugs was reported. When we felt able to speak, there was a lack of interest, and we felt silenced.

As is often the way of these things, news stories about the end of the trial were followed shortly afterwards by newspaper columnists having their say on the subject. The family were particularly distressed when their local paper ran a piece that was critical of Liz and other victims who fought back against criminals. Although a letter putting the family's side of the story was published later, the article had a damaging impact on Janet and her parents:

> That paper arrived on the day that dad had a heart attack. It was waiting on the mat when mum returned from the hospital. Up to that day I'd managed to keep going OK, but after that I went on anti-depressants and sleeping tablets, and the family really struggled. I feel that the newspaper was irresponsible. Did they consider us? I don't know. We were feeling insecure and vulnerable, and it felt like secondary victimisation of Liz and us.

Interestingly, the tiny local newspaper covering the scene of one of the biggest crime stories of recent years – the Soham murders – went out of its way to consider the victims' relatives at the time of the subsequent trial. The *Ely Standard* kept the story off its front page at a time when the case was the splash in virtually all national media. Deputy editor Debbie Davies explained why the paper defied conventional news values:

> It was one of the biggest stories ever for us and the natural instinct was to put it on the front page, but I created a scenario in my head where I could see the parents of the two little girls coming home from the court day after day and they did not want to see our billboards screaming at them or go into the local shop and see front page headlines in the *Standard*.
>
> (Quoted in Pape and Featherstone, 2005: 181)

The result of that newspaper's empathy towards the families may encourage other journalists to realise that things do not always have to be reported in the same old way.

Meanwhile, several years after losing her sister, Janet McKenzie is trying to put her own experiences to good use by helping other families cope with the long-term repercussions of homicide, which can include physical and mental illness and the breakdown of relationships. She trains police family liaison officers to deal with bereaved families; she works with voluntary organisations such as Support After Murder and Manslaughter (SAMM), the Victims of Crime Trust, and Victims' Voice; and she is writing a book about it all. "We're a positive family," she explains, "and we've risen to the challenge."

THE PERILS OF LAZY JOURNALISM

Somebody else who has risen to a challenge is Eric Allison. After giving up on school at the age of 11, he has spent most of his adult life as a career criminal who viewed spells in prison as an occupational hazard. That all changed when, in his sixties, he became a journalist. He had always enjoyed writing, despite his lack of formal schooling, and he discovered the power of the pen whilst in prison:

> I started writing petitions and letters to MPs, mostly about other people's problems, because I wouldn't watch anyone be bullied. I gradually built up a portfolio of contacts among MPs, journalists, prison reform groups, professors of criminology and so on.

One thing led to another and he ended up co-authoring a book about a riot at Strangeways jail, which he observed from outside the prison walls. After leaving prison for the last time in 2000, he saw an advert in the *Guardian* for a job as that newspaper's prisons correspondent:

> It was to be the first prisons correspondent on any national newspaper. They said applications from ex-offenders were welcome, so I wrote them a letter. I've read the paper since 1969 and I've always admired it. I got a lot of education from it and always had an affinity with it. I used to pass it on to a lot of other prisoners after I'd read it.

The letter resulted in an interview and, much to his surprise, he got the job.

Allison loves his new career as a reporter, but he admits to being somewhat disillusioned – angry, even – about what he once imagined to be a noble craft:

> Because I'm very new to journalism, I often look at this job through the eyes of a reader. I'm not running the *Guardian* down particularly, because I'm sure it is one of the best of a bad bunch, but I had perceptions about this job that have been completely shattered. I thought that reporters went out to look for stories, but of course they don't. They sit down and wait for press releases.

He is not impressed by journalists who "don't bother to get off their arses and ask questions", nor by the "random" way in which crime is reported. He recalls a case that has clearly stuck in his mind for decades:

> Something occurred to me 40 odd years ago, when a local woman was caught shoplifting. She was a paragon of virtue in the area, a gossipy woman, and her case was in the paper. It struck me then how unfair that was because there would have been half a dozen cases of shoplifting in that court that week, but the stringer just happened to pick that one, and her punishment was completely out of proportion with the rest of the people who didn't get reported. That struck me, even then at a very early age, as grossly unfair. My view then was that you either report everything or you

> report nothing. To suddenly be selective about one shoplifter ruined that woman's life more than any fine that the court could impose, no question about it.

Selective reporting also results in the demonising of certain types of people and, he believes, in disproportionate public fears about certain categories of crime. "The fact is that the vast majority of child abuse occurs within the home," he explains. "You're far more in danger from a member of your family than you are from a stranger."

Perhaps not surprisingly for someone who has spent so much time on the other side of the law, Allison has little time for journalists who, as he sees it, simply regurgitate police or Home Office handouts:

> They don't question the police. And why would they question them, when they're the supplier of their material all the time? There's a very unhealthy relationship between the police and most journalists; it's an incestuous relationship. I say "most" because there are shining exceptions. Of course you've got to have a working relationship, and you don't expect to be spitting at them, but it becomes too cosy.

One result of this overly cosy relationship, he feels, is that too much prejudicial material is published before cases ever get to court:

> The more shocking the murder, the more they get away with it. Because they work with the police so much, the investigating officer will say to the journalist, "We've got the right geezer here, no question about it." That is dangerous. I've always thought that in high-profile cases, when the jury file in and look at the defendant in the dock, they don't say, "Is that the man who's done this?" they say, "Oh, that's him, is it?" They've already read so much about him and they've already read so much about the crime.

Allison is concerned that prejudicial reporting can lead to miscarriages of justice, in which innocent people are convicted of crimes they did not commit. People wrongly convicted of serious offences may be believed only by members of their own family in the early days, and campaigns to prove their innocence often begin with a desperate parent or other relative writing to a journalist asking for help. Although journalists have a long record of exposing miscarriages of justice, such as in the cases of the Birmingham Six and the Bridgewater Four, Allison feels it is getting harder to arouse the interest of mainstream journalists:

> No-one's interested unless it's massively high profile. The perception of newsdesk is that people have had enough of them, but I'm sorry, I haven't had enough of them. And if the wrong person is inside, it means the real killer is still out there. The law isn't going to put its house in order, the police aren't going to put their house in order, so who does that leave? Journalists. Journalists should go out to see people, make some effort to attend trials every day, not just the opening and closing, get hold of transcripts and read every word, and go beyond the press release. If X didn't do it, then where's the guy who did do it? That's in the public interest to find out.

Someone who did receive such a plea for help was Steve Panter. He recalls being contacted by the mother of Stefan Kiszko, a man who had been jailed for killing an 11-year-old girl:

> She used to ring me and say, "My son's not done it." My cops said, "Oh yeah, he has done it," and I didn't believe her. She eventually got hold of a very good lawyer who did believe her, and her son was proved beyond doubt scientifically to be innocent.

By that time, Stefan Kiszko had spent 16 years in prison for a crime that he had not committed. Panter can't help thinking that, if he and other journalists had looked into the case more closely, an innocent man might not have spent so long behind bars:

> I got involved with the family retrospectively – I was the first reporter his mother rang on the day he died, a year after he came out of prison – I was just so sorry I never looked at it in the first place. I believed my cops rather than her. The cops I spoke to genuinely believed he'd done it, and I was swayed by them. Looking back it was probably lazy journalism. I should have investigated it. I regret that. I always will, really.

If Panter followed the police line on that particular case, he has not always done so, as we saw in the last chapter. His investigations have led to his being arrested twice – once at gunpoint, trying to get close to Myra Hindley on Saddleworth Moor – and he frequently ran stories that embarrassed the police hierarchy. He explains why:

> My loyalty was to the readers, the public, not to the police; they're a publicly funded body. And if there was a cop being disciplined for drink driving, or some sort of internal complaint – what I saw as information the public should have – the police hierarchy would see it as private, internal. They used to hate it if I got anything that wasn't given in a press release, and they would have mole hunts. I was told by one very senior officer that they used to go through all the phones of Greater Manchester Police to find out who was ringing me. It's a balancing act, it's tricky, but ultimately you are respected more as a crime reporter if you are prepared occasionally to write what they might not like. If you're in their pocket all the time, they don't respect that. I get the impression that some current crime reporters are a bit too cosy with the cops and it's a danger, trying to stay onside with them too much you lose your sense of objectivity. I'm quite proud that I was never, ever invited to the CID dinner. I say that because my contacts would never invite me in case they were accused of being one of my moles. It was a backhanded tribute, really.

Eric Allison shares this ethos that journalists should keep their distance from those in positions of authority on whom they are reporting:

> Yes, have a healthy working relationship with the people you have to work with every day – the Crown Prosecution Service, the police press office, police on the ground – but make it a healthy relationship and don't jump into bed with them. It's a cosy little club. Journalists are invited into that club, and the lazy ones join it. Basically, journalists should be outside the club.

A SENSE OF RESPONSIBILITY

Perhaps the final word should come from someone who has experienced crime reporting not as a journalist, but from the other side of the barrage of microphones, cameras and notebooks. Looking back, what advice would Janet McKenzie give to journalists who find themselves covering crimes such as the one that changed her life?

> Journalists in such situations should see themselves almost as social workers, not simply entertaining people or informing people of the bare facts, because there are very few bare facts without a context. They should feel a sense of responsibility to the community. What we want is to have our own say and be faithfully reported, but the impact of being bereaved by homicide was a feeling of complete and utter powerlessness and of being silenced by the media. It was secondary victimisation. They haven't reproduced what we wanted to say, they were in control. Some people want to talk to the press, but if you are told to go away – go away, and leave your card. You can feel for the journalists who have been sent on that job, and perhaps it's the people who send them that are at fault. But it's ridiculous to ask someone how they feel after a murder. How can you put it into words?

She points out that, unlike most celebrities who find themselves at the centre of journalistic feeding-frenzies, "ordinary" people unexpectedly thrust into the limelight do not normally have access to public relations consultants:

> Victims and relatives need an intermediary between themselves and the media, and perhaps that's something that former journalists could do, because without that we don't know who we can trust. When journalists deal with celebrities, the celebrities have teams of people looking after their interests and advising them. We have nobody, and journalists should appreciate that.

Janet adds that journalists could do more to publicise the existence of voluntary organisations such as the Victims of Crime Trust and to include contact details alongside crime stories. Such useful information may not make exciting copy or a dramatic headline, but it may just provide someone with a lifeline when they need it. The trust's website is www.victimsofcrimetrust.com and the telephone number is 0870 8428467.

FURTHER READING

To check out the law on reporting crime and the courts, see the latest edition of Welsh and others (2005), while Hanna (2006) offers a brief but useful guide to court reporting. For academic critiques of the ways in which journalists report crime, see Jewkes (2004), Wykes (2001), and Schlesinger and Tumber (1994). Cohen (2002) is a classic study of the "moral panic" around the Mods and Rockers youth subcultures of the 1960s, Hall and others (1978) explore media coverage of mugging in the 1970s, and Cottle (2005b) is an academic analysis of how the Stephen Lawrence case was reported. Brockes (2000) is a thoughtful journalistic account of the life and times of the so-called Balaclava Boy. For an illuminating personal account of being a crime victim followed by being doorstepped by journalists, see Tulloch (2006).

8 THE REGULATION OF JOURNALISM

"A sick GP who was jailed for downloading and distributing graphic and 'disturbing' images of children has been struck off the medical register," it says in my local newspaper (YEP, 2005). Quite right too. Who wants their doctor to be someone who gets his kicks from viewing and exchanging images of rape and other forms of child abuse? By striking him off its register, the General Medical Council ruled that he could not return to practise as a doctor after his release from jail. A week later, in an unrelated case, the *Daily Telegraph* reports that the General Medical Council has struck off a hospital consultant who took "active measures" to end the life of a patient, against the wishes of the family (Davies, 2005b). Again, who wants to be treated by a doctor who might hasten death when you would prefer them to postpone it? The media report such cases with alarming frequency, although our alarm at the actions of the doctors is assuaged by the knowledge that they will no longer be able to practise their profession.

Suppose for a moment that they were not doctors, but journalists. Journalists who had distributed images of child abuse in their spare time; or journalists who had been cavalier with the facts of a story; or journalists who had entrapped some vulnerable individual in a "sting" operation; or journalists who had accepted bribes; or journalists whose stories had resulted in riots and bloodshed; or journalists who had formed a press pack that camped outside an address and caused someone inside to feel suicidal? A journalist who had done such things may well be sacked from his or her job. And, if they had broken the law of the land, they might face prosecution. But there would be absolutely nothing to stop them from continuing to work as a journalist in the future. They cannot be "struck off" a register, because there is no register. Not in the UK, at least, where we have enjoyed an essentially "free press" since the failure of attempts at more formal regulation in the seventeenth century (Shannon, 2001: 3).

This freedom from official registers contrasts not just with the medical profession, but also with several other occupations, from schoolteachers to gas fitters. Builders who install gas appliances in people's homes can be sent to prison if they have not been registered with Corgi, the Council for Registered Gas Installers. This is a matter of life and death, because an untrained fitter can kill people by exposing them to carbon monoxide poisoning or the risk of an explosion. This registration scheme, which is policed by the Health and Safety Executive, is a way of ensuring that only trained and competent individuals can work as gas fitters (Hopkinson, 2005).

So why are the untrained and incompetent, as well as the unscrupulous, allowed to call themselves journalists as long as they can find an outlet for their work? Partly because the relationship between journalists and "life and death" matters is less obvious than with doctors and gas fitters, although the work of journalists has sometimes been blamed for ruining people's lives, even for prompting suicides or murders. But mainly because of history: the way that journalism developed out of a democratising print culture, as discussed in Chapter 3. The consequences of a system of registration would be rather more disturbing for journalists than for doctors or gas fitters; disturbing, too, for the concept of journalism as a way for citizens to engage in rational discourse with each other in a public sphere. Because, if a journalist has to be officially registered, then that journalist can also be de-registered and classified as a non-journalist. That is a dangerous power to give to the state. It is what has happened in Zimbabwe, for example, where newspapers that have been critical of the government have had their licences to publish withdrawn, and where journalists can be prosecuted and jailed simply for working without state accreditation (Slattery, 2005).

That's why most journalists in most democratic societies have traditionally resisted any suggestion of an official "register" of approved journalists, and that's why the concept of such a register has been rejected as unacceptable in the UK. However, this does not mean that we are above the law of the land. In England and Wales, for example, I have counted around 60 laws that impinge on how journalists may gather or disseminate information (Harcup, 2004: 22), but these laws do not place journalists apart from other citizens. Yes, journalists can be sued for libel or jailed for contempt of court; but so can anyone else. Journalists are citizens with notebooks, tape machines, and/or cameras; and our status in law is the same as that of any other citizen. Which is not to say that journalism is entirely unregulated. Print journalism in the UK is "self-regulated" by the Press Complaints Commission (PCC), an industry-funded body that can tick journalists off but cannot strike them off. And it all works swimmingly, according to proprietors and their editors.

"We are very proud of the PCC definitely and self-regulation," declared *Sun* editor Rebekah Wade in what for her was an extremely rare appearance in public. She was defending the role of the Press Complaints Commission in evidence to a group of MPs, and she continued in similar vein:

> We are very proud of it and the way it has changed our industry over the last 10 years. Self-regulation is working … The PCC and self-regulation has changed the culture in every single newsroom in the land – not just in Fleet Street but every regional newspaper too … The fact that it is quick, fast, free, easy to use and efficient is perfect for ordinary people … The threat of a complaint being upheld by the PCC is what terrifies editors … Self-regulation is not just about an adjudication but it is raising press standards, and that is what the PCC has done, and the last 10 years have seen those press standards steadily become higher and higher and higher … All I can say from starting off as a reporter to becoming the editor of the *Sun* is that all I have seen is constant improvement.
>
> (Select Committee, 2003)

"All is beautiful in the garden, everything is rosy," commented Chris Bryant MP, summarising the Rebekah Wade vision of the press. But there are many people out there who feel that the PCC has proved to be rather a toothless watchdog. Former *Daily Telegraph* editor Max Hastings (2002: 282), for example, who believes that "the PCC sometimes appears to perceive that its function is to provide figleaves of justification for 'redtop' excesses".

Another heavyweight critic is David Seymour, former political editor of the *Daily Mirror*, who told the *Press Gazette* in 2006:

> While I worked at the *Mirror*, I could not say what I really felt about the PCC. The party line for all newspapers is that the PCC is doing a fine job … Now I can say what I really think. And that is that the PCC is doing a hopeless job. It is handing down verdicts which fail to even meet the basic dictates of common sense, let alone justice … If that sort of judgement was handed down by a doctors' professional body, or solicitors', we would all be sitting around our office laughing about it and writing leaders.
>
> (Quoted in Ponsford, 2006b)

Certainly, it is hard to see why Rebekah Wade should be so terrified of having a complaint upheld, when there appears to be so little chance of it actually happening. An examination of the figures reveals that, although the *Sun* is the most complained against newspaper, only 18 complaints against it were upheld in a 10-year period (Frost, 2004: 109). That is an average of just one breach of the code for every 173 issues of the *Sun* published. If things really are that rosy even at the popular redtop end of the garden, then perhaps the proprietors and their editors are right to be so self-congratulatory about self-regulation.

A BRIEF HISTORY OF SELF-REGULATION

The UK press has been subject to this system of self-regulation since the middle of the twentieth century. Following the Second World War, calls for a Royal Commission to investigate the press were initiated by the National Union of Journalists (NUJ) on behalf of members who were concerned both at the political power of the press owners and at what is now called the "dumbing down" of news. A journalist by the name of Preston Benson told the union's 1946 conference in Liverpool that increasing commercialisation "has reduced news to the quality of entertainment and the gathering, reporting, discussing, and commenting on news has lost its social interest" (quoted in Bundock, 1957: 185).

So the NUJ put pressure on the post-war Labour government led by Clement Attlee, and a Royal Commission was duly established in 1947 to enquire into the ownership, finances and management of the press. "For the first time in its embattled history," notes Richard Shannon (2001: 9), the "rough old trade" of journalism was to have "its entrails exposed to searching official examination". When the Commission reported two years later, it declared itself happy with the system of newspaper ownership – "free enterprise is a prerequisite of a free press," it asserted – but not with the way newspapers were fulfilling what was seen as their key role in a democratic society. The Commission proposed the establishment of a General Council of the Press:

> [T]o safeguard the freedom of the press; to encourage the growth of the sense of public responsibility and public service amongst all those engaged in the profession of journalism – that is, in the editorial production of newspapers – whether as directors, editors, or other journalists; and to further the efficiency of the profession and the well-being of those who practise it.
>
> (Quoted in Shannon, 2001: 10)

It further recommended that the new council should be able to deal with complaints.

This report led to the establishment in 1953 of the General Council of the Press, and its first ruling was that a poll in the *Daily Mirror* on whether Princess Margaret should marry Group Captain Townsend was "contrary to the best traditions of British journalism" (Keeble, 2001a: 15). Its membership, although dominated by newspaper editors and proprietors, included representatives of the NUJ and the smaller Institute of Journalists (O'Malley and Soley, 2000: 58). As Shannon (2001: 12) notes, the council was "informal, part-time, and cosy"; although it could consider complaints, it had "no powers of punitive sanction".

The General Council of the Press changed its name to the Press Council in 1963, following a second Royal Commission. Although still dominated by industry representatives, the Press Council did include some members of the public. A third Royal Commission on the Press in the 1970s was critical of the Press Council's performance, and this resulted in the lay representatives becoming a majority (Shannon, 2001: 16). Increasingly, however, Press Council pronouncements were treated with contempt by newspaper editors and owners, who were too busy fighting circulation wars to be bothered by what amounted to an occasional slap on the wrist with a wet lettuce. In 1980 the NUJ withdrew from the Press Council on the grounds that it was "wholly ineffective" (O'Malley and Soley, 2000: 79). The union maintained its boycott for 10 years, deciding to rejoin the Press Council only after a series of reforms had been agreed.

But the Press Council was then hastily disbanded, to be replaced by the Press Complaints Commission (PCC), on which no trades unions were to be offered seats (Frost, 2000: 189–91). The PCC's sudden arrival on the scene in 1991 followed a review of privacy issues that had been ordered by Margaret Thatcher's Conservative government. The mood music of this review was provided by the *Sunday Sport*'s hospital intrusion (see Chapter 6) and by the warning from minister David Mellor that the press was "drinking in the Last Chance Saloon" (quoted in Sanders, 2003: 80). A committee chaired by David Calcutt QC recommended that the new self-regulatory complaints body be given a probationary period of 18 months; if press excesses had not stopped by then, there should be statutory regulation. So, from the start, the PCC was the newspaper proprietors' pre-emptive strike, designed to ward off any possibility of a tougher regulatory regime (Keeble, 2001a: 16). It was dominated by newspaper editors plus a handful of "toffs and profs", as Paul Foot called them (quoted in Frost, 2000: 191); a creature of the industry that funds it, the PCC has the "whiff of the Establishment" about it (Jempson, 2004a: 7). Calcutt reviewed the PCC's performance during its probationary period and concluded in 1993 that it was so ineffective that it should be replaced by a statutory tribunal. However, the government rejected Calcutt's call for a statutory regulation (Sanders, 2003: 81) and the PCC continues to this day, with editors now a minority, albeit a very influential one.

A CUSTOMER COMPLAINTS MODEL

The PCC operates by responding to complaints about breaches of its code of practice, which was drafted – and is occasionally updated – by a committee of editors drawn from national and regional newspapers and magazines. Although few complaints are actually adjudicated, if the PCC finds that a newspaper or magazine has breached its code, then that publication must publish the adjudication. Ian Beales, a former regional newspaper editor who helped draw up the code, explains the thinking here:

> There are no fines or compensation, since these would inevitably involve lawyers, making the system legalistic, slow and expensive ... Adverse adjudications are effective. Editors dislike having to publish them. It means their mistakes are exposed to their own readers, and often to criticism and ridicule in the columns of their commercial rivals, which is doubly damaging.
>
> (Beales, 2005: 8)

It is accepted by many journalists and critics that much of the UK press has improved some of its behaviour since what are perceived as the excesses of the 1970s, 1980s and 1990s. We heard from Steve Panter in Chapter 7 that ethical dimensions of stories are now more likely to be considered within newsrooms than they were in the years before the PCC arrived on the scene. There appear to be fewer media scrums in which packs of journalists camp on people's doorsteps shouting through the letterbox with offers of money or threats of unfavourable coverage. There appear to be fewer examples of casual or calculated homophobia or racism within news coverage. And there appear to be more examples of editors declining to publish intrusive photographs of prurient interest that would have been run without hesitation a few years earlier. We still have the curious phenomenon of the soft-porn "page three" picture that debases the journalism around it, and women in the news are often treated differently from men, but at least these days we see far fewer examples of the automatic use of sexist language in news stories than we saw in previous decades.

How much any of these perceived shifts in newspaper practice are down to the role of the PCC – and how much they reflect wider changes in social attitudes and newsroom composition – is a moot point. But the PCC is gradually building up a large body of cases that journalists can consult, if they are so inclined, to see what might be regarded as acceptable under the code. They can, for example, read that the *News of the World* was found to have breached the privacy of one celebrity, while the *Sun* was justified in publishing personal information about another. Both stories involved alleged affairs, but the difference was that whereas the woman in the *Sun* story "had previously put her own personal details into the public domain in self-promoting articles and interviews", the woman in the *NotW* one "had not compromised her privacy by revealing details of her private life" (Beales, 2005: 34). Journalists can also discover that photographs of a couple on a publicly accessible beach in Majorca seem to be OK, but that a picture of someone in a tearoom in Dorking is quite another matter. The PCC ruled that, whereas nobody could "reasonably" expect privacy in the former case, people should not have to worry about public exposure in a quiet café (Beales, 2005: 38). And journalists can get an idea of when persistence can become harassment, as in this case:

> A couple whose daughter, aged 16, committed suicide declined a weekly newspaper's offer to publish a tribute, saying they would be in touch if they changed their minds. But the reporter, with deadline pressing, called four times in a few days. The PCC said common sense should have dictated that repeated calls in a short time to recently-bereaved parents were inappropriate. The complaint was upheld.
>
> (Beales, 2005: 42)

Most complaints to the PCC are not about intrusions of privacy or harassment, but about inaccurate reporting. In 2005, for example, two-thirds of the 3,654 complaints made to the PCC concerned the accuracy of articles (PCC, 2006a: 3). One such complainant the following year was the Duchess of York, who felt that the *Sun's* coverage of her daughter's 16th birthday party was exaggerated and inaccurate (PCC, 2006b). The complaint was resolved without adjudication when the newspaper published the following correction:

> Following our article on Princess Eugenie's birthday celebrations, we have been asked to point out the party was closely monitored by adults throughout and, while a small amount of mess was cleared away at the end of the evening, there was no damage to furniture, no revellers dived into bedrooms in search of drunken romps and to describe the house as being trashed was incorrect. We are happy to make this clear and regret any distress our report caused.
>
> (*Sun*, 2006)

And the paper was no doubt even happier to have avoided a formal decision against it, not to mention the possibility of legal action.

Although the PCC usually finds complaints about inacurracy too difficult to decide one way or the other, it does sometimes rule against a newspaper on matters of fact, as when the *Sun* stated that gay men had an average life expectancy of just 43 and were 17 times more likely to be paedophiles than were heterosexual men. The newspaper later defended the figures as "broadly accurate", but the PCC upheld a complaint that such claims should not have been presented as fact (Beales, 2005: 26). This was an unusual finding, as the PCC has rarely found fault with press stories about groups of people. Many complaints about alleged racism, for example, have been dismissed on the grounds that no individuals have been named and/or that the report was presented as comment rather than fact. Ian Beales defends the PCC's role in the following terms:

> [T]he code does not cover generalised remarks about groups or categories of people, which would involve subjective views, often based on political correctness or taste, and would be difficult to adjudicate upon without infringing the freedom of expression of others … [T]he PCC … has upheld the press's right to make robust comment, as long as the distinction between opinion and fact is clear.
>
> (Beales, 2005: 71)

One person's "robust comment" might be another's racist diatribe, of course, and many people still feel that our newspapers are too often allowed to get away with inaccurate, intrusive and inflammatory reporting. For its critics, this stems from the PCC's narrow remit and the fact that, from the start, it was based on the model of a customer complaints department rather than on an engagement with journalism and ethics as components of citizenship, social responsibility and democracy.

The PCC's code has been described by academic John Tulloch[1] (1998: 81) as "a set of loopholes bound together with good intentions". Keeble (2001a: 13) notes that such codes of ethical conduct tend to provoke one of two responses: either they are dismissed as "rhetorical devices" to camouflage hypocrisy, or they are lauded as vehicles of increased professionalism. However, a third response is for journalists to behave as if such codes did not exist. James Hipwell – one of the two "city slickers" at the *Daily Mirror* who were convicted of using their articles about share prices to boost their personal investments – told his trial: "To the best of my knowledge, no one at the *Mirror* had a copy [of the PCC code] or had ever seen a copy" (quoted in Daley, 2005). Over at News International, meanwhile, a senior executive spelt out the the fact of corporate life in the following terms:

> If an editor went to Murdoch and said that he had carefully examined the PCC code of conduct on chequebook journalism and had come to the conclusion that to pay to get a story would be a breach of the code and, therefore, he hadn't done it, he would be fired.
>
> (Quoted in Ratcliffe, 2006)

A self-regulatory body as "tightly focused on editors" as the PCC is unlikely to be seen by the public as a truly independent arbiter of media behaviour, argued the NUJ in evidence to a group of MPs considering the issue of privacy. The union called for a wider membership, including representatives of working journalists and the public, and also suggested that journalists should be protected from disciplinary action or dismissal if they refused an employer's instruction to behave unethically. The NUJ told the Culture, Media and Sport Select Committee:

> This approach would offer real support rather than the present system where newspaper proprietors and editors attempt to switch the sole responsibility for good behaviour onto journalists by writing the PCC's code of practice in contracts of employment, allowing editors to sack journalists for breaching the code, but not forcing editors to insist that journalists abide by it. Many journalists believe this forces them to do things that they feel are unethical, knowing that if the matter becomes one of public debate they are likely to be dismissed as a convenient scapegoat.
>
> (NUJ, 2003)

---

1 John Tulloch is a journalism professor at the University of Lincoln and should not be confused with the media studies professor of the same name who was injured in the 7 July 2005 bombings.

MPs on the committee agreed, and their report recommended that journalists should be given the power to refuse assignments that breached the PCC code. In its official response, the PCC rejected this as unnecessary, declaring:

> The Commission has no evidence that journalists are asked to undertake such assignments that would breach the code in the absence of any public interest. This would in any case seem to be a matter for the employer and employee concerned rather than the Commission.
>
> (PCC, 2004)

Such a sanguine view of what goes on within newsrooms ignores the power relationships in the real world, argues Mike Jempson:

> Journalists operate in a hostile employment environment with no formal career structure, and fierce competition for jobs … Like most people, journalists are prone to take the easy way out if it presents itself. Especially now that so many are freelances or on short term contracts, they may feel their personal interests are best served by satisfying the demands of editors whose own security rests upon improving the commercial prospects of their titles.
>
> (Jempson, 2004b: 40)

It is because of such power relationships – and because of a bullying culture within some newsrooms – that this idea of a so-called "conscience clause" has been gaining ground in recent years. Arguing in favour of the concept of the "virtuous journalist" whose behaviour is subject to ethical codes of conduct, Tulloch (2004a: 29) points out that "this is only feasible if journalists establish a right to refuse instructions that breach the code". Similarly, writing in a US context, Bill Kovach and Tom Rosenstiel (2003: 183) argue: "Allowing individuals to voice their consciences in the newsroom makes running the newspaper more difficult. It makes the news more accurate." Journalists at the sharp end of ethical dilemmas in the UK national press have themselves called for such a "conscience clause", as we shall see in Chapter 9.

If the PCC is a customer complaints department, it is one that prides itself on adjudicating very few of the thousands of complaints it receives. This lack of adjudication often leaves complainants frustrated. A detailed study of the PCC's first decade of operation shows that, of almost 23,000 complaints received, fewer than one in 25 were even adjudicated on (3.8 per cent), and just one complaint out of every 60 (1.6 per cent) was actually upheld (Frost, 2004: 106). Throughout this period, the PCC did not uphold even one complaint about press coverage that discriminated on the grounds of race (Frost, 2004: 111). Of more than 600 complaints about alleged racism against Gypsies and Travellers, for example, not a single one was upheld and most were rejected out of hand because the "victims" did not complain personally (Petley, 2004b: 23). Critics point to the small number of adjudications and the smaller number of upheld complaints as evidence of weakness, but "maximising nice conciliation and minimising nasty adjudications" is regarded by the PCC as a sign of success rather than failure (Shannon, 2001: 337). Those who avail of its complaints service do not always agree. One dissatisfied customer who succeeded in obtaining a correction to an inaccurate newspaper story still did not feel that justice had been done:

> The PCC seemed to think I was extraordinarily lucky. But I didn't want to settle for that – I wanted an adjudication and a ruling from the PCC. I wanted the editor to be admonished by his peers. However, I was told that if I declined their offer of an apology, the PCC would probably just chuck my complaint out because it was a reasonable offer. I just felt that the newspaper got away with it, really. What did it cost them? All they had to do was publish a postage-stamp [sized] apology, and they have impunity to do it again.
>
> (Quoted in Cookson, 2004: 13)

Having studied the PCC's record, Chris Frost concludes that it is hardly the unmitigated success story claimed by Wade, Beales and others:

> The PCC makes two main claims about its activities. The first is that self-regulation works and that the PCC is a "first-class complaints handling organisation" that "deals with complaints quickly and effectively" ... and the second is that the PCC "changed the entire culture of British newspapers and magazines" by raising "standards through its adjudications" ... There is no evidence for either of these claims in the data gathered from the PCC's own reports.
>
> (Frost, 2004: 113)

Similarly underwhelmed by the effectiveness of the current system of self-regulation is Stephen Sedley (2006), a Lord Justice of Appeal who argues that "there is no serious case for preserving anything of the PCC" except its code which, he notes, "sets out admirable principles which the more aggressive of its subscribers seem to have very little difficulty in circumventing". It is perhaps no surprise that, as a judge, Sedley would prefer a more legalistic solution to the problem of journalists' "enormous power to wound"; that is, some form of statutory regulation "with rules, legal standards and teeth".

Shannon, in contrast, argues that the PCC is doing a grand job:

> The industry set up the PCC as an evil lesser than legislation. Legislation, it is arguable, would be contrary to the public interest. Does it not then follow that it is publicly beneficial that there be an identity of interest between the industry and its self-regulatory body, always providing that while the industry defines the terms and

> conditions of that interest in its Code, that Code in turn is both validated and administered by the self-regulatory body? It would not serve the public interest if the industry and its self-regulatory body were constantly at odds in the manner of criminals and police. The starting point of the whole arrangement, after all, is the generally accepted axiom that it is in the public interest that the press be free. A free press must persuade itself to be responsible. That is what the PCC does for it. It cannot be other than an intimately internal debate. The more intimate, it might well be argued, the better.
>
> (Shannon, 2001: 335–6)

However, when Shannon refers to "the industry", he – and the PCC itself – appears to be thinking of proprietors and editors. Journalists lower down the hierarchy do not usually get much of a look-in, but we shall hear from some in the next chapter.

DIFFERENT MODELS OF REGULATION

The PCC is not the only form of self-regulation operating within the UK press. Since 1997, the *Guardian* newspaper has pioneered the idea of a readers' editor (Ian Mayes), who deals with complaints independently of the editor and who has a regular space in the paper to correct inaccuracies and discuss wider journalistic issues. More newspapers have since established corrections and clarifications columns and/or appointed people to deal with readers' complaints, and the *Guardian* model has been adopted by the Danish daily *Politiken*, and by the *Hindu* in India, whose editor N Ram explained:

> Freedom of the press is important. So is its social responsibility, which must begin with interaction with and accountability to readers. For a daily newspaper, this must happen on a daily basis.
>
> (Quoted in Mayes, 2006)

This willingness to admit mistakes in public is a relatively new phenomenon, and contrasts with a determination to avoid printing corrections at all costs that was drummed into previous generations of journalists. As the *Guardian*'s assistant readers' editor Helen Hodgson says: "In an industry that calls for accountability in others it seems hypocritical not to be accountable yourself" (quoted in Cookson, 2004: 15). It remains to be seen how many publications will be quite as prepared to admit in public to serious shortcomings. After all, it may be far more palatable to correct simple mistakes in dates and spellings than to publish more substantial corrections, such as the one the *Guardian* (2005) ran in relation to its treatment of a story about the radical intellectual Noam Chomsky. That correction contained words such as, "misleading", "wrong", "unjustified", "misrepresentation" and "misunderstanding". It also led to a complaint about the correction itself, prompting a review of the whole process by the newspaper's external ombudsman. The ombudsman, John Willis, concluded that the readers' editor had been right to publish an apology and correction but that a decision to remove the original article from the newspaper's website had been unnecessary (*Guardian*, 2006).

Painful as it is in the short-term to admit to mistakes, the long-term gain may be that a more open approach leads to an increase in levels of trust. It seems to be working, judging by the newspaper's own research, which suggests that three out of four readers feel the existence of the readers' editor makes the paper more responsive to their views and opinions (Guardian Newspapers Ltd, 2005: 12).

Not all journalists work within a system of self-regulation, however. Broadcast journalists in the UK work under a much stricter regulatory regime, which has the backing of the law. Print and broadcast journalism are both products of the different times in which they developed, and of different technologies, and the regulatory regimes reflect such differences. Hundreds of years ago, the printing press was a new technology that – potentially – allowed anyone to become a publisher. Attempts to control who could have access to this technology proved impossible to enforce. When radio and television came along, in contrast, the new technology depended on the limited number of wavebands available, which allowed the state to restrict the number of broadcasters by issuing licences. There was also a fear of the consequences if broadcast technology fell into the wrong hands. As a committee of MPs reported in 1936, a medium pumped into millions of homes "needs very careful safeguarding if it is not to be abused", because it could allow a controlling party to "influence the whole political thought of the country" (quoted in Marr, 2005: 304).

Such concerns led to the undeniably messy but oddly effective system of broadcast regulation that evolved during the twentieth and into the twenty-first centuries. The BBC is publicly funded by a licence fee but operates at arm's length from government; commercial broadcasters are licensed by the state; and both sectors are regulated more tightly than print media. What this means for journalists is indicated by the stricter wording of both the government's Office of Communications (Ofcom) code for broadcasting (Appendix 5) and the BBC's editorial guidelines (Appendix 6), when compared with the PCC code (Appendix 4). Most obviously, UK broadcasters have to observe the sort of political impartiality that would take much of the fun out of being a newspaper proprietor. And, unlike the press, a broadcasting organisation found to have breached the Ofcom code can be fined and/or have its licence withdrawn.

The contrast with the cosier world of print self-regulation can be seen as soon as you go onto the Ofcom website and browse the adjudications on complaints about broadcasters. For example, Ofcom considered a number of listeners' complaints that Key 103 FM, run by Piccadilly Radio in Manchester, had broadcast offensive comments about the death of British hostage Kenneth Bigley in Iraq, had incited racial hatred, and had given undue prominence to the views of a presenter on a matter of political controversy. Piccadilly, which is owned by Emap, made no attempt to defend the offending broadcasts. Ofcom's Content Sanctions Committee fined the company £125,000 and ordered it to broadcast a summary of the ruling, written by Ofcom, three times every day for a week (Ofcom, 2005). That is very different from anything the PCC could do to an offending newspaper or magazine.

Broadcast regulation in the UK is, in the view of Andrew Marr (2005: 305), a very British compromise, which has turned out to be "an act of political wisdom" because it has (thus far) prevented broadcast news becoming distorted by the sort of party political bias that is evident across the Atlantic:

> In America, Fox News openly avows Rupert Murdoch's politics: but its British cousin Sky News, constrained and influenced by British television culture, does not. A relatively young tradition of politically impartial news was established here and has taken root. And this came about, let us remember, not because British journalists were more virtuous than journalists anywhere else, but because parliament decided to set up a system which was in deliberate tension – a licence fee for the BBC which kept the politicians relevant, and other constraints for the commercial companies, but day-to-day freedom for broadcasters.
>
> (Marr, 2005: 306–7)

Which is not to say that the tension inherent in this "day-to-day freedom" is not stretched to breaking point at times of crisis, such as when the Thatcher government fell out with broadcasters who asked awkward questions about the conflict in Northern Ireland, or when the Blair government turned on the BBC over Andrew Gilligan's reporting of the Iraq war.

Online journalism is something completely new at the same time as being something familiar, a hybrid form of existing journalisms. Some journalists work on web versions of newspapers, which have an orientation towards the PCC model of regulation; some journalists work on web versions of broadcast news, with a consequent orientation towards the BBC/Ofcom model of political impartiality; some journalists work for online-only outlets, some of which are beginning to develop their own models of self-regulation; and some people produce online journalism without necessarily thinking of themselves as journalists at all.

CALLS FOR REFORM

There is no reason to assume that the above systems of self-regulation and regulation will remain in place for all time. Since the Broadcasting Act of 1990 and the Communications Act of 2003, commercial television companies have been allowed to reduce their commitment to public service broadcasting and to chase ratings by cutting back regional output and pushing current affairs programming to the margins. At the same time, the BBC has faced political and economic pressure around the licence fee and the renewal of its charter, prompting media academic Tom O'Malley to warn:

> We now face a future where the government, the elites in the civil service and those at the top of the commercial media industry have embraced a system that will only allow choice to those with privilege and money. For the rest of us it will simply mean we get whatever cheap product can be foisted on us for whatever price the market will bear.
>
> (O'Malley, 2005: 26)

Tom O'Malley is a leading member of the Campaign for Press and Broadcasting Freedom (CPBF), which has lobbied on media issues since 1979. During the last UK general election, the campaign drew up a "manifesto" of proposals for media reform, which included:

- Giving Ofcom the primary task of promoting the public interest and public service values;
- Making the Ofcom board and the BBC governors more democratically representative;
- Allowing journalists to be represented on national media bodies, including the BBC governors and Ofcom;
- Removing the BBC from Ofcom's remit;
- Reducing concentration of media ownership and setting tight limits on cross-media ownership;
- Establishing a statutory right of reply to factual inaccuracies in the press;
- Replacing the Press Complaints Commission with an independent body backed by law and containing both working journalists and lay people;
- Enforcing a statutory "conscience clause" in journalists' contracts, allowing them to refuse to work on unethical material, without fear of reprisal.

(CPBF, 2005)

It is perhaps little surprise that the above calls for media reform were ignored within mainstream media coverage of the election, given that such policies represent the opposite of what most media owners have campaigned for so effectively in recent years. Granville Williams, another leading light in the CPBF, has charted the "easy access" to governments in the UK and elsewhere enjoyed by Rupert Murdoch and other big media players. Williams warns:

> Corporate lobbying plays an ever-increasing role in the development of media policy, and the remorseless growth of global media groups as a result threatens freedom of expression and the presentation of viewpoints and issues inimical to the commercial or political interests of those groups.
>
> (Williams, 2005: 37)

Tackling the power of the global media giants is likely to be a long, slow process; a process that may feel far removed from what goes on in our newsrooms on a daily basis. However, there have been occasions when journalists themselves – acting alone or standing together – have felt compelled to defend ethical standards of journalism against such commercial or political pressures. We shall hear some of their stories in the next chapter.

FURTHER READING

For information on how the law regulates journalists' behaviour in the UK, check out the most recent edition of *McNae's Essential Law for Journalists* by Welsh and others (2005). See Shannon (2001) for a blow-by-blow semi-official history of the Press Complaints Commission, and Beales (2005) for an explanation of the thinking behind each clause of the code and details on the "case law" that has developed. For a more critical account of the history of press self-regulation in the UK, see O'Malley and Soley (2000) or Curran (2000). Curran and Seaton (2003) discuss the wider history, economics and politics of the newspaper, broadcasting and online industries in the UK. Frost (2000), Keeble (2001a), Page (1998) and Sanders (2003) all deal in detail with regulation and the role of codes of ethical conduct. Frost (2004) offers an academic analysis of the first 10 years of PCC adjudications, while Jempson and Cookson (2004) is a collection of critical and anecdotal appraisals of the press complaints system, including the story of the asylum seekers' alleged "swan bake".

A wealth of interesting material, including information on the regulation of journalism in different countries and links to ethical codes around the world, is available on the website of the media ethics charity Mediawise (www.mediawise.org.uk); and the Campaign for Press and Broadcasting Freedom (www.cpbf.org.uk) is a similarly invaluable resource. Much more on press and broadcast regulation, including details of complaints and adjudications, can be found on the websites of the Press Complaints Commission (www.pcc.org.uk) and Ofcom (www.ofcom.org.uk) respectively. For more on the *Guardian* readers' editor, see www.guardian.co.uk/readerseditor, and for further information on readers' editors and "ombudsmen" around the world, see the website of the Organisation of News Ombudsmen (www.newsombudsmen.org).

9 STANDING UP FOR STANDARDS

Newspaper reporters love to see their bylines in print, the more prominent the better. So it was a sign that something was wrong when journalists on a UK national newspaper began to be embarrassed if their name was attached to a splash. Worse, these journalists came to dread receiving the sort of telephone call that is usually very gratifying: a reader calling to say, "You're doing a great job, keep up the good work." Such words of encouragement are not so welcome when spoken by avowed racists who think you are on their wavelength. But that was the experience of some journalists on the *Daily Express* when their newspaper ran a series of front-page stories attacking Gypsies in the run-up to the 2004 enlargement of the European Union (EU), with headlines such as 1.6 MILLION GYPSIES READY TO FLOOD IN – BRITAIN HERE WE COME and WE CAN'T COPE WITH HUGE GYPSY INVASION (Ponsford, 2004a). Although labelled "special investigation", these and other similar stories were following up a smaller item in one of the Sunday newspapers and appeared designed not so much to illuminate the issue as to chime with existing anti-Gypsy sentiments as expressed in readers' telephone polls.

This was neither the first nor the last time that the *Express* had published stories that seemed to some of its staff to be pandering to readers' prejudices; and the *Express* was by no means the only newspaper to go large on the issue. But, after a whole week of such coverage, many *Express* staff were deeply unhappy at their newspaper's apparent obsession with the story of an imminent Gypsy "invasion" of the UK, and several journalists were openly discussing walking out on their jobs. "A few involved in those pieces were very upset and were considering whether to resign," confirms Michelle

Stanistreet, a feature writer on the *Sunday Express* who speaks for the journalists' trade union[1] on the Express titles in London:

> Reporters were being bombarded with calls, some of which were critical but the vast majority of which were praising the coverage, with British National Party-type people ringing up saying "well done, keep it up". It was very upsetting, there was a great deal of anguish.

Some journalists complained that they had been put under pressure to produce stories to fit a pre-conceived editorial line, and this became a late addition to the agenda of what was to have been a routine meeting of National Union of Journalists members at Express Newspapers.

STICKING UP FOR COLLEAGUES

NUJ chapels do not usually concern themselves with editorial content or ethics, being more bothered about "bread and butter" issues. In the early years of the twenty-first century, for example, most meetings of the chapel at the *Express* had been about changes (downwards) in staffing levels or the closure of the staff canteen (a bread and butter issue if ever there was one). But, in late 2003 and early 2004, such traditional trade union issues merged with concerns about the type of journalism that was being produced in their name, when a desire to stick up for colleagues combined with disquiet about the newspaper's editorial line. It resulted in an almost unprecedented collective intervention on ethical journalism, when a crowded and angry meeting of *Express* journalists passed the following motion:

> This chapel is concerned that *Express* journalists are coming under pressure to write anti-Gypsy articles. We call for a letter to be sent to the Press Complaints Commission

1 A note of explanation for the benefit of readers born after 1979: trade unions are "associations of workers for the common representation of their interests", dealing in a collective way with issues such as pay, hours and working conditions (Elliott, 1973: 464). Trade unions were created by working people because, as Robert Taylor (1994: 5) explains, "the worker as an individual in the workplace suffers from having an unequal power relationship vis-à-vis his or her employer". Taylor, who was a longstanding labour correspondent of the *Financial Times*, continues: "Only when workers decide for themselves to combine together collectively can they establish enough unified strength to provide themselves with a strong and credible workplace voice to counter the often arbitrary demands being made upon them by the employer." One such union is the National Union of Journalists, known as the NUJ, which was founded a century ago to represent those whom its first historian described as the "starveling scribes" of journalism, who were working up to 90 hours a week for "the paltriest remuneration" (Mansfield, 1943). As well as a national structure with full-time officials and a leadership elected by the members, the NUJ has workplace organisations – called "chapels" for reasons lost in the mists of time – in which every member at a workplace can have their say.

> reminding it of the need to protect journalists who are unwilling to write racist articles which are contrary to the National Union of Journalists' code of conduct
>
> (Quoted in Ponsford, 2004a)

In other words, *Express* journalists were appealing to the PCC for protection against their *own* newspaper. As one *Express* journalist told the trade magazine *Press Gazette* at the time: "There's a feeling of resentment that people are being pressured into writing articles which they believe to be racist and inflammatory" (quoted in Ponsford, 2004a). The newspaper's editor later defended the stories, telling one interviewer:

> I have never forced anyone to write anything. There were stories at the time that needed running and I have never shrunk from stories that needed to be written. We are not an operation too much concerned with political correctness.
>
> (Quoted in Snoddy, 2006)

Members who spoke at the chapel meeting emphasised that they had no problem with the paper running stories about EU enlargement. The issue was the *way* such stories were being written and presented, and the feeling that staff had been expected to take part in the production of material felt by many to be biased, inaccurate and even pandering to racism. It was also argued that, just because the *Express* was not alone in taking such a stance, it did not excuse the newspaper's journalists from speaking out. So a letter was duly despatched to the PCC asking it to insert a "conscience clause" into its code of practice, whereby journalists who refused unethical assignments would be protected from disciplinary action or dismissal. Michelle Stanistreet recalls how the letter was rejected out of hand by the PCC: "We wrote to them asking for a conscience clause, but they said that journalists don't come under such pressure, so there is no need for one, and it's just a matter between the employer and the employee." This stance was reiterated when the PCC's Professor Robert Pinker told an ethics conference in December 2004 that a conscience clause would be both unnecessary and counter-productive, adding: "It is not our job to become involved in disputes between employers and their staff" (quoted in Bayley and Macaskill, 2004: 17).

Although the proprietors and the PCC regard such issues as being of no concern to a trade union, Stanistreet – as *Express* Mother of Chapel (MoC, workplace union representative) – has a different perspective. For her, raising concerns in a collective way can offer an alternative to the otherwise limited choice between suffering in silence and resigning:

> We didn't see pressure to write anti-Gypsy stories as separate from other workplace issues like job cuts, disciplinaries and so on. It was about sticking up for someone at work, and if we took it to the chapel and stuck together, it would be harder for them to pick on us all than to pick on one. Where does it get us if all the decent people resign? If people leave, who will staff the paper then? People just out of college who will be desperate to do anything to impress? In any case, most people can't just walk out on their jobs, and we can't all work for employers we agree with. After all, we don't agree with them on issues like pay and conditions, so why should it be presumed that we have to agree with them on editorial content?

THE INDIVIDUAL AND THE COLLECTIVE

Sometimes individual journalists feel they have no alternative but to vote with their feet and leave. Such an occasion was 1950 and such a journalist was James Cameron (1968: 85–8), who resigned from his job because he disapproved of the methods used by his newspaper – the *Express*, as it happens – to link a Cabinet minister to an alleged spy scandal. Cameron explained his action by arguing that a journalist who moaned about the ethical shortcomings of his or her employer was like a "rueful whore":

> His [*sic*] condition may be unfortunate but it is hardly irremediable; the journalist who feels that the methods of the organization that pays him are a doleful burden upon his principles can as a rule resolve his dilemma: he can stop taking their money, and get out.
>
> (Cameron, 1968: 84)

Another member of journalism's principled "awkward squad" was George Seldes, who spent most of his long career – he died in 1995 at the age of 104 – working as a freelance or on alternative publications, after walking out on the *Chicago Tribune* in protest at the suppression of a story (Randall, 2005: 71–91). Such resignations continue today. In March 2003, for example, Katy Weitz left her job as a features writer on the *Sun* because she could not square the paper's gung-ho coverage of the Iraq war with her conscience (*Press Gazette*, 2003a); and technology columnist David Hewson quit the *Sunday Times* in 2005 because he felt the paper was too uncritical of the new technology business (Ponsford, 2005).

For Francis Williams, such a willingness to "stand up and be counted" should be a fundamental part of being a journalist, as ethics cannot be trusted in the hands of proprietors:

> [T]he guardianship of journalistic values rests primarily with the journalist ... He [*sic*] cannot dissociate himself from this responsibility without ceasing, in a fundamental sense, to be a journalist. Nor is there any final excuse for him in the claim that he is,

> after all, simply a hired man who must do as he is bid. He must be ready, as must all men when issues of principle arise, to stand up and be counted.
>
> (Williams, 1959: 226)

One editor who did this was Richard Stott (2002: 210–29), an editor of the *Sunday People* and the *Daily Mirror* – when they were owned by Robert Maxwell – who did his best to protect his staff and the newspapers from the proprietor's baleful influence. On being commended for putting his job on the line by running a leader that was critical of Maxwell, who was about to become his boss, Stott writes: "Newspapers and their editors are nothing if they cannot stand up for what is right when it matters personally to them." Editors of *The Lancet* took a similar stance when they published a leader that criticised the medical journal's own publisher – Reed Elsevier – for its involvement with the international arms trade (Fixter, 2005). Such commendable public assertions of editorial independence are relatively few and far between. Far more common is the strategy adopted by individual journalists of using a variety of dodges – diversions, flattery, inertia, making sure they are useless at certain tasks, and so on – to avoid what they see as unethical or just plain bad "suggestions" by their boss. Such everyday ducking and diving may not seem very heroic, and it is rarely acknowledged in the academic literature about journalistic ethics, but it is one of the ways in which journalists strive to do the best they can, often in trying times.

The responsibility of the individual journalist is a recurrent theme in debates about ethics. Ian Hargreaves (2003: 167), for example, argues that journalism is a "highly individualistic" job with ethical responsibility resting "as much with the individual journalist as with any institutional framework". John O'Neill cites "principled resignation" as a form of resistance to the commercial pressures that can compromise a journalistic sense of ethics:

> Journalists, like other workers, are not totally passive in their attitude to their own faculties. They also have the capacity to resist the pressures of the marketplace. The constitutive values of journalism have some power through such resistance, despite the countervailing tendencies of the marketplace.
>
> (O'Neill, 1992: 28)

David Randall (2000: 133) also says that journalists have the "sanction" of changing jobs if they disapprove of the ethical approach of their organisation. True. But is that it? Not according to journalist and campaigner Barry White, who wrote in a review of Randall's otherwise highly regarded book, *The Universal Journalist*:

> Surely the real issue is one of collective action through the trade union. There is some relationship between the decline of ethical standards in the press and the weakening of the media unions. So why no reference to collective action in defence of ethical standards? And what of the journalists overseas who, with union support, stand up to state and media owners' abuses of ethical standards, often at the expense of their own personal freedom and sometimes, their lives?
>
> (White, 2000: 25)

What of them? What of the journalists in the Russian republic of Komi who stuck together and saved the job of newspaper editor Tatiana Borisevich, who was threatened with dismissal for publishing articles critical of the proprietor, who was also president of Komi? Or the Greek journalists who went on strike against censorship? Or the members of the Newspaper Guild in Canada, who took a court case over editorial independence? These cases and others are highlighted by the International Federation of Journalists (IFJ, 2005b) as examples of journalists' trades unions acting as "an important bulwark against undue commercial or political pressure".

Similarly, journalists in Ukraine took collective action against censorship before and during that country's "Orange Revolution" in 2004. Yegor Sobolev, former president of the Kyiv Independent Media Trade Union, recalls:

> I will always remember 25 November 2004 as a happy day. On that day, truthful information was broadcast in the news bulletins of all TV channels … The fight for free speech started, and has to start, with a search for like-minded people who can encourage colleagues at their offices to take a stand. When our publicity campaign began, the journalists seemed to be completely helpless and fearful. But that was only at the start. In each office we found one person who, by their determination and belief, inspired others to resist … Our first serious action in October 2004 – when about 40 journalists from all the TV channels announced that they were being compelled to lie on air, and promised not to do so in future – was preceded by about three months of active campaigning. We talked with our colleagues about the fact that censorship cheapened and degraded their professionalism, as it rendered skills and knowledge unnecessary … The feeling that you are not alone makes people stronger.
>
> (Sobolev, 2005: 52–4)

In the UK and Ireland, the organisation with the most potential to help journalists stand up and be counted collectively is the National Union of Journalists (NUJ). Yet the union tends to be ignored in most discussion of the ethics of journalism, during which more individualistic arguments tend to be privileged. As Michael Bromley (1997: 331) notes: "In the extensive and expanding body of literature addressing journalism which has been produced over the past 40 years, journalists appear only rarely as workers." Instead, resistance to the pressures of the marketplace tends to be seen purely in individual terms, with no reference to the possibility of any form of *collective* intervention. But ethical responsibility should not be assumed to be the sole responsibility of the individual journalist, argues journalism lecturer Deirdre O'Neill:

> In an uncertain job market where you are only as good as your last byline, journalists are not likely to question news gathering techniques or the news values or news agenda in operation ... To expect individuals to make a stand at the expense of their careers is unrealistic – what is needed is a collective response.
>
> (O'Neill, 2004: 48)

A collective response does not have to mean getting together in a trade union, of course. Back in the 1970s, for example, contributors to the *Guardian* women's page banded together to defeat the editor's plan to scrap what was seen as an important public space for women. A more recent example was the spontaneous protest campaign staged by thousands of BBC staff – including journalists – in 2004, after the corporation's governors reacted to the Hutton Report by sacking Director-General Greg Dyke and issuing "the most grovelling of apologies" for unspecified mistakes (Dyke, 2004: 22–26). Two years later, journalists on the German *Berliner Zeitung* newspaper responded to the appointment of a new editor by holding a disruptive meeting and refusing to produce a normal edition of the paper; instead they put out an emergency edition carrying criticism of the appointment and expressing fears that their controversial proprietor intended to "sacrifice journalistic quality and high standards for the sake of short-term money-making ambitions" (Harding, 2006). Also in 2006, a collective intervention of a different kind occurred when around 50 journalists held up an international cricket match in Bangladesh by staging a sit-in on the pitch to protest at the beating of a local photographer by the police (Ahmed, 2006).

Some people have expressed their dissatisfaction with mainstream journalism by working collectively to establish alternative forms of media – print, broadcast or online – that challenge the accepted news values and ethical frameworks of dominant media. Sometimes such media have been created by journalists unhappy at what they have been asked to produce by their employers (Whitaker, 1981); more often alternative media have been created by disgruntled consumers of journalism, some of whom may go on to work as journalists in the mainstream as well (Harcup, 2005b). However, the role of alternative media also tends to be ignored within "the dominant media (and academic) discourse" (Keeble, 2005: 62–3).

ETHICS AND ECONOMICS

As with principled resignation, the creation of alternative media is likely to remain a minority option for journalists. When it comes to standing up for ethical standards within mainstream journalism itself, it is the NUJ that offers the most likely platform. Earlier, I described the actions of the *Express* NUJ chapel in 2003/2004 as almost unprecedented. In 2001 *Express* staff had also reported their own newspaper to the PCC following a series of front-page headlines such as: ASYLUM: WE'RE BEING INVADED. "That was all to do with the headlines," recalls Michelle Stanistreet, "not the stories themselves, which weren't changed and which therefore didn't reflect the headlines put on them." After the *Express* had splashed on asylum seekers for six days in a row, journalists' alarm at the "inflammatory" tone of such headlines coalesced with separate claims that the business pages had been used to promote the proprietor's interests, hardly a complaint unique to that newspaper. One journalist insisted: "We are not the proprietors' stenographers" (quoted in Morgan, 2001).

Such concerns came to the fore at a chapel meeting that had been called to discuss proposed job cuts. After debating the spate of recent headlines, the journalists voted to express their disapproval of what they saw as a "sustained campaign against asylum seekers", and their motion continued: "This chapel believes the media has an important role to play in a democratic society and should not distort or whip up confrontational racist hatred, in pursuit of increased circulation" (*Journalist*, 2001b). The NUJ complained to the PCC on behalf of its members at the *Express*, alleging that the asylum stories breached the PCC's own code of practice which says the press should avoid prejudicial references to race. The complaint was rejected on the grounds that no individuals had been named in the copy, prompting NUJ organiser John Toner to comment: "This is absurd. If you make pejorative references to a particular group or race you are applying those remarks to every individual within that group or race" (*Journalist*, 2002).

Express staff were not the first journalists to use their trade union as a mechanism to raise ethics as well as economics, as Mansfield records:

> In 1931, as the result of journalists being asked to behave in a distasteful and unseemly manner in getting news, the union issued a strong protest and appealed to proprietors, editors and managements to endeavour to come to an understanding as to the limits of licence which should be allowed to, or imposed upon, reporters and photographers ... The union suggested that reporters should not be expected or permitted to intrude into the private lives of private people, that they should not usurp the function of official or private detectives, and that they should confine their activities to the reporting of, and commenting upon, facts. Moreover, to give practical effect to

> these views, the union promised to treat the case of a member who was dismissed for refusing to carry out instructions repugnant to his sense of decency, as one of victimization, ie to maintain him while getting fresh employment.
>
> (Mansfield, 1936: 372)

Five years later the NUJ became the first body in the UK to establish a code of ethical conduct for journalists, more than 50 years before the industry's self-regulators got around to it (Bundock, 1957: 128–9; Frost, 2000: 175, 224). The union code pledged backing for journalists who refused to do work "incompatible with the honour and interests of the profession", and asserted: "In obtaining news or pictures, reporters and press photographers should do nothing that will cause pain or humiliation to innocent, bereaved, or otherwise distressed persons. News, pictures and documents should be acquired by honest methods only" (quoted in O'Malley and Soley, 2000: 43). The NUJ code became an appendix to the NUJ rule book, and members found guilty of breaking it could – in theory, at least – be reprimanded, fined, or even expelled (Frost, 2000: 224).

Roy Greenslade (2003: 247, 282–4) notes that newspaper proprietors feared that increasing NUJ influence within newsrooms – particularly in the form of de facto "closed shops" whereby only union members would be employed – could lead to frequent battles over editorial content as well as wages. However, he adds, there were no cases in which editors were prevented by NUJ members from publishing what they wanted. In fact, despite the wishes of a minority of members – including Greenslade (2003: 282) himself at one time – the NUJ has hardly ever attempted to use whatever industrial muscle it possesses to influence editorial content. But it has attempted to improve journalistic standards by other means.

THE ETHICS COUNCIL

During its period of exile from the Press Council (see Chapter 8), the NUJ created its own Ethics Council in 1986. This had two functions: to promote higher ethical standards through a process of education, and to hear complaints against members who were alleged to have breached the union's code (Frost, 2000: 224). The Ethics Council began life as the "custodian" of the union's code of conduct at an unfortunate time, against the backdrop of the 1986 News International dispute. Rupert Murdoch moved his national newspaper titles to Wapping, sacking thousands of workers in the process, and his eventual victory encouraged other media employers to take advantage of the anti-union legislation introduced by Margaret Thatcher's government – a government that had been cheered on within the pages of Murdoch's newspapers.

There was early suspicion of the Ethics Council among many journalists, with some critics dismissing it as the "thought police" (quoted in NUJ, 1988: 32). Its first chairperson was Wapping "refusenik" Pat Healy, a journalist on *The Times* who had declined Murdoch's invitation to cross the sacked printworkers' picket lines. She conceded that many journalists saw the role of the Ethics Council as representing "undue interference in their working lives" (NUJ, 1987: 19). Undeterred, in its first nine months the Ethics Council received 62 complaints, three of which resulted in members being reprimanded and one of which saw a member being fined £100; several other complaints were resolved by conciliation. The following year the Ethics Council received 132 complaints, of which 25 went to formal hearings. Four journalists were fined, two of whom were later expelled for non-payment while two others had their fines reduced to reprimands on appeal. Another case resulted in a reprimand and two resulted in no penalty being imposed. The remaining complaints were withdrawn, dropped after investigation, or resolved through conciliation. After this high-water mark, the number of complaints gradually declined (NUJ, 1989: 31; 1990: 30). One member of the union's national executive was quoted as saying that such attempts at enforcing the code of conduct had not been "a happy experience", adding: "Journalists say they want a union to represent them, not to tell them how to do their jobs" (quoted in Snoddy, 1992: 197).

The work of the Ethics Council during its early years was not helped by the Thatcherite industrial relations climate within most of the media at the time; a climate of intense employer hostility to trade unions in general and to the NUJ in particular. The 1980s and 1990s saw the temporary ending of collective bargaining for a majority of journalists, the forcing down of wage and staffing levels, the denial of union representation on disciplinary and other issues such as health and safety, the removal of union facilities including noticeboards, and the sacking of some union activists (Gall, 1993; Gall and McKay, 1994; Smith and Morton, 1994). Journalist Paul Foot (cited in Keeble, 2001a: 6) claimed that this employers' onslaught on wages, conditions and union organisation led to an atmosphere of fear, obsequiousness and conformity within newsrooms that also seeped into editorial content by making journalists more compliant:

> My own strong view is that the smashing of the trade unions [ie at Wapping and its aftermath] was part of the centralizing of control and bureaucratization in the press which have done so much to damage investigative journalism. The purpose of an organized union in a newspaper office is not just to look after wages, conditions and employment practices – or even to organize against the widespread nepotism and corruption in

> recruitment which is now commonplace in the national press. It is also to provide a centre where journalists can collect and discuss their common problems, free from the management hierarchy. A recognized trade union adds to the spirit of independence inside a newspaper which is so crucial to successful investigative journalism.
>
> (Foot, 2000: 86)

Journalist David Walker (2000: 242) also observed that the "nakedly authoritarian occupational culture" within UK newspapers after Wapping created a climate in which "editorial whims go unchallenged". As Chris Frost records:

> The anti-union stance of the government during the 1980s and 1990s led to a general weakening of union power and this played a part in reducing the role of the Ethics Council. No longer did journalists have to have an NUJ card in order to work in the more prestigious jobs in television and what used to be Fleet Street. This meant that breaching the NUJ code, with the consequent risk of discipline and possible expulsion, was no longer the risk it once might have been. The union, too, was less inclined to deal harshly with members as workers became less confident of the benefits of belonging to a union.
>
> (Frost, 2000: 224)

This situation has resulted in the Ethics Council focusing increasingly in recent years on raising awareness about ethical issues, and trying to create a more ethical climate within newsrooms, rather than acting as a form of "policing" body. This change of emphasis was articulated when an NUJ spokesperson described the union's code of conduct as "a beacon for journalists to aim for rather than a means to punish" (quoted in Keeble, 2001a: 15).

OFF THE AGENDA

The union's activity on ethical issues has not been confined to its Ethics Council, however. The NUJ has also been involved in a range of free speech issues and has worked with the Campaign for Press and Broadcasting Freedom and the Campaign for Freedom of Information to defend the fourth estate concept of journalism as a check on the powerful, and with the charity Mediawise and others to encourage a more ethical approach to journalism. Other interventions have included condemnation of a "homophobic scare campaign" waged in much of the Scottish press (*Journalist*, 2000a), the production of guidelines on the reporting of mental health, AIDS, race, disability, and on avoiding sexist language (Frost, 2000: 78, 93), and bringing together journalists and refugees to discuss media coverage of the asylum issue (*Journalist*, 2001a). The union also has a long record of supporting individual journalists who have been threatened with jail for protecting confidential sources, from

EDG Lewis who was prosecuted under the Official Secrets Act in 1937 (Bundock, 1957: 145) to Robin Ackroyd and others who have similarly stood by their principles in the twenty-first century (Gopsill, 2005).

Yet a trawl through the union's publications reveals relatively few examples of journalists doing what those at the *Express* did in the early years of this century; that is, voicing ethical concerns collectively within the workplace. Not that all such incidents will have been recorded. I was told by one veteran FoC (Father of Chapel), for example, that his chapel had intervened on ethical matters several times over the years "on the quiet", but he did not wish to go on the record about it because it might damage the relationship with management that it had taken so long to build. Notwithstanding this, however, it cannot be denied that, as Mark Hollingsworth notes:

> British journalists have rarely, if ever, taken any kind of industrial action to protest at political bias and distortion in their papers' news columns. The nearest came during the 1983 general election when the *Daily Mail*'s NUJ chapel passed a motion expressing their concern at the one-sided coverage of the campaign. Sir David English, the editor since 1970, replied that the content of the paper was the sole responsibility of the editor and of no concern to the National Union of Journalists.
>
> (Hollingsworth, 1986: 25)

Similarly, in the wake of the *Sunday Times* publishing what turned out to be fake diaries by Adolf Hitler, the NUJ chapel on the newspaper demanded that editor Frank Giles come and speak to them en masse; he declined, arguing that it was not an appropriate matter for a trade union meeting (Greenslade, 2003: 465). Historically, many NUJ members appear to agree that the topic of editorial content should be off the union agenda. Hollingsworth (1986: 29) reports that, on the *Sun*, just one journalist attempted to discuss editorial issues during chapel meetings throughout the 1980s. During the 1984–5 miners' strike, the *Sun*'s NUJ chapel sided with management rather than the print unions when the latter objected to the publication of a photograph of miners' leader Arthur Scargill raising his right arm beneath the banner headline MINE FUHRER. The NUJ FoC at the paper said: "Our chapel believes we should not interfere in editorial matters, and must remain neutral" (quoted in Hollingsworth, 1986: 276).

Around the same time, the *Guardian* NUJ chapel intervened to secure a correction – long before its famed Corrections and Clarifications column made such things routine – after the newspaper had mistakenly labelled a striking miner a strikebreaker (Hollingsworth, 1986: 260). The NUJ chapel at the *Guardian* has also involved itself in editorial matters by organising hustings to allow members to question candidates for the job of editor (Greenslade, 2003: 586). But the same chapel refused to come down hard on the then editor who, in 1983, handed over a leaked memo to the authorities, resulting in the jailing of civil servant Sarah Tisdall, who had blown the whistle on what she saw as government deception over nuclear missiles (see Chapter 6). NUJ members on the paper did, however, raise a collection and bought Ms Tisdall a bike when she came out of prison after several months (Taylor, 1993: 253). Bless.

Occasionally – very occasionally – ethical issues have sparked off strikes or other forms of industrial action by journalists. When an *Oxford Mail* photographer was disciplined after refusing to take a snatch picture of a disabled 5-year-old outside school, following appeals by the child's mother for an end to media attention, the NUJ chapel walked out for a one-day strike in protest (McIntyre, 2004). Industrial action on a much larger scale occurred in July 1985, when NUJ members in the broadcasting sector staged a one-day strike in protest at censorship of a BBC *Real Lives* television documentary concerning Northern Ireland (NUJ, 1989: 6; Bolton, 1990: 166–7; Schlesinger, 1987: xx). *The Times* reported that the 24-hour walkout "represented the most serious industrial action ever undertaken in British television, and attracted more support than has ever been won by a pay claim" (quoted in Curtis, 1996: 279).

Over the years, reporting "the Troubles" in Northern Ireland resulted in numerous small local ethical difficulties punctuated by the occasional full-scale battle, such as when the UK government banned broadcast journalists from using the voices of Sinn Fein leaders and certain other political activists between 1988 and 1994 (Miller, 1994; Rolston and Miller, 1996). The broadcasting ban resulted in repeated protests by the NUJ but was eventually lifted after the IRA declared a ceasefire. Another high-profile row over journalistic ethics was prompted by an attack by sections of the UK press on the Thames TV documentary *Death on the Rock* concerning the killing of three Irish republicans in Gibraltar in 1988. After the *Sunday Times* attempted to rubbish the programme makers, the newspaper's own journalists used their NUJ chapel to call for an independent inquiry into the *Sunday Times*' own reporting of the subject; meanwhile, a number of journalists left the paper, unhappy at its treatment of the story (NUJ, 1989: 5; Bolton, 1990: 292).

Remarkably, when *Sunday World* reporter Martin O'Hagan was shot dead – apparently by "loyalist" paramilitaries – in September 2001, he became the first journalist to be killed during the Troubles. "For 30 years there was an 'unwritten rule' in Northern Ireland that journalists were not shot," notes Michael Foley, former media correspondent of the *Irish Times* and now a journalism lecturer. One factor in this was that all sides in the conflict saw the need to influence public opinion via the media, argues Foley:

> Another factor was the NUJ. Journalists in Northern Ireland were always members of a union that offered solidarity and a bridge across the sectarian divide, regardless of the editorial stance of their publications. They stood together, loyalist and nationalists, in their opposition to censorship – notably, with very few exceptions, against the UK broadcasting ban introduced in 1988. They carried the same press card ... Even when working for highly sectarian outlets, journalists were able to demonstrate a professional detachment that allowed the media to be viewed as something between a necessary evil and a trusted conduit.
>
> (Foley, 2001)

For NUJ members in a divided society, their membership of the journalists' trade union – a union that predates partition and so organises throughout the island of Ireland – was one way of asserting their journalistic independence and integrity at a time of political and military conflict. Those journalists in the rest of Ireland as well as England, Scotland and Wales who joined their colleagues in protesting against broadcasting bans and other forms of overt censorship also asserted their independence; independence from governments that sometimes seemed to expect journalists to act as state propagandists.

A COLLECTIVE VOICE IN THE NEWSROOM

Most western journalists, most of the time, will not find themselves engaged in such high-profile ethical confrontations as strikes against government-imposed censorship. That does not mean they don't face ethical issues every day. To what extent have journalists looked for support from their fellow journalists, through the NUJ, when faced with ethical dilemmas large or small? Not a lot, according to a small survey conducted at provincial newspapers in the north of England and the English Midlands. Journalists in six chapels reported just three modest instances of ethical interventions, including the following macabre tale:

> The *Newcastle Evening Chronicle* compiled a Death League where staff were rated on their performance during death knocks. For example, a full story and collect pics was worth, say, ten points and a total knockback zero points ... Bearing in mind the editor is a member of the PCC, the chapel raised this issue. We were told it was only a bit of fun organised by the reporters themselves. However, immediately after chapel intervention the scheme was abandoned and the Death League tables taken down from offices.
>
> (Quoted in Harcup, 2002: 110)

When asked to assess the extent to which journalists were aware of the NUJ code of conduct, and whether they thought it had any impact on members' daily work, most chapels reported that there was a general awareness of its existence but that few journalists conscientiously tailored their work to comply with its detailed provisions. One reported: "In 10 years as FoC I have never had an issue raised citing the code of conduct." That study, which was conducted before the *Express* chapel's interventions discussed above, concluded:

> An examination of the NUJ's engagement with ethical issues suggests that, if ethics are not to remain a marginal concern for working journalists, journalists do not need their trade union to act as a form of "thought police", but they do need a collective voice in the workplace, and the confidence to use it. Without a collective voice and collective confidence, control of the ethics of journalism will remain largely in the hands of editors and proprietors, with individual journalists being left with little choice but to do what they are told or resign – conditions of production hardly conducive to a journalism that contributes to a well-informed citizenry … [J]ournalistic ethics cannot be divorced from everyday economic realities such as understaffing, job insecurity, casualised labour, bullying and unconstrained management prerogative.
>
> (Harcup, 2002: 111–12)

AN ALTERNATIVE TO SAYING NOTHING

The way in which journalists on the *Express* gave confidence to each other by sticking together – confidence enough to question their own newspaper's ethics – has only added weight to that conclusion. But what, if anything, has their stance achieved? Michelle Stanistreet doesn't make any great claims. Indeed, she seems rather embarrassed at the fact that, on the surface at least, not a lot has changed:

> Obviously the company finds it embarrassing to have its staff make complaints about it, and the editor certainly didn't want to be labelled as racist. In the short-term, there was some effect in that there was discussion at editorial conferences about being seen to be more even-handed in the paper's coverage of Gypsy and asylum issues. But I certainly wouldn't claim it as a great success and, in the long term, who knows? I wouldn't be at all surprised if this is an issue the chapel has to confront again in the future.

The long-term impact may be difficult to predict, but it could be profound. It is possible, for example, that the actions of the *Express* journalists, modest as they were, will act as an example to inspire others; to show that doing something together can be an alternative to saying nothing alone. Maybe, as a result, a journalist coming under what he or she regards as unethical pressure might be more likely to look for support from colleagues rather than simply obey or resign.

Listening to descriptions of discussions within the *Express* chapel, I am reminded of a story Paul Foot once told me about his early days in journalism about 40 years earlier. Apparently, several Scottish newspapers were at each other's throats over who had "bought up" a man involved in a notorious Glasgow murder case that had just ended. This resulted in an undignified scramble outside the court followed by a high-speed chase through the city, during which one set of reporters tried physically to drag the man from a rival newspaper's car. Competing journalists complained about each other's behaviour and matters came to a head at the next NUJ meeting, as Paul Foot recalled:

> The monthly meeting of the branch, usually six people and a cup of tea, turned into a mass meeting of 200 or 300 people. Most came to say *their* newspaper had behaved properly. It developed into the most fascinating argument between those who were putting the point of view of their proprietors and those few active trade unionists who argued that the whole thing was a disgraceful episode and chequebook journalism of the worst kind. What I remember was how the mood changed. The meeting started off: "You bastard, you seized our man." Then the alternative view: "This is rubbish, we're all doing this job together and we're being made into hooligans by our newspapers." As a result of that discussion, the resolution passed was that the NUJ, representing *all* these journalists, was absolutely opposed to chequebook journalism. You can only have an alternative to the control of the editorial hierarchy and the proprietor if you've got the discipline of being in a collective body behind you.

Collective discussion may not always result in collective wisdom; individuals may still feel the need to stand out against the crowd, and newsrooms should have room for maverick characters. But a workplace climate in which ethical concerns can be discussed openly by journalists – informally and/or formally, individually and/or collectively – can only be good for journalistic standards. This lesson may have been learned the hard way at the *New York Times* where, as discussed in Chapter 2, a culture that discouraged people from speaking out contributed directly to the Jayson Blair scandal. When Joe Lelyveld stepped in as interim editor to help rescue the paper's credibility, he promised his staff: "The cure for what has ailed us is called journalism. The only way to communicate is to speak up in an atmosphere where outspokenness is sometimes rewarded and never penalized" (quoted in Mnookin, 2005: 213).

The willingness of *Express* journalists to question the editorial line of their employer, as discussed in this chapter, may have been in the minds of colleagues on its sister paper the *Daily Star* when they look a stand against what many saw as "deliberately offensive" copy that made fun of Muslims. At an emergency meeting of the paper's NUJ chapel, called as the *Daily Star* was being put to bed on the night of 17 October 2006, journalists voted to urge management to withdraw a spoof version of a supposed Islamic *Daily*

Fatwa that was due to run in the following day's edition complete with a "page three burkha babes special". Journalists' concerns for their own safety and about the offensive nature of the material were passed on to the editor and the spoof was promptly pulled (Burrell, 2006).

Who can tell what long-term effect on journalistic standards there might be if journalists gain more confidence to reflect on what they are doing, to discuss it openly with colleagues, and – every now and then – to stand up and be counted? The Chinese leader Chou En-lai was once asked to assess the impact of the French Revolution which had taken place a couple of hundred years earlier. He replied: "It's too early to tell."

FURTHER READING

Little has been written specifically on the subject of journalists taking a collective approach to ethical issues, but two relevant research articles were published in *Journalism Studies* in 2002. Harcup (2002) traces the history of the NUJ Ethics Council in more detail than in this chapter and also presents more fully the findings of a survey of NUJ chapels, while Horgan (2002) explores the sometimes contradictory response of journalists in the Republic of Ireland to the Dublin government's imposition of censorship during the Troubles. The possibility of journalists acting collectively to influence editorial content is the subject of a study by industrial relations professor Gregor Gall (2006; see also 1993, 2004). For the most up-to-date history of the NUJ see Gopsill and Neale (2007).

Harcup (1994, 2005b) and Atton (2002) explore the motivations behind the creation of alternative media, while Harcup (2005c) discusses the role of journalists as "citizens in the newsroom".

10 ETHICAL JOURNALISM IS GOOD JOURNALISM

Respect for truth is the first principle in the international journalists' code reprinted in Appendix 1. There are two key words here. The one that gets most attention is "truth". What truth might be, how we can identify it, whether it exists, and whether there might be occasions when it is better not told, are all subjects of discussion. But every bit as important is the word "respect". If journalists have no respect for their journalism and for their fellow citizens, then they will probably have little respect for truth either. Ethical journalism, as a former crime reporter puts it in Chapter 7, involves respect for people's human rights. Without such respect, who knows what horrors might be committed, from the thoughtless intrusion into an individual's grief to disturbing actions on a far greater scale? Consider what happened in the central African state of Rwanda in 1994, when journalists working on a Hutu radio station described the Tutsi population as devils, snakes and cockroaches, inciting Hutus to go out and kill Tutsis. Names, addresses and vehicle number plates of Tutsi people were read out on air, and listeners were even encouraged to phone in with details of where Tutsis were hiding (Melvern, [2000] 2004: 442–56). An estimated 800,000 people were massacred in the resulting bloodshed. Almost 10 years later a number of journalists were jailed for "incitement to genocide and crimes against humanity" (Reporters Without Borders, 2004).

Rwanda is an extreme example, but extreme examples help make the point that our actions and our words can have consequences. That is true whether we are reporting from a war zone or reviewing the latest Hollywood movie. The codes of ethical conduct gathered in the appendices of this book represent different attempts to anticipate and take account of such consequences; their purpose is to encourage the good that journalists can achieve while minimising or eliminating any harm that may be done in the name of journalism. Such codes can be useful reference points for journalists, but they do not stand on their own. We need a newsroom culture in which journalists are aware of, and have the freedom to discuss, the ethical issues involved in their work. And journalists need some kind of guiding principles beyond the specifics of the codes' provisions. Some people will look to religion, philosophy or political ideology to steer them through potential ethical conflicts. I prefer the idea that, fundamentally, journalism is about informing and empowering the citizens of a society, holding the powerful to account, and facilitating a public sphere of rational discussion.

A DEMOCRATIC DEFICIT?

The healthy functioning of such a public sphere – space in which informed citizens can engage with one another in reasoned debate and critical reflection (Habermas, 1989) – depends on a diversity of people and perspectives having access to the media. Not the type of limited access offered by vox pops, letters' pages or phone-ins, but access on a more equitable basis. As James Bohman (2004: 152–3) argues, people can exercise citizenship in a public sphere "only if they stand as equals". Thus, widening "democratic inclusion" is fundamental to creating a more just society (Young, 2000: 17). However, the less powerful groups in society can face structural obstacles in gaining access to mainstream journalism (Manning, 2001: 137, 226–7). The perspectives of people living in poorer societies, and poorer areas of wealthy societies, are often marginalised in favour of the powerful and glamorous, just as the sharp tongues of anti-globalisation protesters, peace activists, eco-warriors and other critics of the new world order are only rarely allowed to puncture the complacency of a mainstream journalism that too often allows its agenda to be set by the slick PR operations of resource-rich organisations. This results in what has been described as a "democratic deficit" (Hackett, 2005: 95).

"An eerie silence pervades the contemporary public sphere," argues Stephen Coleman (1997: 135, 153) in his history of struggles around the idea of free speech. He continues: "The unaccountable power to relegate public ideas and events to the margins or beyond the scope of the media agenda is a matter for democratic concern." One result of this appears to be that many people disengage from mainstream media that too often seem to have disengaged from them. In contrast, some of the marginalised have found their voices through the "democratised media practices" of what are termed alternative media, many of which are now online (Atton, 2004: 7); and others have been sought out by journalists within mainstream media who go beyond the press release and the soundbite. One way of addressing the democratic deficit is for journalists to recognise that their primary duty is to a society's citizens. This was the approach taken by the veteran American journalist Martha Gellhorn who, after receiving praise for her coverage of the Vietnam war, said: "All I did was report from the ground up, not the other way round" (quoted in Pilger, 2004: 1). Doing journalism from the bottom up is not simply interesting and illuminating; it is vital.

As Bill Kovach and Tom Rosenstiel (2003: 18) point out, the concepts of journalism and democracy are so entwined that "societies that want to suppress freedom must first suppress the press". Journalism, they argue, owes its first loyalty to citizens and has as its primary purpose providing those citizens "with the information they need to be free and self-governing" (2003: 12–17). Yet journalists are citizens too, and do not cease to be so upon entering a newsroom. For Kovach and Rosenstiel (2003: 52), journalists are not like employees in other industries because they "have a social obligation that can actually override their employers' immediate interests at times". This social obligation means that journalism is not just about entertaining people, though it might do that as well. Nor should it primarily be about making money, though it might do that too. Reflecting on his brief period as editor of the *Independent*, Andrew Marr (2005: 197) recalls being told by his boss that there should be fewer dreary scenes of poverty and "dead black babies" in his newspaper; instead, there should be more aspirational stories about fashionable people driving Porsches and wearing Rolex watches. Although proprietors do not necessarily spell out what they want in such an unsubtle manner, their values may become "internalised" by journalists over time (Tracy, 2004: 454); hence the importance of external reference points to remind us that there are other perspectives, other expectations, and other loyalties.

As argued elsewhere, journalism matters because knowledge is power. We have heard a lot about journalism's claim to be a fourth estate acting in the public interest as a check on the powerful; yet we have heard counterclaims that too much journalism fails to live up to this ideal. Some critics, such as John Lloyd (2004: 22), bemoan a journalism that damages democracy by displaying "constant suspicion towards politicians and public officials". Others argue that most journalists display not too much suspicion towards those in power, but too little (Baker and McLaughlin, 2005: 5). David Leigh, investigations editor of the *Guardian*, rejects the Lloyd thesis out of hand and calls for a greater degree of scepticism:

> [W]hen a journalist asks members of British institutions uncomfortable questions about what is going on, they respond with more or less polished evasions or with downright lies… [W]e do not need to reduce the quantity of confrontational and mistrustful journalism. We need to encourage a good deal more of it.
>
> (Leigh, 2005)

It is not only investigative journalists who want to see more muck-raking; and let's face it, they would, wouldn't they? Journalism professor John Tulloch (2004b: 5) has highlighted the need for "active mischief-making, and scepticism and suspicion of the motives of the powerful, even if some of that mischief is damaging and even dangerous to the body politic". A prominent public relations consultant has also defended the validity of journalism's "central defence, that it does what it does in a mucky, imprecise way but with the best intentions, namely to uncover truth that those in power might prefer to remain hidden" (Hobsbawm, 2004). Contrary to what some doom-sayers seem to think, media criticism of the ruling elite does not necessarily stir up apathy, according to research by Pippa Norris:

> A citizenry that is better informed and more highly educated, with higher cognitive skills and more sources of information, may well become increasingly critical of governing institutions, with declining affective loyalties towards traditional representative bodies such as parties and parliaments. But increasing criticism from citizens does not necessarily reduce civic engagement; indeed, it can have the contrary effect.
>
> (Norris, 2000: 319)

If the health of a public sphere can be judged on "how well it functions as a space of opposition and accountability, on the one hand, and policy influence, on the other" (Young, 2000: 173), then it is likely to be improved by the actions of journalists who scrutinise the actions of the powerful, including those whose power lies in the media.

This role need not be the sole preserve of those who style themselves "investigative journalists," as has been pointed out by James Ettema and Theodore Glasser (1998: 189–200), among others. They identify three achievements of investigative reporting. First, bringing instances of systems failures to public attention. Second, demanding an account from those responsible. Third, establishing an empathetic link between people who have suffered in the situation and the rest of us. Although these roles – or ideals – have emerged specifically from investigative journalism, they could legitimately be held up as "a new set of values to all others who practise the reporter's craft".

TIME FOR A FIFTH ESTATE?

Journalists try to shine a small torch into a very large, very dark cupboard. But a torch will not work if the batteries are not replaced when they run out, and that is what happens when those in charge cut editorial budgets and under-invest in journalism by reducing the number of reporters, closing local offices and turning journalists into churnalists. Nor will a torch illuminate a cupboard if it is pointed somewhere else. That is why journalist Ignacio Ramonet, of *Le Monde Diplomatique* in France, has called for the creation of a "fifth estate" – made up of journalists and other concerned citizens – to rescue the idea of socially responsible journalism from the clutches of giant media corporations:

> Over the past 15 years, with the acceleration of globalisation, this fourth estate has been stripped of its potential, and has gradually ceased to function as a counter-power … We have to create a new estate, a fifth estate, that will let us pit a civic force against this new coalition of rulers. A fifth estate to denounce the hyperpower of the media conglomerates which are complicit in, and diffusers of, neoliberal globalisation … Press freedom is no more than the extension of collective freedom of expression, which is the foundation of democracy. We cannot allow it to be hijacked by the rich and powerful.
>
> (Ramonet, 2003)

There are fears that it may already be too late for journalists working in some of the more profit-hungry sectors of the media. Academic Bob Franklin (2005: 148) uses the term "McJournalism" to characterise the predictable, standardised and "flavourless mush" produced when journalists have to work in conditions that are more commonly associated with the fast food sector: conditions produced by the relentless drive for economic efficiency. Interestingly, the founder of the international *Metro* chain of free newspapers – not to be confused with the UK *Metro* – once described his product as the "Big Mac" of the press (Marriner, 2005). It is not exactly the healthiest of diets and, just as the prevalence of fast food is now being countered by a Slow movement that puts quality above speed (Honoré, 2004), so "time is needed to prepare, publish and understand careful journalism which explains the working of society to its citizens" (Lloyd, 2004: 188). A campaign for slow journalism may be unlikely to set pulses racing, but the point is well made that journalists need time and space within which to function properly. Journalists are far more likely to get things wrong, or to behave unethically, when they are denied the necessary time and space: time to get out of the office, time to nurture a range of sources, time to build trust, time to check things out, time to read documents properly, time to think, and the space to discuss with colleagues any ethical implications without the fear of being ridiculed.

Despite changes in technology and ownership, a journalist's basic responsibility remains what it has always been: "It is to report honestly, to comment fearlessly, and to hold fast to independence" (Williams, 1959: 247). It was to protect this role that, in 2006, journalists in the UK launched a "Journalism Matters" campaign highlighting the threat to the democratic process posed by constant reductions in editorial budgets, closure of offices and shedding of jobs (Morley, 2006). There are also movements in many countries attempting to resist and reverse the takeover of media outlets by corporate giants. In the UK and US, respectively, the Campaign for Press and Broadcasting Freedom (CPBF) and Fairness and Accuracy in Reporting (Fair) have both worked over the years to highlight trends, spark public debates and counteract the lobbying of the big commercial players. Of necessity, they are playing a long game. Yet journalists do not need to – indeed, cannot afford to – wait for structural changes to media institutions before trying to improve our journalism. Individually and collectively, we can reflect on and improve our practice despite the constraints in the way the industry currently operates.

REFLECTIVE PRACTICE

Every day, in little ways and in big ways, with quiet words or grand gestures, journalists make decisions to act in a more ethical manner. Not all journalists and not always, but more often than many of the harshest critics of journalism seem to believe. Women in the news are – mostly – no longer crudely labelled according to their appearance or assumed to be housewives in the way that they tended to be just a few years ago, because for one reason or another most journalists stopped doing it. A contributory factor to this change was that many women journalists, and some men, spoke up and challenged what had previously been accepted practice. It is not just practice that can be changed: people can change too. Steve Panter, for example, looks back on some of his actions as a younger reporter with embarrassment, even shame, conceding that the desire for a story often meant that ethical considerations were either brushed aside or not even noticed. Having thought deeply about such stories in recent years, he has become a more reflective practitioner. And he is not alone.

We saw in the previous chapter that some individual journalists have resigned on matters of conscience when they disapproved of what was being done in their names. We have also seen evidence of a growing groundswell behind the idea of a "conscience clause" in journalists' contracts of employment, whereby an individual would have the right to refuse an unethical assignment. On rare occasions, groups of journalists have intervened collectively, standing up for standards of journalism and ethical conduct alike. Such outspoken responses are likely to remain the exception rather than the rule.

A concept of ethical journalism influences the actions of countless journalists in innumerable ways, whether they are thinking about which word to use in a headline or deciding whether to knock one more time on the door of a bereaved family. It is true that journalists have sometimes been willing to trample on the feelings of people to get a story, using tricks of the trade to obtain quotes or pictures; that prevailing news values can give us a distorted vision of society; and that easy labels can result in people being stereotyped. But it is equally true that journalists sometimes go out of their way to give the "ordinary" people on whom they are reporting an opportunity to understand and comment upon the way in which their words are going to be used; that journalists have been prepared to go to prison to protect whistleblowers; and that journalists have sometimes agonised over whether keeping a promise to a confidential source is always right, in every circumstance. Journalists have been willing to take personal risks, going undercover to bring to light matters that are in the public interest to know; yet journalists cannot always agree on what the public interest is. Journalists have reported from below as well as from on high, taking seriously the trust placed in them by sources and audiences alike – their fellow citizens.

Ethical journalism is not an oxymoron. Ethical journalism is not only possible, it is essential; not just for journalists' sense of self-worth, but for the health and well-being of society. It requires journalists – wherever they work – to be reflective practitioners, engaged in a constant process of reflection and learning while doing their job. And it requires journalists to be prepared to voice their concerns within the newsroom, as Kovach and Rosenstiel argue:

> Innumerable hurdles make it difficult to produce news that is accurate, fair, balanced, citizen focused, independent-minded, and courageous. But the effort is smothered in its crib without an open atmosphere that allows people to challenge one another's assumptions, perceptions, and prejudices.
>
> (Kovach and Rosenstiel, 2003: 181)

Far from being a luxury, ethics are integral to being a good journalist. An ethical journalist is one who cares: cares about accuracy, cares about people, cares about journalism, cares enough to speak out, and cares enough to challenge preconceptions and prejudices.

Which brings us back to where this book began: the story of Hattie Carroll, a crime victim from nearly half a century ago. You may recall that the story was from a local newspaper but became something else when Bob Dylan got hold of it. Although the songwriter later received some flak for making the facts fit "his preconceived notions of injustice and corruption" (Heylin, 2001: 124–5), the facts as presented in the lyrics tally with newspaper reports of the time. Today, we know the story of Hattie Carroll, if we know it at all, only because Dylan turned it into a song all those years ago. Ian Frazier points out:

> On the long and sad list of victims of racial violence, from Emmett Till to Amadou Diallo, most names are forgotten after the news moves on. Dylan's poetry has caused Hattie Carroll's name, and the sorrow and true lonesomeness of her death, to stick in some people's minds.
>
> (Frazier, 2004)

It sticks in people's minds because it tells the story from the bottom up – from the perspective of an individual victim of injustice – while subtly placing events within a wider social context. Although written as "a piece of reportage that describes a real event", according to Nigel Williamson (2004: 262), the song "transcends the 'who, what, when, where and why' role of the journalist". Maybe the songwriter transcended journalism, and maybe the story is alive today only because it stopped being journalism and became something else. But neither Dylan nor the rest of us would ever have heard of Hattie Carroll without the efforts of the journalists who found out about the case, who checked it out, and who decided it was worth reporting. They did this despite the fact that many of their readers at the time may not have cared two cents about a poor black mother-of-10 being killed by a wealthy white man. Bringing such stories to public attention is in the public interest. Not only is it ethical journalism it is good journalism.

FURTHER READING

For an introduction to the practice of journalism, and for consideration of concepts such as objectivity, impartiality and news values, see Harcup (2004), which attempts to bridge the divide between theory and practice and also offers extensive suggestions for further reading. Randall (2000) and Sheridan Burns (2002) are thoughtful companions for any journalist or journalism student, while Allan (2005) features contributions from a range of journalism academics. Sanders (2003), Kovach and Rosenstiel (2003), Keeble (2001a) and Frost (2000) all discuss different approaches to the ethics of journalism. For a feminist account of journalistic practice in the UK and US, see Chambers and others (2004). In a thought-provoking and challenging book, Lynch and McGoldrick (2005) contrast what they term "war journalism" with "peace journalism" and draw lessons that extend far beyond the way in which conflicts are covered. Reflective journalists discuss their craft in *British Journalism Review* (Sage) and the *Columbia Journalism*

Review (www.cjr.org), and academic research into journalism is published in the journals *Journalism Studies* (Routledge), *Journalism: Theory, Practice and Criticism* (Sage) and *Ethical Space* (Institute of Communication Ethics).

Useful websites include those of the media ethics charity Mediawise (www.mediawise.org.uk), the National Union of Journalists (www.nuj.org.uk), the Campaign for Press and Broadcasting Freedom (www.cpbf. org.uk) and Fairness and Accuracy in Reporting (www.fair.org). There are also more and more individual blogs dealing specifically with journalism, and ones worth checking out for discussion of ethical issues include those by Roy Greenslade (http://blogs.guardian.co.uk/greenslade), Jay Rosen (http://journalism.nyu.edu/pubzone/weblogs/pressthink), and Danny Schechter (http://www.newsdissector.org/blog).

Journalists' memoirs are always worth reading, although some are more reflective than others. Interesting volumes in recent years include Marr (2005), Snow (2005), Hastings (2002), Stott (2002), Simpson (1999), Adie (2002) and Knightley (1998). One of the most illuminating of the lot has recently been republished by Granta after nearly 40 years: James Cameron's (1968) *Point of Departure* virtually defined the concept of the reflective practitioner, and is also a great read.

APPENDICES

1 International Federation of Journalists Code of Conduct

2 National Union of Journalists Code of Conduct

3 National Union of Journalists Guidelines on Race Reporting

4 Press Complaints Commission Code of Practice

5 Ofcom Broadcasting Code: selected extracts

6 BBC Editorial Guidelines: selected extracts

7 Committee of Concerned Journalists Statement of Journalism Principles

8 Al-Jazeera Code of Ethics

9 Indymedia UK Mission Statement

APPENDIX 1

International Federation of Journalists Declaration of Principles on the Conduct of Journalists

Adopted in 1954, last amended by the 1986 World Congress of the IFJ.

This international declaration is proclaimed as a standard of professional conduct for journalists engaged in gathering, transmitting, disseminating and commenting on news and information in describing events.

1 Respect for truth and for the right of the public to truth is the first duty of the journalist.
2 In pursuance of this duty, the journalist shall at all times defend the principles of freedom in the honest collection and publication of news, and of the right to fair comment and criticism.
3 The journalist shall report only in accordance with facts of which he/she knows the origin. The journalist shall not suppress essential information or falsify documents.
4 The journalist shall only use fair methods to obtain news, photographs and documents.
5 The journalist shall do the utmost to rectify any published information which is found to be harmfully inaccurate.
6 The journalist shall observe professional secrecy regarding the source of information obtained in confidence.
7 The journalist shall be alert to the danger of discrimination being furthered by media, and shall do the utmost to avoid facilitating such discriminations based on, among other things, race, sex, sexual orientation, language, religion, political or other opinions, and national and social origins.
8 The journalist shall regard as grave professional offences the following: plagiarism; malicious misinterpretation; calumny; libel; slander; unfounded

accusations; acceptance of a bribe in any form in consideration of either publication or suppression.

9 Journalists worthy of the name shall deem it their duty to observe faithfully the principles stated above. Within the general law of each country the journalist shall recognise in matters of professional matters the jurisdiction of colleagues only, to the exclusion of any kind of interference by governments or others.

(www.ifj.org)

APPENDIX 2

National Union of Journalists Code of Conduct

Adopted in 1936, last amended in 2004, under review in 2007.

1 A journalist has a duty to maintain the highest professional and ethical standards.

2 A journalist shall at all times defend the principle of the freedom of the press and other media in relation to the collection of information and the expression of comment and criticism. He/she shall strive to eliminate distortion, news suppression and censorship.

3 A journalist shall strive to ensure that the information he/she disseminates is fair and accurate, avoid the expression of comment and conjecture as established fact and falsification by distortion, selection or misrepresentation.

4 A journalist shall rectify promptly any harmful inaccuracies, ensure that correction and apologies receive due prominence and afford the right of reply to persons criticised when the issue is of sufficient importance.

5 A journalist shall obtain information, photographs and illustrations only by straightforward means. The use of other means can be justified only by overriding considerations of the public interest. The journalist is entitled to exercise a personal conscientious objection to the use of such means.

6 A journalist shall do nothing which entails intrusion into anybody's private life, grief or distress, subject to justification by overriding considerations of the public interest.

7 A journalist shall protect confidential sources of information.

8 A journalist shall not accept bribes nor shall he/she allow other inducements to influence the performance of his/her professional duties.

9 A journalist shall not lend himself/herself to the distortion or suppression of the truth because of advertising or other considerations.

10 A journalist shall mention a person's age, sex, race, colour, creed, illegitimacy, disability, marital status, or sexual orientation only if this information is strictly relevant. A journalist shall neither originate nor process material which encourages discrimination, ridicule, prejudice or hatred on any of the above-mentioned grounds.

11 A journalist shall not interview or photograph children in connection with stories concerning their welfare without the permission of a parent or other adult responsible for their welfare.

12 No journalist shall knowingly cause or allow the publication or broadcast of a photograph that has been manipulated unless that photograph is clearly labelled as such. Manipulation does not include normal dodging, burning, colour balancing, spotting, contrast adjustment, cropping and obvious masking for legal or safety reasons.

13 A journalist shall not take private advantage of information gained in the course of his/her duties before the information is public knowledge.

14 A journalist shall not by way of statement, voice or appearance endorse by advertisement any commercial product or service save for the promotion of his/her own work or of the medium by which he/she is employed.

THE PUBLIC INTEREST

The above Code of Conduct uses the concept of 'the public interest' as a yardstick to justify publication of sensitive material. This is the definition of the public interest drawn up by the NUJ Ethics Council:

1 The public interest includes:

a) Detecting or exposing crime or a serious misdemeanour;

b) Protecting public health and safety;

c) Preventing the public from being misled by some statement or action of an individual or organisation;

d) Exposing misuse of public funds or other forms of corruption by public bodies;

e) Revealing potential conflicts of interest by those in positions of power and influence;

f) Exposing corporate greed;

g) Exposing hypocritical behaviour by those holding high office.

2 There is a public interest in the freedom of expression itself.

3 In cases involving children, journalists must demonstrate an exceptional public interest to over-ride the normally paramount interests of the child.

(www.nuj.org.uk)

APPENDIX 3

NUJ Guidelines on Race Reporting

STATEMENT

1 The NUJ believes that the development of racist attitudes and the growth of fascist parties pose a threat to democracy, the rights of trade union organisations, a free press and the development of social harmony and well-being.

2 The NUJ believes that its members cannot avoid a measure of responsibility in fighting the evil of racism as expressed through the mass media.

3 The NUJ reaffirms its total opposition to censorship but equally reaffirms its belief that press freedom must be conditioned by responsibility and an acknowledgement by all media workers of the need not to allow press freedom to be abused to slander a section of the community or to promote the evil of racism.

4 The NUJ believes the methods and lies of the racists should be publicly and vigorously exposed.

5 The NUJ believes that newspapers and magazines should not originate material which encourages discrimination on grounds of race or colour, as expressed in the NUJ's rule book and code of conduct.

6 The NUJ recognises the right of members to withhold their labour on grounds of conscience where employers are providing a platform for racist propaganda.

7 The NUJ believes that editors should ensure that coverage of race stories should be placed in a balanced context.

8 The NUJ will continue to monitor the development of media coverage in this area and give support to members seeking to enforce the above aims.

RACE REPORTING

Only mention someone's race if it is strictly relevant. Check to make sure you have it right. Would you mention race if the person was white?

Do not sensationalise race relations issues; it harms black people and it could harm you.

Think carefully about the words you use. Words which were once in common usage are now considered offensive, eg half-caste and coloured. Use mixed-race and black instead. Black can cover people of Arab, Asian, Chinese and African origin. Ask people how they define themselves.

Immigrant is often used as a term of abuse. Do not use it unless the person really is an immigrant. Most black people in Britain were born here and most immigrants are white.

Do not make assumptions about a person's cultural background – whether it is their name or religious detail. Ask them or where it is not possible check with the local race equality council.

Investigate the treatment of black people in education, health, employment and housing. Do not forget travellers and gypsies. Cover their lives and concerns. Seek the views of their representatives.

Remember that black communities are culturally diverse. Get a full and correct view from representative organisations.

Press for equal opportunities for employment for black staff.

Be wary of disinformation. Just because a source is traditional does not mean it is accurate.

REPORTING RACIST ORGANISATIONS

When interviewing representatives of racist organisations or reporting meetings or statements or claims, journalists should carefully check all reports for accuracy and seek rebutting or opposing comments. The anti-social nature of such views should be exposed.

Do not sensationalise by reports, photographs, film or presentation the activities of racist organisations.

Seek to publish or broadcast material exposing the myths and lies of racist organisations and their anti-social behaviour.

Do not allow the letters column or 'phone-in' programmes to be used to spread racial hatred in whatever guise.

(www.nuj.org.uk)

APPENDIX 4

Press Complaints Commission Code of Practice

The Press Complaints Commission is charged with enforcing the following code of practice which was framed by the newspaper and periodical industry and was last amended by the PCC in August 2006.

THE CODE

All members of the press have a duty to maintain the highest professional standards. This Code sets the benchmark for those ethical standards, protecting both the rights of the individual and the public's right to know. It is the cornerstone of the system of self-regulation to which the industry has made a binding commitment.

It is essential that an agreed code be honoured not only to the letter but in the full spirit. It should not be interpreted so narrowly as to compromise its commitment to respect the rights of the individual, nor so broadly that it constitutes an unnecessary interference with freedom of expression or prevents publication in the public interest.

It is the responsibility of editors and publishers to implement the Code and they should take care to ensure it is observed rigorously by all editorial staff and external contributors, including non-journalists, in printed and online versions of publications.

Editors should co-operate swiftly with the PCC in the resolution of complaints. Any publication judged to have breached the Code must print the adjudication in full and with due prominence, including headline reference to the PCC.

1. ACCURACY

i) The Press must take care not to publish inaccurate, misleading or distorted information, including pictures.
ii) A significant inaccuracy, misleading statement or distortion once recognised must be corrected, promptly and with due prominence, and – where appropriate – an apology published.
iii) The Press, whilst free to be partisan, must distinguish clearly between comment, conjecture and fact.
iv) A publication must report fairly and accurately the outcome of an action for defamation to which it has been a party, unless an agreed settlement states otherwise, or an agreed statement is published.

2. OPPORTUNITY TO REPLY

A fair opportunity for reply to inaccuracies must be given when reasonably called for.

3. *PRIVACY

i) Everyone is entitled to respect for his or her private and family life, home, health and correspondence, including digital communications. Editors will be expected to justify intrusions into any individual's private life without consent.
ii) It is unacceptable to photograph individuals in private places without their consent.

Note – Private places are public or private property where there is a reasonable expectation of privacy.

4. *HARASSMENT

i) Journalists must not engage in intimidation, harassment or persistent pursuit.
ii) They must not persist in questioning, telephoning, pursuing or photographing individuals once asked to desist; nor remain on their property when asked to leave and must not follow them.
iii) Editors must ensure these principles are observed by those working for them and take care not to use non-compliant material from other sources.

5. INTRUSION INTO GRIEF OR SHOCK

i) In cases involving grief or shock, enquiries must be carried out and approaches made with sympathy and discretion. Publication must be handled sensitively at such times but this should not be interpreted as restricting the right to report judicial proceedings.

ii) When reporting suicide, care should be taken to avoid excessive detail about the method used.*

6. *CHILDREN

i) Young people should be free to complete their time at school without unnecessary intrusion.

ii) A child under 16 must not be interviewed or photographed on issues involving their own or another child's welfare unless a custodial parent or similarly responsible adult consents.

iii) Pupils must not be approached or photographed at school without the permission of the school authorities.

iv) Minors must not be paid for material involving children's welfare, nor parents or guardians for material about their children or wards, unless it is clearly in the child's interest.

v) Editors must not use the fame, notoriety or position of a parent or guardian as sole justification for publishing details of a child's private life.

7. *CHILDREN IN SEX CASES

1. The press must not, even if legally free to do so, identify children under 16 who are victims or witnesses in cases involving sex offences.
2. In any press report of a case involving a sexual offence against a child -

i) The child must not be identified.

ii) The adult may be identified.

iii) The word "incest" must not be used where a child victim might be identified.

iv) Care must be taken that nothing in the report implies the relationship between the accused and the child.

8. *HOSPITALS

i) Journalists must identify themselves and obtain permission from a responsible executive before entering non-public areas of hospitals or similar institutions to pursue enquiries.

ii) The restrictions on intruding into privacy are particularly relevant to enquiries about individuals in hospitals or similar institutions.

9. *REPORTING OF CRIME

i) Relatives or friends of persons convicted or accused of crime should not generally be identified without their consent, unless they are genuinely relevant to the story.
ii) Particular regard should be paid to the potentially vulnerable position of children who witness, or are victims of, crime. This should not restrict the right to report legal proceedings.

10. *CLANDESTINE DEVICES AND SUBTERFUGE

i) The press must not seek to obtain or publish material acquired by using hidden cameras or clandestine listening devices; or by intercepting private or mobile telephone calls, messages or emails; or by the unauthorised removal of documents or photographs.
ii) Engaging in misrepresentation or subterfuge can generally be justified only in the public interest and then only when the material cannot be obtained by other means.

11. VICTIMS OF SEXUAL ASSAULT

The press must not identify victims of sexual assault or publish material likely to contribute to such identification unless there is adequate justification and they are legally free to do so.

12. DISCRIMINATION

i) The press must avoid prejudicial or pejorative reference to an individual's race, colour, religion, gender, sexual orientation or to any physical or mental illness or disability.
ii) Details of an individual's race, colour, religion, sexual orientation, physical or mental illness or disability must be avoided unless genuinely relevant to the story.

13. FINANCIAL JOURNALISM

i) Even where the law does not prohibit it, journalists must not use for their own profit financial information they receive in advance of its general publication, nor should they pass such information to others.
ii) They must not write about shares or securities in whose performance they know that they or their close families have a significant financial interest without disclosing the interest to the editor or financial editor.
iii) They must not buy or sell, either directly or through nominees or agents, shares or securities about which they have written recently or about which they intend to write in the near future.

14. CONFIDENTIAL SOURCES

Journalists have a moral obligation to protect confidential sources of information.

15. WITNESS PAYMENTS IN CRIMINAL TRIALS

i) No payment or offer of payment to a witness – or any person who may reasonably be expected to be called as a witness – should be made in any case once proceedings are active as defined by the Contempt of Court Act 1981.

This prohibition lasts until the suspect has been freed unconditionally by police without charge or bail or the proceedings are otherwise discontinued; or has entered a guilty plea to the court; or, in the event of a not guilty plea, the court has announced its verdict.

*ii) Where proceedings are not yet active but are likely and foreseeable, editors must not make or offer payment to any person who may reasonably be expected to be called as a witness, unless the information concerned ought demonstrably to be published in the public interest and there is an overriding need to make or promise payment for this to be done; and all reasonable steps have been taken to ensure no financial dealings influence the evidence those witnesses give. In no circumstances should such payment be conditional on the outcome of a trial.

*iii) Any payment or offer of payment made to a person later cited to give evidence in proceedings must be disclosed to the prosecution and defence. The witness must be advised of this requirement.

16. *PAYMENT TO CRIMINALS

i) Payment or offers of payment for stories, pictures or information, which seek to exploit a particular crime or to glorify or glamorise crime in general, must not be made directly or via agents to convicted or confessed criminals or to their associates – who may include family, friends and colleagues.

ii) Editors invoking the public interest to justify payment or offers would need to demonstrate that there was good reason to believe the public interest would be served. If, despite payment, no public interest emerged, then the material should not be published.

THE PUBLIC INTEREST

There may be exceptions to the clauses marked * where they can be demonstrated to be in the public interest.

1. The public interest includes, but is not confined to:
   - i) Detecting or exposing crime or serious impropriety.
   - ii) Protecting public health and safety.
   - iii) Preventing the public from being misled by an action or statement of an individual or organisation.
2. There is a public interest in freedom of expression itself.
3. Whenever the public interest is invoked, the PCC will require editors to demonstrate fully how the public interest was served.
4. The PCC will consider the extent to which material is already in the public domain, or will become so.
5. In cases involving children under 16, editors must demonstrate an exceptional public interest to over-ride the normally paramount interest of the child.

(www.pcc.org.uk)

APPENDIX 5

Selected Extracts from the Ofcom Broadcasting Code

This code came into effect on 25 July 2005.

[…]

CRIME

PRINCIPLE

To ensure that material likely to encourage or incite the commission of crime or to lead to disorder is not included in television or radio services.

RULES

3.1 Material likely to encourage or incite the commission of crime or to lead to disorder must not be included in television or radio services.

3.2 Descriptions or demonstrations of criminal techniques which contain essential details which could enable the commission of crime must not be broadcast unless editorially justified.

3.3 No payment, promise of payment, or payment in kind, may be made to convicted or confessed criminals whether directly for an interview or other programme contribution by the criminal (or any other person) relating to his/her crime/s. The only exception is where it is in the public interest.

3.4 While criminal proceedings are active, no payment or promise of payment may be made, directly or indirectly, to any witness or any person who may reasonably be expected to be called as a witness. Nor should any payment be suggested or made dependent on the outcome of the trial. Only actual expenditure or loss of earnings necessarily incurred during the making of a programme contribution may be reimbursed.

3.5 Where criminal proceedings are likely and foreseeable, payments should not be made to people who might reasonably be expected to be witnesses unless there is a clear public interest, such as investigating crime or serious wrongdoing, and the payment is necessary to elicit the information. Where such a payment is made it will be appropriate to disclose the payment to both defence and prosecution if the person becomes a witness in any subsequent trial.

3.6 Broadcasters must use their best endeavours so as not to broadcast material that could endanger lives or prejudice the success of attempts to deal with a hijack or kidnapping.

[…]

DUE IMPARTIALITY AND DUE ACCURACY IN NEWS

PRINCIPLES

To ensure that news, in whatever form, is reported with due accuracy and presented with due impartiality…

RULES

5.1 News, in whatever form, must be reported with due accuracy and presented with due impartiality.

MEANING OF "DUE IMPARTIALITY"

"Due" is an important qualification to the concept of impartiality. Impartiality itself means not favouring one side over another. "Due" means adequate or appropriate to the subject and nature of the programme. So "due impartiality" does not mean an equal division of time has to be given to every view, or that every argument and every facet of every argument has to be represented. The approach to due impartiality may vary according to the nature of the subject, the type of programme and channel, the likely expectation of the audience as to content, and the extent to which the content and approach is signalled to the audience.

[…]

5.5 Due impartiality on matters of political or industrial controversy and matters relating to current public policy must be preserved… This may be achieved within a programme or over a series of programmes taken as a whole.

[…]

5.8 Any personal interest of a reporter or presenter, which would call into question the due impartiality of the programme, must be made clear to the audience.

[…]

FAIRNESS

PRINCIPLE

To ensure that broadcasters avoid unjust or unfair treatment of individuals or organisations in programmes.

RULE

7.1 Broadcasters must avoid unjust or unfair treatment of individuals or organisations in programmes.

PRACTICES TO BE FOLLOWED

Dealing fairly with contributors and obtaining informed consent:

7.2 Broadcasters and programme makers should normally be fair in their dealings with potential contributors to programmes unless, exceptionally, it is justified to do otherwise.

[…]

7.7 Guarantees given to contributors, for example relating to the content of a programme, confidentiality or anonymity, should normally be honoured.

7.8 Broadcasters should ensure that the re-use of material, ie use of material originally filmed or recorded for one purpose and then used in a programme for another purpose or used in a later or different programme, does not create unfairness. This applies both to material obtained from others and the broadcaster's own material.

OPPORTUNITY TO CONTRIBUTE AND PROPER CONSIDERATION OF FACTS:

7.9 Before broadcasting a factual programme, including programmes examining past events, broadcasters should take reasonable care to satisfy themselves that:

- material facts have not been presented, disregarded or omitted in a way that is unfair to an individual or organisation; and
- anyone whose omission could be unfair to an individual or organisation has been offered an opportunity to contribute.

7.10 Programmes … should not portray facts, events, individuals or organisations in a way which is unfair to an individual or organisation.

7.11 If a programme alleges wrongdoing or incompetence or makes other significant allegations, those concerned should normally be given an appropriate and timely opportunity to respond.

7.12 Where a person approached to contribute to a programme chooses to make no comment or refuses to appear in a broadcast, the broadcast should make clear that the individual concerned has chosen not to appear and should give their explanation if it would be unfair not to do so.

7.13 Where it is appropriate to represent the views of a person or organisation that is not participating in the programme, this must be done in a fair manner.

DECEPTION, SET-UPS AND 'WIND-UP' CALLS:

7.14 Broadcasters or programme makers should not normally obtain or seek information, audio, pictures or an agreement to contribute through misrepresentation or deception. (Deception includes surreptitious filming or recording.) However:

- it may be warranted to use material obtained through misrepresentation or deception without consent if it is in the public interest and cannot reasonably be obtained by other means;
- where there is no adequate public interest justification, for example some unsolicited wind-up calls or entertainment set-ups, consent should be obtained from the individual and/or organisation concerned before the material is broadcast;
- if the individual and/or organisation is/are not identifiable in the programme then consent for broadcast will not be required;
- material involving celebrities and those in the public eye can be used without consent for broadcast, but it should not be used without a public interest justification if it is likely to result in

unjustified public ridicule or personal distress. (Normally, therefore such contributions should be pre-recorded.)

[...]

PRIVACY

PRINCIPLE

To ensure that broadcasters avoid any unwarranted infringement of privacy in programmes and in connection with obtaining material included in programmes.

RULE

8.1 Any infringement of privacy in programmes, or in connection with obtaining material included in programmes, must be warranted.

MEANING OF "WARRANTED":

In this section "warranted" has a particular meaning. It means that where broadcasters wish to justify an infringement of privacy as warranted, they should be able to demonstrate why in the particular circumstances of the case, it is warranted. If the reason is that it is in the public interest, then the broadcaster should be able to demonstrate that the public interest outweighs the right to privacy. Examples of public interest would include revealing or detecting crime, protecting public health or safety, exposing misleading claims made by individuals or organisations or disclosing incompetence that affects the public.

PRACTICES TO BE FOLLOWED

PRIVATE LIVES, PUBLIC PLACES AND LEGITIMATE EXPECTATION OF PRIVACY:

MEANING OF "LEGITIMATE EXPECTATION OF PRIVACY":

Legitimate expectations of privacy will vary according to the place and nature of the information, activity or condition in question, the extent to which it is in the public domain (if at all) and whether the individual concerned is already in the public eye. There may be circumstances where people can reasonably expect privacy even in a public place. Some activities and conditions may be of such a private nature that filming or recording, even in a public place, could involve an infringement of privacy. People under investigation or in the public eye, and their immediate family and friends, retain the right to a private life, although private behaviour can raise issues of legitimate public interest.

8.2 Information which discloses the location of a person's home or family should not be revealed without permission, unless it is warranted.

8.3 When people are caught up in events which are covered by the news they still have a right to privacy in both the making and the broadcast of a programme, unless it is warranted to infringe it. This applies both to the time when these events are taking place and to any later programmes that revisit those events.

[...]

8.11 Doorstepping for factual programmes should not take place unless a request for an interview has been refused or it has not been possible to request an interview, or there is good reason to believe that an investigation will be frustrated if the subject is approached openly, and it is warranted to doorstep. However, normally broadcasters may, without prior warning interview, film or record people in the news when in public places.

MEANING OF "DOORSTEPPING":
Doorstepping is the filming or recording of an interview or attempted interview with someone, or announcing that a call is being filmed or recorded for broadcast purposes, without any prior warning. It does not, however, include vox-pops (sampling the views of random members of the public).

8.12 Broadcasters can record telephone calls between the broadcaster and the other party if they have, from the outset of the call, identified themselves, explained the purpose of the call and that the call is being recorded for possible broadcast (if that is the case) unless it is warranted not to do one or more of these practices.

If at a later stage it becomes clear that a call that has been recorded will be broadcast (but this was not explained to the other party at the time of the call) then the broadcaster must obtain consent before broadcast from the other party, unless it is warranted not to do so.

8.13 Surreptitious filming or recording should only be used where it is warranted.

Normally, it will only be warranted if:

- there is prima facie evidence of a story in the public interest; and
- there are reasonable grounds to suspect that further material evidence could be obtained; and
- it is necessary to the credibility and authenticity of the programme.

MEANING OF "SURREPTITIOUS FILMING OR RECORDING":
Surreptitious filming or recording includes the use of long lenses or recording devices, as well as leaving an unattended camera or recording device on private property without the full and informed consent of the occupiers or their agent. It may also include recording telephone conversations without the knowledge of the other party, or deliberately continuing a recording when the other party thinks that it has come to an end.

8.14 Material gained by surreptitious filming and recording should only be broadcast when it is warranted.

[...]

SUFFERING AND DISTRESS:

8.16 Broadcasters should not take or broadcast footage or audio of people caught up in emergencies, victims of accidents or those suffering a personal tragedy, even in a public place, where that results in an infringement of privacy, unless it is warranted or the people concerned have given consent.

8.17 People in a state of distress should not be put under pressure to take part in a programme or provide interviews, unless it is warranted.

8.18 Broadcasters should take care not to reveal the identity of a person who has died or of victims of accidents or violent crimes, unless and until it is clear that the next of kin have been informed of the event or unless it is warranted.

8.19 Broadcasters should try to reduce the potential distress to victims and/or relatives when making or broadcasting programmes intended to examine past events that involve trauma to individuals (including crime) unless it is warranted to do otherwise. This applies to dramatic reconstructions and factual dramas, as well as factual programmes.

- In particular, so far as is reasonably practicable, surviving victims, and/or the immediate families of those whose experience is to feature in a programme, should be informed of the plans for the programme and its intended broadcast, even if the events or material to be broadcast have been in the public domain in the past.

PEOPLE UNDER SIXTEEN AND VULNERABLE PEOPLE:

8.20 Broadcasters should pay particular attention to the privacy of people under sixteen. They do not lose their rights to privacy because, for example, of the fame or notoriety of their parents or because of events in their schools.

8.21 Where a programme features an individual under sixteen or a vulnerable person in a way that infringes privacy, consent must be obtained from:

- a parent, guardian or other person of eighteen or over in loco parentis; and
- wherever possible, the individual concerned;

unless the subject matter is trivial or uncontroversial and the participation minor, or it is warranted to proceed without consent.

8.22 Persons under sixteen and vulnerable people should not be questioned about private matters without the consent of a parent, guardian or other person of eighteen or over in loco parentis (in the case of persons under sixteen), or a person with primary responsibility for their care (in the case of a vulnerable person), unless it is warranted to proceed without consent.

MEANING OF "VULNERABLE PEOPLE":

This varies, but may include those with learning difficulties, those with mental health problems, the bereaved, people with brain damage or forms of dementia, people who have been traumatised or who are sick or terminally ill.

[...]

(www.ofcom.org.uk)

APPENDIX 6

Selected Extracts from the BBC Editorial Guidelines

The latest edition of the BBC editorial guidelines were published in June 2005 and apply across all BBC content on radio, television, new media and magazines.

[…]

3. ACCURACY

… For the BBC accuracy is more important than speed and it is often more than a question of getting the facts right. All the relevant facts and information should be weighed to get at the truth. If an issue is controversial, relevant opinions as well as facts may need to be considered.

We aim to achieve it by:

- the accurate gathering of material using first hand sources wherever possible.
- checking and cross checking the facts.
- validating the authenticity of documentary evidence and digital material.
- corroborating claims and allegations made by contributors wherever possible.

GATHERING MATERIAL

We should try to witness events and gather information first hand.

Where this is not possible, we should talk to first hand sources and, where necessary, corroborate their evidence.

We should be reluctant to rely on a single source. If we do rely on a single source, a named on the record source is always preferable.

[…]

NOTE-TAKING

We must take accurate, reliable and contemporaneous notes of all significant research conversations and other relevant information.

We must keep records of research including written and electronic correspondence, background notes and documents. It should be kept in a way that allows double checking, particularly at the scripting stage, and if necessary by another member of the team.

We must keep accurate notes of conversations with sources and contributors about anonymity. A recording is preferable where possible.

When we broadcast serious allegations made by an anonymous source, full notes of interviews, conversations and information which provide the basis for the story must be kept.

When anonymity is essential no document, computer file, or other record should identify a source. This includes notebooks and administrative paperwork as well as video and audio tapes.

FACT CHECKING

We must check and verify information, facts and documents, particularly those researched on the internet. This may include confirming with an individual or organisation that they posted material and that it is accurate.

Even the most convincing material on the web may not be what it seems.

DIGITAL MANIPULATION

The ability to digitally create, manipulate and copy audio-visual material, including still photographs, video and documents, poses ethical dilemmas and creates the potential for hoaxing.

We should ensure that any digital manipulation … does not distort the meaning of events, alter the impact of genuine material or otherwise seriously mislead our audiences.

IDENTIFYING SOURCES

We should normally identify on air and online sources of information and significant contributors, as well as providing their credentials, so that our audiences can judge their status.

ANONYMOUS SOURCES

Sometimes information the public needs to know is only available through anonymous sources or contributors, generally on an "off the record" basis.

Protecting sources is a key principle of journalism for which some journalists have gone to jail. We must take care when we promise anonymity that we are in a position to honour it, including the need to resist a court order.

When a source asks for anonymity as a condition of giving information, or a contributor demands anonymity when taking part, we must agree with them precisely the way they are to be described. However, with an anonymous source, especially a source making serious allegations, we must give the audience as much information about them as is compatible with protecting their identity, and in a way that does not mislead the audience about their status.

[…]

REPORTING ALLEGATIONS

We should not normally use live unscripted two-ways to report allegations. It must be the editor's decision as to whether they are an appropriate way to break a story. When BBC colleagues follow up a story they must ensure they understand the terms in which the allegations are to be reported and do so accurately.

Any proposal to rely on a single unnamed source making a serious allegation or to grant anonymity to a significant contributor must be referred to a senior editorial level, or for Independents to the commissioning editor. In the most serious cases it may also be necessary to refer to Controller Editorial Policy and Programme Legal Advice. We will need to consider:

- whether the story is of significant public interest.
- whether the source is of proven credibility and reliability and in a position to have sufficient knowledge of the events featured.
- any legal issues.
- safety concerns eg whistleblowers.
- whether a response to serious allegations has been sought from the people or organisations concerned.
- sensitive and personal issues such as whether the serious allegation was made or substantiated "off the record".

We should script carefully the reporting of allegations made by an anonymous source to explain:

- the nature of the allegation.
- that the allegation is being made by an anonymous source and not the BBC.
- whether the allegation has been independently corroborated.

[...]

REPORTING STATISTICS AND RISKS

We should report statistics and risks in context, taking care not to worry the audience unduly, especially about health or crime. It may also be appropriate to report the margin of error and the source of figures to enable people to judge their significance. This may involve giving trends, taking care to avoid giving figures more weight than can stand scrutiny. If reporting a change, consideration should be given to making the baseline figure clear. For example, a doubling of a problem affecting one in two million people will still only affect one in a million.

We should consider the emotional impact pictures and personal testimony can have on perceptions of risk when not supported by the balance of argument. If a contributor's view is contrary to majority scientific or professional opinion, the demands of accuracy may require us to make this clear.

CORRECTING MISTAKES

We should normally acknowledge serious factual errors and correct mistakes quickly and clearly. Inaccuracy may lead to a complaint of unfairness.

An effective way of correcting a mistake is saying what was wrong as well as putting it right …

[…]

6. PRIVACY

The BBC must not infringe privacy without good reason wherever in the world it is operating. It is essential in order to exercise our rights of freedom of expression and information that we work within a framework which respects an individual's privacy and treats them fairly, while investigating and establishing matters which it is in the public interest to reveal. Private behaviour, correspondence and conversation should not be brought into the public domain unless there is a clear public interest …

PRIVACY EDITORIAL PRINCIPLES

The BBC seeks to:

- balance the public interest in freedom of expression with the legitimate expectation of privacy by individuals.
- balance the public interest in the full and accurate reporting of stories involving human suffering and distress with an individual's privacy and respect for their human dignity.
- justify intrusions into an individual's private life without consent by demonstrating a clear public interest.
- normally only report the private legal behaviour of public figures where broader public issues are raised either by the behaviour itself or by the consequences of its becoming widely known. The fact of publication by other media may not justify the BBC reporting it.

PUBLIC INTEREST

There is no single definition of public interest, it includes but is not confined to:

- exposing or detecting crime.
- exposing significantly anti-social behaviour.
- exposing corruption or injustice.
- disclosing significant incompetence or negligence.
- protecting people's health and safety.
- preventing people from being misled by some statement or action of an individual or organisation.
- disclosing information that allows people to make a significantly more informed decision about matters of public importance.

There is also a public interest in freedom of expression itself. When considering what is in the public interest we also need to take account of information already in the public domain or about to become available to the public.

PUBLIC AND SEMI-PUBLIC PLACES

An individual's right to privacy is qualified by location.

We should therefore not normally reveal information which discloses the precise location of a person's home or family without their consent, unless it is editorially justified.

People in public places or in semi-public places such as airports, railway stations and shopping malls cannot expect the same degree of privacy as in their own homes.

However, there may be circumstances where people can reasonably expect privacy even in a public place, for example, there is a greater expectation of privacy when someone is receiving medical treatment in a public or semi-public place.

[...]

BEHAVIOUR

An individual's right to privacy is also qualified by their behaviour. People are less entitled to privacy where their behaviour is criminal or seriously anti-social.

[...]

SECRET RECORDING

Secret recording must be justified by a clear public interest. It is a valuable tool for the BBC because it enables the capture of evidence or behaviour that our audiences would otherwise not see or hear. However, secret recording should normally be a method of last resort – misuse or overuse could discredit or devalue its impact.

The BBC will normally only use secret recording for the following purposes:

- as an investigative tool to expose issues of public interest where:
  - there is clear existing documentary or other evidence of such behaviour or of an intention to commit an offence.
  - it can be shown that an open approach would be unlikely to succeed.
  - the recording is necessary for evidential purposes.
- to obtain material outside the UK where a country's laws make the normal and responsible gathering of material extraordinarily difficult or impossible.

[...]

Secret recording is defined as:

- the use of hidden cameras and microphones.
- the deliberate use of audio-video equipment including long lenses, small video cameras, mobile phone cameras or radio microphones, either to conceal the equipment from targeted individuals or to give the impression of recording for purposes other than broadcasting, for example, a holiday video.
- the general use of audio-video equipment including long lenses, small video cameras, mobile phone cameras, webcams and radio microphones when people are unaware they are being recorded.
- recording phone calls for broadcast without asking permission.
- deliberately continuing a recording when the other party thinks that it has come to an end.

[...]

- The BBC requires a higher public interest test for secretly recording in a private place where the public do not have access.
- The BBC requires a higher public interest test for secretly recording medical treatments.

- The BBC requires a higher public interest test for secretly recording identifiable people in grief or under extremes of stress both in public and semi-public places.
- We must not go on "fishing expeditions" – that is secretly recording on private property in search of crime or anti-social behaviour by identifiable individuals or a group when there is no clear or current evidence against them of that behaviour.

[…]

ELECTRONIC NOTE-TAKING

We can record our conversations in both audio and video, for example, by using small cameras or telephones, for note-taking purposes without obtaining consent. Electronic note-taking can ensure accuracy in our reporting, or enable us to gather evidence to defend the BBC against possible legal action or complaints. The intention of such recordings must be for note-taking and research, not for broadcast.

We do not normally broadcast any recordings originally made for note-taking purposes … Retrospective permission to broadcast material gathered in this way will only be granted in exceptional circumstances.

DOOR-STEPPING

Door-stepping is when we confront and record, or attempt to record, an interview with someone for broadcast, or announce that a phone call is being recorded for broadcast, when that person is not expecting to be interviewed because we have not made an arrangement with them to do so.

Door-stepping can be in person or on the phone. It can take place on public or private property. It can be for news and factual programmes as well as comedy and entertainment.

The BBC has rules about door-stepping that all content producers must follow. This is because door-stepping should normally be a last resort.

However, the rules are not intended to prevent the legitimate gathering of material either for the daily news agenda or for research purposes.

DAILY NEWS GATHERING

When public figures and other people are the subject of news stories they must expect media attention and may be asked questions and their answers recorded for broadcast, without prior arrangement, as they come and go from buildings, airports and so on.

MEDIA SCRUMS

We should be aware that when media representatives congregate in large numbers to cover a news story the resulting media scrum can become intimidating or unreasonably intrusive. Sometimes it will be appropriate to make pooling arrangements with other media organisations, at other times we may judge it proper to withdraw.

RESEARCH

The BBC's rules on door-stepping are not intended to prevent researchers, who are not recording for broadcast, from making cold calls to people, either by phone or in person, or approaching people opportunistically, for example, when conducting vox pops.

[…]

REPORTING SUFFERING AND DISTRESS

We must always balance the public interest in full and accurate reporting against the need to be compassionate and to avoid any unjustified infringement of privacy when we report accidents, disasters, disturbances or war.

We will always need to consider carefully the editorial justification for portraying graphic material of human suffering and distress. There are almost no circumstances in which it is justified to show executions and very few circumstances in which it is justified to broadcast other scenes in which people are being killed. It is always important to respect the privacy and dignity of the dead.

We should never show them gratuitously. We should also avoid the gratuitous use of close-ups of faces and serious injuries or other violent material.

The passage of time is an important factor when it comes to making difficult judgements about the broadcasting of graphic material. In the immediate aftermath of an event the use of more graphic material is normally justified to provide a reasonable illustration of the full horror, although a good script is equally important in conveying the reality of tragedy. However, as the story unfolds it may become more difficult to justify its continued use. Then when it comes to marking the anniversary of an event or when considering it in a contemporary historical context, it may again be editorially justified to re-use it.

We also need to consider the cumulative effect of the use of graphic material on our continuous news channels.

We should normally request interviews with people who are injured or grieving following an accident or disaster by approaching them through friends, relatives or advisers. We should not:

- put them under pressure to provide interviews.
- harass them with repeated phone calls, emails, text messages or knocks at the door.
- stay on their property if asked to leave.
- normally follow them if they move on.

However, it is important that we do not inadvertently censor our reporting. For example, public expressions of grief and the extent to which it is regarded as an intrusion into someone's private life to show them, vary around the world. There are two key considerations when judging what to broadcast, the people we record and our audience. Graphic scenes of grief are unlikely to offend or distress those victims and relatives who consented to our recording them, but they may upset or anger some of our audience. A few words of explanation when introducing scenes of extreme distress or suffering may help to prevent misunderstandings.

[...]

(www.bbc.co.uk/editorialguidelines)

APPENDIX 7

Committee of Concerned Journalists Statement of Journalism Principles

1. Journalism's first obligation is to the truth.
2. Its first loyalty is to citizens.
3. Its essence is a discipline of verification.
4. Its practitioners must maintain an independence from those they cover.
5. It must serve as an independent monitor of power.
6. It must provide a forum for public criticism and compromise.
7. It must strive to make the significant interesting and relevant.
8. It must keep the news comprehensive and proportional.
9. Its practitioners must be allowed to exercise their personal conscience.

(www.journalism.org)

APPENDIX 8

Al-Jazeera Code of Ethics

This code was adopted on 12 July 2004.

Being a globally oriented media service, Al-Jazeera shall determinedly adopt the following code of ethics in pursuance of the vision and mission it has set for itself:

1. Adhere to the journalistic values of honesty, courage, fairness, balance, independence, credibility and diversity, giving no priority to commercial or political considerations over professional ones.

2. Endeavour to get to the truth and declare it in our dispatches, programmes and news bulletins unequivocally in a manner which leaves no doubt about its validity and accuracy.

3. Treat our audiences with due respect and address every issue or story with due attention to present a clear, factual and accurate picture while giving full consideration to the feelings of victims of crime, war, persecution and disaster, their relatives and our viewers, and to individual privacy and public decorum.

4. Welcome fair and honest media competition without allowing it to affect adversely our standards of performance so that getting a "scoop" will not become an end in itself.

5. Present diverse points of view and opinions without bias or partiality.

6. Recognise diversity in human societies with all their races, cultures and beliefs and their values and intrinsic individualities in order to present unbiased and faithful reflection of them.

7. Acknowledge a mistake when it occurs, promptly correct it and ensure it does not recur.

8. Observe transparency in dealing with news and news sources while adhering to internationally established practices concerning the rights of these sources.

9. Distinguish between news material, opinion and analysis to avoid the pitfalls of speculation and propaganda.

10. Stand by colleagues in the profession and offer them support when required, particularly in light of the acts of aggression and harassment to which journalists are subjected at times. Cooperate with Arab and international journalistic unions and associations to defend freedom of the press.

(www.aljazeera.co.uk)

APPENDIX 9

Indymedia UK Mission Statement

The Indymedia UK website provides an interactive platform for reports from the struggles for a world based on freedom, cooperation, justice and solidarity, and against environmental degradation, neoliberal exploitation, racism and patriarchy. The reports cover a wide range of issues and social movements – from neighbourhood campaigns to grassroots mobilisations, from critical analysis to direct action.

The content of the Indymedia UK website is created through a system of open publishing: anyone can upload a written, audio and video report or a picture directly to the site through an openly accessible web interface. Through this system of "Direct Media", Indymedia erodes the dividing line between reporters and reported, between active producers and passive audience: people are enabled to speak for themselves. At bigger actions, Indymedia UK volunteers extend this participatory model by establishing "Public Access Terminals" on the streets, and facilitating direct access to the technical equipment that enables participants to upload to the website.

Indymedia UK stands for Indymedia United Kollektives. An increasing number of IMC collectives in the UK have their own pages on the IMC UK website or elsewhere. IMC UK is part of the worldwide network of Independent Media Centres (IMCs), focuses on Britain, and is also an intermediary for information from other parts of the world. IMC groups in the UK collaborate on sharing contents and resources amongst themselves and with the global IMC network. The main element of Indymedia UK is the website; this platform generates a variety of other activities including video-production, film-screenings, printed materials and public interventions.

The DIY media workers of the Indymedia United Kollektives operate within a network of radical UK media groups, individual contributors and IMC supporters. Volunteers of Indymedia United Kollektives act as moderators on the IMC UK website. We aim to live up to the following principles:

- Indymedia United Kollektives works on a non-hierarchical basis
- We reject all systems of domination and discrimination
- We acknowledge that the struggle for a better world takes many forms. The focus of the Indymedia UK collective is on grassroots politics, actions and campaigns
- Indymedia United Kollektives does not have any ties with political parties or larger NGOs
- We understand that by lobbying there will be no radical change. As a collective our attitude is assertive, and where necessary confrontational.

Inherent in the mainstream corporate media is a strong bias towards Capitalism's power structures, and it is an important tool in propagating these structures around the globe. While the mainstream media conceal their manifold biases and alignments, we clearly state our position. Indymedia UK does not attempt to take an objective and impartial standpoint: Indymedia UK clearly states its subjectivity.

(www.indymedia.org.uk)

REFERENCES

INTERVIEWS

Unless otherwise indicated in the text, comments by the following are taken from interviews conducted by the author during 2005 and 2006:

Eric Allison
Andrew Gilligan
Janet McKenzie
Steve Panter
Ryan Parry
Kevin Peachey
Michelle Stanistreet

Comments by Paul Foot are taken from an interview conducted in 2001 for the book *Journalism: principles and practice*.

Adie, Kate (2002) *The Kindness of Strangers*. London: Headline.

Ahmed, Nabila (2006) 'Police-media brawl at Test', *Guardian,* 17 April.

Airs, Gordon (2003) 'The last one in', *Journalist,* July.

Allan, Stuart (2004) *News Culture*. Maidenhead: Open University Press.

Allan, Stuart (2005) (ed) *Journalism: critical issues*. Maidenhead: Open University Press.

Armstrong, Stephen (2005) 'It's going to get a lot worse before it gets worse still', *Guardian*, 31 October.

Atton, Chris (2002) *Alternative Media*. London: Sage.

Atton, Chris (2004) *An Alternative Internet: radical media, politics and creativity*. Edinburgh: Edinburgh University Press.

Baker, Stephen and Greg McLaughlin (2005) 'News. What is it good for?', *Variant* 22 (Spring): 5, at: www.variant.org.uk

Barnett, Steven (2005) 'Opportunity or threat? The BBC, investigative journalism and the Hutton Report', in Stuart Allan (ed) *Journalism: critical issues*. Maidenhead: Open University Press, pp 328–41.

Bayley, Ros and Hilary Macaskill (2004) *Journalism and Public Trust*. London: NUJ.

BBC (2003a) 'Kelly 22.5.03', *BBC evidence to the Hutton Inquiry,* at: http://www.the-hutton-inquiry.org.uk/content/bbc/bbc_1_0054to0055.pdf

BBC (2003b) BBC Radio Four *Today* programme broadcast 29 May 2003, *BBC evidence to the Hutton Inquiry Today*, at: http://www.the-hutton-inquiry.org.uk/content/bbc/bbc_1_0004to0017.pdf

BBC (2003c) 'Extract from Susan Watts' notebook', at: http://www.the-hutton-inquiry.org.uk/content/bbc/bbc_1_0051to0053.pdf

BBC (2003d) 'Copy of a tape recording and transcript of telephone conversation: Susan Watts/Dr Kelly 30/05/03', at: http://www.the-hutton-inquiry.org.uk/content/bbc/bbc_1_0058to0063.pdf

BBC (2003e) 'Extract from the notebook of Gavin Hewitt – telephone conversation with Dr Kelly 29/05/03', at: http://www.the-hutton-inquiry.org.uk/content/bbc/bbc_1_0056to0057.pdf

BBC (2004) 'Dog's death order is overturned', 15 October, at: http://news.bbc.co.uk/go/pr/fr/-/hi/england/northamptonshire/3744866.stm

BBC (2005) 'BBC editorial guidelines', published June 2005, at: http://www.bbc.co.uk/guidelines/editorialguidelines/

BBC (2006) 'Met chief accuses media of racism', BBC News, 26 January, at: http://news.bbc.co.uk/go/pr/fr/-/1/hi/england/london/4651368.stm

BBC Board of Governors (2005) 'Programme complaints: appeals to the governors, July to September 2005', published November, at: www.bbcgovernors.co.uk/docs/complaints/apps_julsept2005.txt

Beales, Ian (2005) *The Editors' Codebook*. London: Newspaper Publishers Association, Newspaper Society, Periodical Publishers Association, Scottish Daily Newspaper Society, and Scottish Newspaper Publishers Association.

Benn, Tony (2001) 'The media and the political process', in Hugh Stephenson (ed) *Media Voices: the James Cameron memorial lectures*. London: Politico's, pp 327–45.

Bernstein, Carl and Bob Woodward (1974) *All the President's Men*. New York: Simon & Schuster.

Blair, Jayson (2004) *Burning Down My Masters' House*. Beverly Hills: New Millennium Press.

Bohman, James (2004) 'Expanding dialogue: the internet, the public sphere and the prospects for transnational democracy', in Nick Crossley and John Michael Roberts (eds), *After Habermas: new perspectives on the public sphere*. Oxford: Blackwell, pp 131–55.

Bolton, Roger (1990) *Death on the Rock and Other Stories*. London: WH Allen.

Borger, Julian (2005) 'Miller's twisted tale', *Guardian*, 10 October.

Born, Matt (2003) 'Sky fined £50,000 over fake news film that led to suicide', *Daily Telegraph,* 17 December.

Bradlee, Ben [1987] (2001) 'Why governments lie', in Hugh Stephenson (ed) *Media Voices: the James Cameron memorial lectures*. London: Politico's, pp 7–20.

British Press Awards (2005) *2005 Winners Collection*. Croydon: Quantum Business Media.

Brockes, Emma (2000) 'Chronicle of a death foretold', *Guardian*, 15 May.

Bromley, Michael (1997) 'The end of journalism? Changes in workplace practices in the press and broadcasting in the 1990s', in Michael Bromley and Tom O'Malley (eds), *A Journalism Reader*. London: Routledge, pp 330–50.

Brown, Gerry (1995) *Exposed!* London: Virgin.

Bundock, Clement J (1957) *The National Union of Journalists: a jubilee history*. Oxford: Oxford University Press for the NUJ.

Burrell, Ian (2006) 'Newsroom revolt forces "Star" to drop its "Daily Fatwa" spoof', *Independent*, 19 October.

Butt, Riazat (2005) 'Robbie Williams calls journalists hypocrites for criticising Moss', *Guardian*, 8 October.

Cameron, James (1968) *Point of Departure*. London: Readers Union.

Capote, Truman [1965] (2000) *In Cold Blood*. London: Penguin.

Carter, Helen (2003a) 'Five resign as police chiefs promise action against racism', *Guardian*, 23 October.

Carter, Helen (2003b) 'BBC racism exposé case dropped', *Guardian*, 5 November.

Chambers, Deborah, Linda Steiner and Carole Fleming (2004) *Women and Journalism*. London: Routledge.

Channel Four News (2002) 'How real is the risk?', 19 August, www.channel4.com/news

Clarke, Bob (2004) *From Grub Street to Fleet Street: an illustrated history of English newspapers to 1889*. Aldershot: Ashgate.

Clough, Sue (2001) '"Wicked" killer who showed no remorse gets life', *Daily Telegraph*, 22 December.

Coates, Tim (2004) (ed) *The Hutton Inquiry, 2003*. London: Tim Coates Books.

Cohen, Stanley (2002) *Folk Devils and Moral Panics*. London: Routledge.

Cole, Peter (2005) 'Medium earthquake in far off place. Few interested', *Independent on Sunday*, 16 October.

Cole, Peter (2006) 'Journalism or voyeurism?', *Independent on Sunday*, 8 January.

Coleman, Stephen (1997) *Stilled Tongues: from soapbox to soundbite*. London: Porcupine Press.

Coles, John and Mike Sullivan (2001) 'Murdered for £20', *Sun*, 18 April.

Conboy, Martin (2004) *Journalism: a critical history*. London: Sage.

Conboy, Martin (2006) *Tabloid Britain: constructing a community through language*. London: Routledge.

Cookson, Rich (2004) 'Satisfaction guaranteed?', in Mike Jempson and Rich Cookson (eds), *Satisfaction Guaranteed? Press complaints systems under scrutiny*. Bristol: Mediawise, pp 13–20.

Corcoran, Neil (2003) 'Death's Honesty', in Neil Corcoran (ed) *Do You, Mr Jones? Bob Dylan with the poets and professors*. London: Pimlico, pp 143–74.

Cottle, Simon (2000) 'Rethinking news access', *Journalism Studies* 1(3): 427–48.

Cottle, Simon (2005a) 'In defence of "thick" journalism; or how television journalism can be good for us', in Stuart Allan (ed) *Journalism: critical issues*. Maidenhead: Open University Press, pp 109–24.

Cottle, Simon (2005b) 'Mediatized public crisis and civil society renewal: the racist murder of Stephen Lawrence', *Crime, Media, Culture* (1): 49–71.

Coulter, John (2005) 'The moral reason never to tell', *British Journalism Review*, 16(1): 65–9.

CPBF (2005) *Media Manifesto 2005*. London: Campaign for Press and Broadcasting Freedom.

CPJ (2005a) 'China, Cuba, two African nations are top jailers of journalists', Committee to Protect Journalists, 13 December, at: http://www.cpj.org/Briefings/2005/imprisoned_05/imprisoned_05.html#more

CPJ (2005b) 'Marked for death: the five most murderous countries for journalists', Committee to Protect Journalists, 2 May, at: http://www.cpj.org/Briefings/2005/murderous_05/murderous_05.html

Curran, James (2000) 'Press reformism 1918–98: a study of failure', in Howard Tumber (ed) *Media Power, Professionals and Policies*. London: Routledge, pp 35–55.

Curran, James and Jean Seaton (2003) *Power without Responsibility: the press, broadcasting and new media in Britain*. London: Routledge.

Curtis, Liz (1996) 'A catalogue of censorship 1959–1993', in Bill Rolston and David Miller (eds) *War and Words: the Northern Ireland Media Reader*. Belfast: Beyond the Pale, pp 265–304.

Daily Mirror (1912) 'Story Mr Stead could have told', *Daily Mirror*, 18 April, at: www.attackingthedevil.co.uk/titanic/mirror1.php

Daley, James (2005) '*Mirror* editor "encouraged City Slicker to buy shares he tipped"', *Independent*, 15 November.

Daly, Mark (2003) 'My life as a secret policeman', BBC News, 21 October, at: http://news.bbc.co.uk/go/pr/fr/-/1/hi/magazine/3210614.stm

Davies, Nick (2005a) 'No direction home', *Guardian*, 19 October.

Davies, Caroline (2005b) 'Consultant struck off for "actively" ending patient's life', *Daily Telegraph*, 17 November.

de Burgh, Hugo (2000) (ed) *Investigative Journalism: context and practice*. London: Routledge.

Dodd, Vikram (2004) 'The walk' in Simon Rogers (ed) *The Hutton Inquiry and its Impact*. London: Politico's, pp 67–83.

Donnelly, Claire (2003) 'Asylum: the truth', *Daily Mirror*, 3 March.

Dorling, Danny (2006) 'Inequality kills', *Red Pepper*, January.

Dyke, Greg (2004) *Inside Story*. London: HarperCollins.

Edwards, Jeff (2005) 'Bish! Bash! Bosh!', *Daily Mirror*, 4 November.

Elliott, Florence (1973) *A Dictionary of Politics*. Harmondsworth: Penguin.

Elliott, Geoff (2005) *Reporting Diversity: how journalists can contribute to community cohesion*. Cambridge: Society of Editors.

Ettema, James S and Theodore L Glasser (1998) *Custodians of Conscience: investigative journalism and public virtue*. New York: Columbia University Press.

FAC (2003) 'Oral Evidence to Foreign Affairs Committee: Dr David Kelly, 15 July 2003', at: http://www.the-hutton-inquiry.org.uk/content/fac/fac_4_0001to0027.pdf

Fisk, Robert (2005) 'Secrets of the morgue: Baghdad's body count', *Independent*, 17 August.

Fixter, Alyson (2005) '*Lancet* hits out at its publisher over Docklands arms exhibition', *Press Gazette*, 16 September.

Foley, Michael (2001) 'Charmed lives on the streets of Northern Ireland', *Journalist*, November/December.

Foley, Michael (2004a) 'Absolutism and the confidential controversy', *Ethical Space*, 1(2): 18–19.

Foley, Michael (2004b) 'Colonialism and journalism in Ireland', *Journalism Studies* 5(3): 373–385.

Foot, Paul (1999) 'The slow death of investigative journalism', in Stephen Glover (ed) *The Penguin Book of Journalism*. London: Penguin, pp 79–89.

Foot, Paul [1994] (2000) 'Up the Levellers', in Paul Foot, *Articles of Resistance*, London: Bookmarks, pp 62–7.

Franklin, Bob (2004) *Packaging Politics: political communications in Britain's media democracy*. London: Arnold.

Franklin, Bob (2005) 'McJournalism: the local press and the McDonaldization thesis', in Stuart Allan (ed) *Journalism: critical issues*. Maidenhead: Open University Press, pp 137–50.

Frazier, Ian (2004) 'The legacy of a lonesome death', in *Mother Jones*, November/December 2004. [An edited version was reprinted as 'Life after a lonesome death' in the *Guardian*, 25 February 2005.]

Frost, Chris (2000) *Media Ethics and Self-Regulation*. Harlow: Longman.

Frost, Chris (2004) 'The Press Complaints Commission: a study of ten years of adjudications on press complaints', *Journalism Studies* 5(1): 101–14.

Gall, Gregor (1993) 'The employers' offensive in the provincial newspaper industry', *British Journal of Industrial Relations* 31(4): 615–24.

Gall, Gregor (2004) 'State of the union', *British Journalism Review* 15(3): 34–9.

Gall, Gregor (2006) 'Journalists' collective representation and editorial content in British newspapers: never the twain', *Union Ideas Network,* 9 February 2006, www.uin.org.uk/content/view/54/5/

Gall, Gregor and Sonia McKay (1994) 'Trade union derecognition in Britain 1988–1994', *British Journal of Industrial Relations* 32(3): 433–48.

Galtung, Johan and Mari Ruge (1965) 'The structure of foreign news: the presentation of the Congo, Cuba and Cyprus crises in four Norwegian newspapers', *Journal of International Peace Research* 1: 64–91.

Gans, Herbert (1980) *Deciding What's News*. New York: Vintage.

Gerodimos, Roman (2004) 'Journalists in the eye of the storm: balancing ethics and competition', in *Journalism and Public Trust*, published by the NUJ

Ethics Council and Mediawise for a conference in London on 4 December 2004, pp 19–21.

Gibson, Owen (2005) 'Bringing the *Times* to book', *Guardian*, 17 October.

Gibson, Owen (2006) '*Mirror* man held over palace ploy', *Guardian*, 16 February.

Gilligan, Andrew (2004) 'Speech to Edinburgh TV Festival, 29 August 2004', at: www.mgeitf.co.uk/MGEITF/pressoffice/news.asp?view=0&style=mgeitf&year=2004

Glees, Anthony and Philip HJ Davies (2004) *Spinning the Spies: intelligence, open government and the Hutton inquiry*. London: Social Affairs Unit.

Gopsill, Tim (2005) 'Five-year stretch', *Journalist*, March.

Gopsill, Tim and Greg Neale (2007) *Journalists: a hundred years of the National Union of Journalists*. London: Profile.

Grant, Kath (2006) 'Stories of life and death', *Journalist*, April/May.

Grant, Tony (2005) (ed) *From Our Own Correspondent*. London: Profile.

Greenslade, Roy (2003) *Press Gang: how newspapers make profits from propaganda*. London: Macmillan.

Greenslade, Roy (2005) 'Dear judges, how could you?', *Guardian*, 4 April.

Greenslade, Roy (2006) 'Royal stunts that diminish the concept of the public interest', *Daily Telegraph*, 21 February.

Gregg, Pauline (2000) *Free-Born John: the biography of John Lilburne*. London: Phoenix.

Guardian (2005) 'Corrections and clarifications', *Guardian*, 17 November.

Guardian (2006) 'Readers' editor right to publish apology, external review finds', *Guardian*, 25 May.

Guardian Newspapers Ltd (2005) *Living Our Values: social, ethical and environmental audit 2005*. Available online at: www.guardian.co.uk/socialaudit

Habermas, Jürgen (1989) *The Structural Transformation of the Public Sphere: an inquiry into a category of bourgeois society*. Cambridge: Polity.

Hackett, Robert A (2005) 'Is there a democratic deficit in US and UK journalism?', in Stuart Allan (ed) *Journalism: critical issues*. Maidenhead: Open University Press, pp 85–97.

Hajdu, David (2001) *Positively 4th Street: the lives and times of Bob Dylan, Joan Baez, Mimi Baez Farina & Richard Farina*. London: Bloomsbury.

Hall, Sarah (2003) 'Downing Street losing voters' trust', *Guardian*, 19 August.

Hall, Stuart (1973) 'The determination of news photographs', in Stanley Cohen and Jock Young (eds), *The Manufacture of News: deviance, social problems and the mass media*. London: Constable, pp 176–90.

Hall, Stuart, Chas Critcher, Tony Jefferson, John Clarke and Brian Roberts (1978) *Policing the Crisis: mugging, the state, law and order*. London: Macmillan.

Hanna, Mark (2006) 'All human life: covering the courts', in Richard Keeble (ed) *The Newspapers Handbook*, fourth edition. Abingdon: Routledge, pp 192–203.

Hanson, Christopher (2004) 'Blair, Kelley, Glass, and Cooke: scoundrels or scapegoats, symptoms or flukes?', *Journalism Studies* 5(3): 399–403.

Harcup, Tony (1994) *A Northern Star: Leeds Other Paper and the alternative press 1974–1994*. London and Pontefract: Campaign for Press and Broadcasting Freedom.

Harcup, Tony (2002) 'Journalists and ethics: the quest for a collective voice', *Journalism Studies* 3(1): 101–14.

Harcup, Tony (2003a) 'Adding an ethical dimension', *Press Gazette Journalism Training Supplement*, March: 29.

Harcup, Tony (2003b) 'The unspoken – said. The journalism of alternative media', *Journalism: theory, practice and criticism* 4(3): 356–76.

Harcup, Tony (2004) *Journalism: principles and practice*. London: Sage.

Harcup, Tony (2005a) 'Siren voices of war must not fool us again', *Press Gazette*, 28 January.

Harcup, Tony (2005b) '"I'm doing this to change the world: journalism in alternative and mainstream media"', *Journalism Studies* 6(3): 361–74.

Harcup, Tony (2005c) 'Citizens in the newsroom: democracy, ethics and journalism', *Ethical Space* 2(3): 25–31.

Harcup, Tony (2006) 'The local alternative press', in Bob Franklin (ed) *Local Journalism and Local Media: making the local news*. London: Routledge.

Harcup, Tony and Deirdre O'Neill (2001) 'What is news? Galtung and Ruge revisited', *Journalism Studies* 2(2): 261–80.

Harding, Luke (2006) 'Revolt in the newsroom', *Guardian,* 5 June.

Hargreaves, Ian (2003) *Journalism: truth or dare?* Oxford: Oxford University Press.

Harrabin, Roger, Anna Coote and Jessica Allen (2003) *Health in the News: risk, reporting and media influence*, Executive Summary. London: King's Fund.

Harrison, Jackie (2006) *News*. London: Routledge.

Harrison, Stanley (1974) *Poor Men's Guardians: a survey of the struggles for a democratic newspaper press 1763–1973*. London: Lawrence & Wishart.

Harvey, Oliver (2006) '*Sun* buys sex slave for £450', *Sun*, 18 January.

Hastings, Max (2000) *Going to the Wars*. London: Macmillan.

Hastings, Max (2002) *Editor*. London: Macmillan.

Hattenstone, Simon (2005) 'Looking for trouble', *Guardian Weekend* magazine, 5 March.

Hazards (2006) 'Asbestos trade's lingering death', *Hazards* 93 (January/March).

Henderson, Mark (2003) 'Junk medicine: don't believe the hype', *Times*, 20 September.

Heylin, Clinton (2001) *Bob Dylan: behind the Shades, take two*. London: Penguin.

Hill, Christopher (1975) *The World Turned Upside Down: radical ideas during the English revolution*. Middlesex: Peregrine.

HM Government (2002) *Iraq's Weapons of Mass Destruction: the assessment of the British government*. London: HMSO.

Hobsbawm, Julia (2004) 'Heroes can still make the news', *Independent*, 18 October.

Hollingsworth, Mark (1986) *The Press and Political Dissent: a question of censorship*. London: Pluto.

Honoré, Carl (2004) *In Praise of Slow: how a worldwide movement is challenging the cult of speed*. London: Orion.

Hooper, John (2005) 'Italian journalist posing as migrant reports abuse at detention camp', *Guardian*, 8 October.

Hopkinson, Rod (2005) 'Workman jailed for breaching gas ban', *Yorkshire Evening Post*, 10 December.

Horgan, John (2002) 'Journalists and censorship: a case history of the NUJ in Ireland and the broadcasting ban 1971–94', *Journalism Studies* 3(3): 377–92.

Humphries, Paul (2005) 'A dying breed', *Journalist*, September.

Hunter, Caroline and Yvonne Bolouri (2005) 'Every week two women are killed by their partners', *Sun*, 21 September.

Hutton, Lord (2004) *Report of the Inquiry into the Circumstances Surrounding the Death of Dr David Kelly CMG*, at: http://www.the-hutton-inquiry.org.uk/content/report/index.htm

IFJ (2005a) *Journalists and Media Staff Killed in 2004: an IFJ report on media casualties in the field of journalism and newsgathering*. Brussels: International Federation of Journalists, www.ifj.org

IFJ (2005b) *Let's Organise: a union handbook for journalists*. Brussels: International Federation of Journalists, www.ifj.org

Iggulden, Caroline (2006) 'Fancy a nibble of my donut?', *Sun*, 15 February.

IPI (2005) *World Press Freedom Report 2004*. Vienna: International Press Institute.

Independent (2004) 'Editor resigns after caption gaffe', *Independent*, 28 July.

Independent (2005) 'War criminals', *Independent*, 8 December.

Ingrams, Richard (2005) *My Friend Footy: a memoir of Paul Foot*. London: Private Eye.

Jack, Ian (2004) 'Introduction', in Janet Malcolm, *The Journalist and the Murderer*. London: Granta, pp ix–xvii.

Jempson, Mike (2004a) 'Memo to Meyer' in Mike Jempson and Rich Cookson (eds) *Satisfaction Guaranteed? Press complaints systems under scrutiny*. Bristol: Mediawise, pp 7–11.

Jempson, Mike (2004b) 'Time for a culture change', in Mike Jempson and Rich Cookson (eds) *Satisfaction Guaranteed? Press complaints systems under scrutiny*. Bristol: Mediawise, pp 31–40.

Jempson, Mike (2006) 'PCC and editor's code committee must act on suicide coverage', *Mediawise Bulletin* 115, 5 January 2006, www.mediawise.org.uk

Jempson, Mike and Rich Cookson (2004) (eds) *Satisfaction Guaranteed? Press complaints systems under scrutiny*. Bristol: Mediawise.

Jenkins, Simon (2006) 'Three cheers for Gutenberg – and long live dead trees', *Guardian*, 6 January.

Jewkes, Yvonne (2004) *Media & Crime*. London: Sage.

Journalist (2000a) 'Stop anti-gay propaganda in Scottish press, urges NUJ', *Journalist*, April.

Journalist (2001a) 'Why don't we listen to refugee stories?', *Journalist*, March.

Journalist (2001b) 'Outrage at "racist" refugee coverage', *Journalist*, September.

Journalist (2002) 'PCC snubs an NUJ complaint', *Journalist*, January/ February.

Journalist (2004a) '*Express* journalists complain again about "racist" pressure', *Journalist*, March.

Journalist (2004b) 'It makes me ashamed', *Journalist*, November/December.

Journalist (2004c) 'Mystery surrounds raid on Indymedia servers', *Journalist*, November/December.

Keane, John (1996) *Tom Paine: a political life*. London: Bloomsbury.

Keeble, Richard (2001a) *Ethics for Journalists*. London: Routledge.

Keeble, Richard (2001b) *The Newspapers Handbook*. London: Routledge.

Keeble, Richard (2005) 'Journalism ethics: towards an Orwellian critique', in Stuart Allan (ed) *Journalism: critical issues*. Maidenhead: Open University Press, pp 54–66.

Kinsey, Marie, David Holmes and Katie Stewart (2006) 'The videojournalism revolution: quality television news?' Paper presented to the MeCCSA/AMPE conference at Leeds Metropolitan University, 13–15 January.

Kiss, Jemima (2006) 'Changing Media Summit: citizen media will unlock the secret society, says Jon Snow', 28 March, at: www.journalism.co.uk/news/story1779.shtml,

Klein, Peter (2006) 'Film *Capote* raises disturbing ethical questions', at http://www.journalismethics.ca/book_reviews/capote.htm

Knightley, Phillip (1998) *A Hack's Progress*. London: Vintage.

Knightley, Phillip (2000) *The First Casualty*. London: Prion.

Kovach, Bill and Tom Rosenstiel (2003) *The Elements of Journalism*. London: Atlantic.

Krajicek, David J (1998) 'The bad, the ugly and the worse', *Guardian*, 11 May.

Lagan, Sarah (2005) 'Hoax kidnapper picked pupils' names from paper', *Press Gazette*, 25 March.

Leeds Alternative Publications (1980s, nd) *Views on the News*, internal discussion paper.

Leigh, David (2005) 'The cliché is right – the lying bastards lie to us', *Guardian*, 10 January.

Lewis, Justin (2004) 'At the service of politicians', *Guardian*, 4 August.

Lewis, Justin, Terry Threadgold, Rod Brookes, Nick Mosdell, Kirsten Brander, Sadie Clifford, Ehab Bessaiso and Zahera Harb (2004) *Too Close for Comfort? The role of embedded reporting during the 2003 Iraq war*. Cardiff: School of Journalism, Media and Cultural Studies.

Lewis, Justin, Stephen Cushion and James Thomas (2005) 'Immediacy, convenience or engagement? An analysis of 24-hour news channels in the UK', *Journalism Studies* 6(4): 461–77.

Lloyd, John (2004) *What the Media Are Doing to Our Politics*. London: Constable.

Luscombe, Richard (2005) 'Pranksters hijack "banal" TV news', *Observer*, 3 July.

Lynch, Jake and Annabel McGoldrick (2005) *Peace Journalism*. Stroud: Hawthorn Press.

Mackay, Hamish and Caitlin Pike (2005) 'GB8', *Press Gazette*, 8 July.

Maguire, Kevin and Andy Lines (2005) 'Bush plot to bomb his Arab ally', *Daily Mirror*, 22 November.

Malcolm, Janet (2004) *The Journalist and the Murderer*. London: Granta.

Mangold, Tom (2006) 'Let the hacks attack', *Guardian*, 6 March.

Manning, Paul (2001) *News and News Sources: a critical introduction*. London: Sage.

Mansfield, FJ (1936) *The Complete Journalist: a study of the principles and practice of newspaper-making*. London: Sir Isaac Pitman and Sons.

Mansfield, FJ (1943) *Gentlemen, the Press! Chronicles of a Crusade: official history of the National Union of Journalists*. London: WH Allen.

Marr, Andrew (2005) *My Trade: a short history of British journalism*. London: Pan.

Marriner, Cosima (2005) 'Pelle the conqueror', *Guardian*, 28 November.

Martin-Clark, Nick (2003) 'When a journalist must tell', *British Journalism Review*, 14(2): 35–9.

Mason, Paul (2005) 'Newsnig8t' weblog, July 2005, at: www.paulmason.typepad.com

Mayes, Ian (2006) 'Open door: the readers' editor on … a significant move by a major Indian newspaper', *Guardian*, 23 January.

McChesney, Robert (2000) *Rich Media, Poor Democracy: communication politics in dubious times*. New York: New Press.

McIntyre, Peter (2004) 'An example to so many', *Journalist*, November/December.

McLaughlin, Greg (2002) *The War Correspondent*. London: Pluto.

McMasters, Paul (2004) 'Commentary', *Journalism Studies* 5(3): 399–403.

Mediawise (2003) *The Media and Suicide: guidance for journalists from journalists*, at: www.mediawise.org.uk

Melvern, Linda [2000] (2004) 'A people betrayed', extract published in John Pilger (ed) *Tell Me No Lies: investigative journalism and its triumphs*. London: Jonathan Cape, pp 434–64.

Michael, Neil and Alyson Fixter (2005) 'London terror: "I have never come across such outrageous reporting practices"', *Press Gazette*, 15 July.

Miles, Hugh (2005) *Al-Jazeera: how Arab TV news challenged the world*. London: Abacus.

Mill, John Stuart [1859] (1997) 'Essay on liberty', in Michael Bromley and Tom O'Malley (eds) *A Journalism Reader*. London: Routledge, pp 22–7.

Miller, David (1994) *Don't Mention the War: Northern Ireland, propaganda and the media*. London: Pluto.

Milton, John [1644] (2005) 'Areopagitica: a speech for the liberty of unlicensed printing', in John Milton and Granville Williams, *Milton and the Modern Media: a defence of a free press*. Accrington: B&D.

Mnookin, Seth (2005) *Hard News: twenty-one brutal months at the New York Times and how they changed the American media*. New York: Random House.

Morgan, Jean (2001) 'Hellier on sick leave as row over Desmond stance grows', *Press Gazette*, 14 September.

Morley, Chris (2006) 'Journalism matters', *Journalist*, June.

National Conference of Alternative Papers (1984) Leeds, Spring. Editorial and Workshop Reports.

Neil, Ronald (2004) *The BBC's Journalism After Hutton: the report of the Neill Review Team*, June 2004, at: www.bbc.co.uk/info/policies/pdf/neil_report.pdf

Newsbreakers (2005) 'Evangelist exorcises Clear Channel newscast', 15 April, at: www.newsbreakers.org

Nicholas, Sian, David Povey, Alison Walker and Chris Kershaw (2005) *Crime in England and Wales 2004/2005*. London: Home Office, at: www.homeoffice.gov.uk/rds/bcs1.html

Norris, Pippa (2000) *A Virtuous Circle: political communications in postindustrial societies*. Cambridge: Cambridge University Press.

Norton-Taylor, Richard (2004) 'Introduction' in Simon Rogers (ed) *The Hutton Inquiry and its Impact*. London: Politico's, pp 1–9.

NUJ (1987) *NUJ Annual Report 1986–1987*. London: National Union of Journalists.

NUJ (1988) *NUJ Annual Report 1987–1988*. London: National Union of Journalists.

NUJ (1989) *NUJ Annual Report 1988–1989*. London: National Union of Journalists.

NUJ (1990) *NUJ Annual Report 1989–1990*. London: National Union of Journalists.

NUJ (2003) 'Memorandum submitted by the National Union of Journalists to the Select Committee on Culture, Media and Sport', at: http://www.publications.parliament.uk/pa/cm200203/cmselect/cmcumeds/458/3030407.htm

NUJ (2005) *The Reporting of Mental Health and Suicide by the Media: a practical guide for journalists*. Glasgow: National Union of Journalists.

Number Ten (2003) 'Press Briefing: 11am Monday 4 August 2003', at: http://www.numberten.gov.uk/output/Page4314.asp

Nyaira, Sandra (2004) 'Losing faith in colleagues I thought would help', in *Journalism and Public Trust*, published by the NUJ Ethics Council and Mediawise for a conference in London on 4 December, pp 34–6.

Ofcom (2005) *Consideration of Piccadilly Radio, in respect of its service 'Key 103' FM*, Ofcom Content Sanctions Committee, 24 November, at: www.ofcom.org.uk/tv/obb/ocsc_adjud/key103.pdf

O'Malley, Tom (1997) 'Labour and the 1947–9 Royal Commission on the Press', in Michael Bromley and Tom O'Malley (eds), *A Journalism Reader*. London: Routledge, pp 126–58.

O'Malley, Tom (2005) *Keeping Broadcasting Public: the BBC and the 2006 charter review*. London: Campaign for Press and Broadcasting Freedom.

O'Malley, Tom and Clive Soley (2000) *Regulating the Press*. London: Pluto.
O'Neill, Deirdre (2004) 'The challenge for journalism educators', in NUJ Ethics Council and Mediawise, *Journalism and Public Trust*, pp 47–9.
O'Neill, John (1992) 'Journalism in the market place', in Andrew Belsey and Ruth Chadwick (eds) *Ethical Issues in Journalism and the Media*. London: Routledge, pp 15–32.
O'Neill, Onora (2002), Reith Lectures 2002: A Question of Trust, lecture 5: *Licence to Deceive*, at: www.bbc.co.uk/radio4/reith2002/lecture5.shtml
Page, Adrian (1998) 'Interpreting codes of conduct', in Michael Bromley and Hugh Stephenson (eds) *Sex, Lies and Democracy: the press and the public*. Harlow: Longman, pp 127–35.
Palmer, Jerry (2000) *Spinning into Control: news values and source strategies*. London: Leicester University Press.
Pape, Susan and Sue Featherstone (2005) *Newspaper Journalism: a practical introduction*. London: Sage.
Parry, Ryan (2003) 'A right royal fiasco', *Daily Mirror*, 19 November.
PCC (2004) *PCC Response to the Culture, Media and Sport Select Committee's Recommendations Following its Inquiry into Privacy and Media Intrusion*. London: Press Complaints Commission.
PCC (2006a) *Annual Review 2005*. London: Press Complaints Commission.
PCC (2006b) 'Resolved – the Duchess of York v the *Sun*', Press Complaints Commission, 30 May, www.pcc.org.uk/news/index.html?article=Mzk1Ng==
PCC (2006c) 'Petetin v the *Times*', at: www.pcc.org.uk/news/index.html?article=Mzg4Nw
Petley, Julian (2004a) 'Fourth-rate estate', *Index on Censorship* 33(2): 68–75.
Petley, Julian (2004b) 'A modern day Circumlocution Office?', in Mike Jempson and Rich Cookson (eds) *Satisfaction Guaranteed? Press complaints systems under scrutiny*. Bristol: Mediawise, pp 21–6.
Phillips, Peter (2004) *Censored 25: the top 25 censored stories*. New York: Seven Stories Press.
Pilger, John (2004) (ed) *Tell Me No Lies: investigative journalism and its triumphs*. London: Jonathan Cape.
Plett, Barbara (2004) 'Yasser Arafat's unrelenting journey', *From our own Correspondent*, BBC Radio Four, 30 October, at: http://news.bbc.co.uk/1/hi/programmes/from_our_own_correspondent/3966139.stm
Ponsford, Dominic (2004a) '*Express* staff call in PCC over anti-gypsy articles', *Press Gazette*, 30 January.
Ponsford, Dominic (2004b) 'Notts weekly forces NHS care trust to end secret meetings', *Press Gazette*, 27 August.
Ponsford, Dominic (2005) 'Columnist quits after row', *Press Gazette*, 19 August.
Ponsford, Dominic (2006a) 'Ackroyd victory strikes blow for protection of sources', *Press Gazette*, 10 February.
Ponsford, Dominic (2006b) 'PCC branded "hopeless" by ex *Mirror* political chief…', *Press Gazette,* 26 May.

Porter, Roy (2000) *Enlightenment: Britain and the creation of the modern world*. London: Allen Lane.

Press Gazette (2003a) '*Sun* writer quits over "pro-war bias"', *Press Gazette*, 28 March.

Press Gazette (2003b) 'Local papers match nationals for insensitivity', *Press Gazette*, 31 October.

Press Gazette (2006a) 'Climate change journey for ITV News' McGinty', *Press Gazette*, 24 February.

Press Gazette (2006b) 'The British press awards 2006', *Press Gazette*, 24 March.

Preston, Peter (2005) 'How not to defend your source', *British Journalism Review*, 16(3): 47–52.

Private Eye (2004) 'Paul Foot' and 'More Foot', at: www.private-eye.co.uk

Procter, Harry (1958) *The Street of Disillusion: confessions of a journalist*. London: Allan Wingate.

Ramonet, Ignacio (2003) 'Set the media free', *Le Monde Diplomatique*, October, at: www.mondediplo.com/2003/10/01media

Randall, David (2000) *The Universal Journalist*. London: Pluto.

Randall, David (2005) *The Great Reporters*. London: Pluto.

Ratcliffe, Roger (2006) 'Cash for questions', *Guardian,* 8 May.

Reporters Without Borders (2004) *Rwanda – 2004 Annual Report*, at: http://www.rsf.org/article.php3?id_article=10193

Rogers, Simon (2004) (ed) *The Hutton Inquiry and Its Impact*. London: Politico's.

Rolston, Bill and David Miller (1996) (eds) *War and Words: the Northern Ireland media reader*. Belfast: Beyond the Pale.

Rose, Jonathan (2002) *The Intellectual Life of the British Working Classes*. New Haven and London: Yale Nota Bene.

Rusbridger, Alan (2004) 'Foreword' in Simon Rogers (ed) *The Hutton Inquiry and Its Impact*. London: Politico's.

Rusbridger, Alan (2005) 'What are newspapers for?', the Hugo Young Lecture, University of Sheffield, 9 March, at: http://doj.shef.ac.uk/hugo1.doc

Sambrook, Richard (2004) 'Tragedy in the fog of war', *British Journalism Review* 15(3): 7–13.

Sanders, Karen (2003) *Ethics & Journalism*. London: Sage.

Sands, Phillipe (2006) *Lawless World*. London: Penguin.

Schechter, Danny [1994] (2001) 'Helicopter journalism and its limits: why reporters who only look down tend to cover up', in *News Dissector: passions, pieces and polemics 1960–2000.* New York: Akashic Books.

Schlesinger, Philip (1987) *Putting 'Reality' Together*. London: Routledge.

Schlesinger, Philip and Howard Tumber (1994) *Reporting Crime: the media politics of criminal justice*. Oxford: Clarendon.

Schuffels, Klaus (1979) 'Introduction', in Günter Wallraff, *The Undesirable Journalist*. New York: Overlook Press.

Scott, Kirsty (2004) 'Why a 29–0 "trouncing" was victory for the press', *Guardian*, 30 March.

Seale, Clive (2002) *Media & Health*. London: Sage.

Security Commission (2004) *Report of the Security Commission, May 2004, Presented to Parliament by the Prime Minister by Command of Her Majesty*. Norwich: The Stationery Office.

Sedley, Stephen (2006) 'Towards a right to privacy', *London Review of Books,* 8 June, 28(11): 20–3.

Select Committee (2003) House of Commons Select Committee on Culture, Media and Sport, Minutes of Evidence, 11 March, at: http://www.publications.parliament.uk/pa/cm200203/cmselect/cmcumeds/458/3031112.htm

Shannon, Richard (2001) *A Press Free and Responsible: self-regulation and the Press Complaints Commission, 1991–2001*. London: John Murray.

Shaw, Chris (2005) 'Medialand: Local news is a source of profit for ITV, not subsidy', *Press Gazette*, 15 July.

Shaw, Danny (2004) 'Crimes, surveys and statistics', BBC News, 10 November, at: http://news.bbc.co.uk/go/pr/fr/-/1/hi/uk/3733542.stm

Sheridan Burns, Lynette (2002) *Understanding Journalism*. London: Sage.

Shift (2006) *Mind Over Matter: improving media reporting of mental health*. London: Shift, at: www.shift.org.uk

Simpson, John (1999) *Strange Places, Questionable People*. London: Pan.

Simpson, John (2005) 'The foreign legion', *Guardian*, 6 September.

Slattery, Jon (2005) '*Daily News* "will return to streets of Zimbabwe"', *Press Gazette*, 26 August.

Smith, Paul and Gary Morton (1994) 'Union exclusion – next steps', *Industrial Relations Journal*, March.

Snoddy, Raymond (1992) *The Good, the Bad and the Unacceptable: the hard news about the British press*. London: Faber & Faber.

Snoddy, Raymond (2006) 'A mountain to climb for Hill', *Independent*, 20 February.

Snow, Jon (2005) *Shooting History: a personal journey*. London: Harper Perennial.

Sobolev, Yegor (2005) 'The fight against censorship: how we put an end to it on Ukrainian television', in *Getting It Together! Workplace trade union organisation in Britain and Ukraine*. Brussels: International Federation of Journalists, pp 52–5.

SOTCAA (2000) 'Comment: stop press', *Some Of The Corpses Are Amusing,* December. at: http://web.ukonline.co.uk/sotcaa/comment/stoppress.html

Sounes, Howard (2002) *Down the Highway: the life of Bob Dylan*. London: Black Swan.

Spark, David (1999) *Investigative Reporting: a study in technique*. Oxford: Focal.

Starck, Nigel (2005) 'Posthumous parallel and parallax: the obituary revival on three continents', *Journalism Studies* 6(3): 267–83.

Steed, Henry Wickham (1938) *The Press*. Harmondsworth: Penguin.

Stott, Richard (2002) *Dogs and Lampposts*. London: Metro.

Stromback, Jesper (2005) 'In search of a standard: four models of democracy and their normative implications for journalism', *Journalism Studies* 6(3): 331–45.

Sun (2005) 'Cops go to Ross row', *Sun*, 4 November.

Sun (2006) 'Princess Eugenie – correction', *Sun,* 1 May.

Taylor, Geoffrey (1993) *Changing Faces: a history of the Guardian 1956–88*. London: Fourth Estate.

Taylor, Robert (1994) *The Future of the Trade Unions*. London: Andre Deutsch.

Time (1963) 'The Murder of Hattie Carroll' at: http://www.stmarystoday.com/this_account_of_what_took__place.htm

Tomalin, Nicholas (1997) 'Stop the press I want to get on', in Michael Bromley and Tom O'Malley (eds), *A Journalism Reader*. London: Routledge, pp 174–8.

Tomlin, Julie and Caitlin Pike (2005) 'How many more must die?', *Press Gazette*, 6 May.

Toomey, Christine (2003) 'A moment of madness that did for poor James', *Sunday Times*, 12 October.

Tracy, James F (2004) 'The news about the newsmakers: press coverage of the 1965 American Newspaper Guild strike against *The New York Times*', *Journalism Studies* 5(4): 451–67.

Travis, Alan (2003) 'Blunkett apologises for slating BBC film', *Guardian*, 25 October.

Tulloch, John (1998) 'Managing the press in a medium-sized European power', in Michael Bromley and Hugh Stephenson (eds), *Sex, Lies and Democracy: the press and the public*. Harlow: Longman, pp 63–83.

Tulloch, John (2004a) 'What moral universe are you from? Everyday tragedies and the ethics of press intrusion into grief', *Ethical Space* 1(3): 25–30.

Tulloch, John (2004b) 'Journalism: the myth of trust', *Media Education Journal* 36 (Winter 2004/2005): 4–5.

Tulloch, John (2006) *One Day in July: experiencing 7/7*. London: Little, Brown.

Tunstall, Jeremy (1996) *Newspaper Power: the new national press in Britain*. Oxford: Oxford University Press.

Turner, Janice (2005) 'Dirty young men', *Guardian*, 22 October.

Tweedale, Geoffrey (2001) *Magic Mineral to Killer Dust: Turner & Newall and the asbestos hazard*. Oxford: Oxford University Press.

Vasagar, Jeevan (2006) 'Kenya clamps down on media freedom', *Guardian*, 3 March.

Walker, David (2000) 'Newspaper power: a practitioner's account', in Howard Tumber (ed) *Media Power, Professionals and Policies*. London: Routledge, pp 236–46.

Wallraff, Günter [1985] (2004) 'Lowest of the low', extract published in John Pilger (ed) *Tell Me No Lies: investigative journalism and its triumphs*. London: Jonathan Cape.

Walsh, Nick Paton (2004) 'Highly-trained militants left almost nothing to chance', *Guardian*, 7 September.

Ward, David (2004) 'Training use for exposé of racism', *Guardian*, 7 April.

Waugh, Paul (2003) 'No 10 dismisses Kelly as a "Walter Mitty"', *Independent*, 4 August.

Welsh, Tom, Walter Greenwood and David Banks (2005) *McNae's Essential Law for Journalists*, 18th edition. Oxford: Oxford University Press.

Wheen, Francis (2004) *How Mumbo-Jumbo Conquered the World*. London: Harper Perennial.

Whitaker, Brian (1981) *News Ltd: why you can't read all about it*. London: Minority Press Group.

White, Barry (2000) 'Competitive, but collective as well', *Journalist*, December.

Wilkinson, Nick (2004) 'Letter' in *British Journalism Review* 15(4): 86.

Willey, Jo (2005) 'The school where they speak 58 languages', *Daily Express*, 21 April.

Williams, Francis (1959) *Dangerous Estate: the anatomy of newspapers*. London: Arrow.

Williams, Granville (2005) 'A text for our times', in John Milton and Granville Williams, *Milton and the Modern Media: a defence of a free press*. Accrington: B&D.

Williams, Kevin (1998) *Get Me a Murder a Day! A history of mass communication in Britain*. London: Arnold.

Williamson, Nigel (2004) *The Rough Guide to Bob Dylan*. London: Rough Guides.

Wood, Roy H (1963) 'Rich brute slays negro mother of 10', *Baltimore Sun*, 10 February, at: http://pool.dylantree.com/pool_view_image.php?image=4954

Wykes, Maggie (2001) *News, Crime and Culture*. London: Pluto.

YEP (2005) 'Child porn doctor is struck off', *Yorkshire Evening Post*, 12 November.

Young, Iris Marion (2000) *Inclusion and Democracy*, Oxford: Oxford University Press.

Younge, Gary (2004) '*Washington Post* apologises for underplaying WMD scepticism', *Guardian*, 13 August.

Younge, Gary (2005) 'Eyewitness 21.12.56: Montgomery, Alabama', *Guardian*, 26 October.

Zelizer, Barbie (2004) *Taking Journalism Seriously: news and the academy*. London: Sage.

INDEX